Solar Fire®

Gold

v. 7

for Microsoft® *Windows*™

User Guide

ASTROLABE   ESOTERIC TECHNOLOGIES

Before you open the disk package... Please read the End User Agreement that comes with your program disks. Breaking the wrapper signifies that you agree to the terms of this contract. This means you will not sell or give away copies of *Solar Fire* or its documentation and manuals while still using a copy on your own computer. *Buying a copy of this program entitles its use on only one computer at a time.* If you do not agree to these terms, return the manual and unopened disk package, and your money will be refunded. No refunds are available on opened disk packages.

Producing this program has taken many months of development time, testing, and documenting. To continue to supply astrologers with top-grade astrology software, its makers need to recoup costs and keep staff on hand to give service and technical support. Please make sure that those you know have only licensed copies of these programs. That way, you can ensure continued technical support and new programs in the future.

ISBN 978-0-87199-151-5

1. Astrology   2. Computer Software   1. Title

Printed in the United States of America

Published by: Astrolabe, Inc.
350 Underpass Road • PO Box 1750 • Brewster, MA 02631 USA
Tel.: (508) 896-5081 • Fax: (508) 896-5289
www.alabe.com • email: astrolabe@alabe.com

Table of Contents

Chapter 1: Solar Fire and Its Authors

Solar Fire is a state-of-the-art astrology software package for Windows on a PC. Solar Fire is intuitive, easy-to-use calculation software, designed for both novice and expert astrologers alike, and it provides easy access to high-quality chart production using the Windows visual interface.

Solar Fire includes natal, progressed, directed, solar, lunar and any planet or asteroid return, composite, harmonic, lunar phase, rise/set and prenatal charts, with a flexible selection of aspect sets, chart point sets, and database files for chart and place detail storage. It also includes flexible and powerful dynamic transit and progression reporting over any specified time period, plus novel options for sorting and viewing output graphically for maximized readability.

It is possible to view interpretations of any natal chart or of any dynamic report event interactively on the screen, by simply clicking on items in the chart or report. Synastry interpretations are also included for any pair of charts. Both interpretations of individual charts plus general definitions of a large variety of astrological categories are included. It is possible to edit or append your own text to that supplied with the program.

Chart viewing includes an aspectarian inside the chart wheel (or as a separate tabulation, if preferred), plus dual wheels, biwheels, triwheels or even quadriwheels for displaying combinations of two or more charts, and synastry grids. Chart points can be viewed in color, as can the zodiac sign glyphs.

Reports include sorted listings of standard chart analysis details, lunar phasing, modalities and elements, plus additional listings of aspects, rulerships and dispositorships, both traditional and esoteric, and midpoints listings, midpoint trees and axes, fixed star and Arabic Parts positions and aspects.

There are 50 standard chart points to choose from, including planets, moons, chart angles, trans-neptunians, asteroids and other minor bodies. There are also additional sets of asteroids, fixed stars, arabic parts, and midpoints, for example.

Solar Fire has aspect sets selectable from the 1st to the 12th harmonic, with glyphs and colors for each, plus the ability to accept user defined aspect of any type.

Selected Features

- Holds up to 15 chart pages in "video memory" for instantaneous viewing.

- Allows on-screen viewing of a large variety of astrological definitions and interpretations, including interpretations of each planet and asteroid in each sign and house, plus interpretations of each planet in aspect to every other planet (using six different aspect types). There is also information relating to decanates and individual degrees of the chart, amongst many other categories.

- Displays high-clarity, high-resolution charts on the screen using the maximum resolution of any screen device.

- Chart point and aspect colors are user selectable.

- Includes all commonly used chart-type calculation methods.

- Computes composite charts for a pair of individuals or for an entire family or group of up to 15 individuals.

- Includes 30 different house systems.

- Creates any number of named aspect sets with user-definable orbs. Any one of these can be selected to be used in computing charts by simple mouse operation.

- Prints charts to the maximum resolution of any printer, including high-resolution laser printers and inkjet printers.

- Contains an atlas with more than 250,000 location names, positions and time zones with full daylight savings history, accessible by simple mouse operation.

- Allows creation of any number of chart database files from which records can be retrieved, copied or deleted.

- Supports color printers. Aspect lines, planets and signs can be printed in color.

- Copies charts to the Windows clipboard for use in word-processing or drawing programs, and can also export as a PDF file.

- Charts, chart data and page displays and may be emailed in one step, when used with a MAPI compliant email program.

Esoteric Technologies Pty Ltd

Esoteric Technologies is an Australian company specializing in technology for the harnessing and beneficial use of esoteric knowledge. In addition to the development of astrological software, it offers various astrological services, including chart printing and consultations.

Esoteric Technologies' directors are Stephanie Johnson and Neville Lang.

Stephanie is one of the founders of Esoteric Technologies and has a major role in the ongoing development of Solar Fire including authoring Solar Fire's Interpretation text files. Stephanie is the Marketing Director of Esoteric Technologies and is also a consulting astrologer. She holds a Practitioner's Certificate and Diploma from the Federation of Australian Astrologers and holds a B.A. in journalism and has been a freelance journalist reporting on current affairs, women's issues, the environment, politics and the arts.

Neville is the Technical Director of Esoteric Technologies, starting his role of developing the Solar suite of products in 2007. He is also the author of Astracadabra, the astrology program for Pocket PCs. Neville has been a keen student of astrology since 1970 studying the various techniques of western and vedic astrology. He has also been in the computer industry since 1970 and has been a full-time software developer since 1986.

Graham Dawson was one of the founders of Esoteric Technologies and one of the authors of the Solar suite of astrology programs. He holds a Practitioner's Certificate and Diploma from the Federation of Australian Astrologers and holds a B.Sc. in Physics and Meteorology and a Ph.D. in Coastal Oceanography.

Chapter 2: Finding the Information You Need

If you are new to the Solar Fire program, then you should first read the sections Installing Solar Fire and Finding Your Way Around Solar Fire. This presents some basic information about the manner in which the program operates.

If you are familiar with the basic concepts and method of operation, but you wish to find out how to achieve a specific task, then you may like to refer to relevant chapters in the body of the manual as the need arises.

If you are upgrading your version of Solar Fire from earlier versions, then you may wish to refer to the section that contains a summary of differences between this version and older versions.

If you wish to find out by which methods charts have been calculated, or how certain information in a report has been produced, and other advanced topics, then you will need to refer to the on-line user guide instead of the printed (or PDF) manual. Due to the very comprehensive nature of Solar Fire, the printed manual cannot contain detailed information on every aspect of the program. The most detailed (and generally most up-to-date) information and help can always be obtained through Solar Fire's on-line help facilities.

>> To get context sensitive information or help anywhere in Solar Fire

Use the **F1** key.

>> To get access to the full on-line user guide and help

• Use the **F1** key from anywhere in Solar Fire – this opens the on-line guide to a location relevant to your current location in Solar Fire.

• Use **Solar Fire User Guide...** from the **Help** menu – this opens the on-line user guide at the contents page, and you can look through the list of contents to find what you need.

Chapter 3: Installing Solar Fire

Computer System Requirements

Before installing the program, ensure that you have all the hardware and software you need to run Solar Fire:

- An PC or compatible computer with a Pentium processor or equivalent

- A CD or DVD drive

- Windows 98, 98SE, ME, NT4, 2000, XP, Vista or later. (Windows XP or Vista recommended)

- For Windows 98, 98SE - 32 MB of RAM minimum (64 MB of RAM or more recommended)

- For Windows ME, NT4 - 40 MB of RAM minimum (80 MB of RAM or more recommended)

- For Windows 2000 - 72 MB of RAM minimum (144 MB of RAM or more recommended)

- For Windows XP - 128 MB of RAM minimum (256 MB of RAM or more recommended)

- For Windows Vista - 256 MB of RAM minimum (512 MB of RAM or more recommended)

- A SVGA (800x600) monitor and adapter with 256 or more colors (XGA 1024x768 or higher resolution modes with True Color is recommended)

- A hard disk drive with at least 130Mb of free disk space (or about 60Mb for a compact installation with minimal features installed)

- Internet access is recommended

Installation
>> To Install Solar Fire

1. Insert the Solar Fire installation CD into you CD ROM drive

2. After a short delay, the installation will start. (If it does not start automatically then use Start/Run/Browse to find INSTALL.EXE on the CD, and then click on the OK button to run it.)

3. The installation program will guide you through the subsequent steps. You will be shown licensing information and any other important last minute information before the installation goes ahead.

4. You will also be prompted to enter your name, serial number and password as supplied to you by your vendor. Note that you must enter these three items exactly as they as given to you, including the same spelling and spacing.

5. You may then choose the location for your installation. Unless you are familiar with folders and directories, and have a reason for altering the suggested location, then it is recommended that you proceed without altering the suggested location.

6. You can then choose one of the following setup types

•   **Typical** – This installs the entire program with all options included. This is the recommended option for most users.

•   **Compact** – This installs the program with a reduced ephemeris range and no additional asteroid ephemerides. This option is recommended for those users who wish to conserve space on their computers, and have no interest in charts prior to 1200BC or after 3000AD, or in the additional asteroids.

•   **Custom** – This allows you to choose exactly which items to install. This option is only recommended for expert users who are re-installing parts of the program.

If You are Re-installing Solar Fire

The installation program will find your existing installation location and suggest that you re-install it there.

If You are Upgrading from an Earlier Version of Solar Fire

It is recommended that you install Solar Fire into its own new folder instead of into the same folder of your earlier version. Note that Solar Fire allows you to import copies of your old charts, files and other settings from your earlier version. Solar Fire will ask you if you wish to do this when it first runs.

If You Own a Copy of Solar Maps v3

This version of Solar Fire includes Solar Maps v2 Lite. However, if you already have a full version of Solar Maps installed on your computer, then Solar Fire will use your full copy of Solar Maps in preference to its less powerful built-in version. (You will need to install the latest patch update to Solar Maps v3 if your existing version is v3.0.12 or earlier.)

If You Own a Copy of Solar Maps v1

Solar Maps v1 can be used on its own (or with an earlier version of Solar Fire) but cannot be used interactively with Solar Fire Gold v7. If you wish to get the benefit of a full version of Solar Maps working interactively with Solar Fire Gold v7, then you will need to upgrade to Solar Maps v3 or higher, which works seamlessly with Solar FireGold v7.

First Run Setup Tasks

The first time that Solar Fire runs after it has been installed, you will be prompted to allow some initial setup tasks to be performed.

These initial tasks are

• Checking for program updates via the Internet – if an update it found, then it is recommended that you download and install it before proceeding further. If you do not have an Internet connection, or you would prefer not to do this now, you can do so at any later time by choosing the appropriate option from the Help menu.

• Importing Charts, Files and Settings from an earlier version of Solar Fire – this option is available only if you still have an earlier version of Solar Fire on your computer. If you prefer not to do this now, you can do it at any later time by selecting the appropriate option from the Utilities menu.

• Obtaining the "Solar Live" list of links via the Internet – this will ensure that you have the latest available information. If you prefer not to do this now, you can do so at any later time by choosing the appropriate option from the Help menu.

Further Manual Setup

Connecting to the ACS Atlas

Besides having its own place database and its own built-in ACS Atlas, Solar Fire interfaces seamlessly with the stand-alone ACS atlases if you have one of them installed on your computer. Solar Fire works with:

- ACS PC Atlas, version 2.x or 3.x

- ACS PC Atlas for Windows

- ACS PC Mini Atlas

Solar Fire does not work with the ACS PC Atlas version 1.x for DOS. If you try to use an ACS Atlas while running Solar Fire and get the error message "Invalid TIMZON.BIN file", it means that you have the ACS PC Atlas version 1. In this case, contact your dealer to have it upgraded to a current version.

>> To connect to an ACS Atlas

If you have a standalone ACS Atlas already on your hard disk, then Solar Fire will connect with it automatically in preference to Solar Fire's built-in atlas. However, you can select any of up to three different atlases in Solar Fire by clicking on the Places tab of the Preferences dialog. See Places for more details.

Setting Your Computers Internal Clock

On its Main Screen, Solar Fire has a constantly updated display of current planetary positions. In several of its data-input screens it has a "Now" button that automatically inserts the current date and time. For these features to work correctly, you should ensure that your computer's internal clock is correctly set.

Most modern computers with internet connections will not need adjusting, as they automatically check and synchronize their clocks via the internet. However, some older computers may not keep accurate time, or you may want to change from Standard to Daylight or Summer time or vice-versa, if Windows has not done this for you automatically.

>> To set the computer's internal clock

Click on the current date or time panel of the status bar across the top of the main screen of Solar Fire. This will open up the Control Panel dialog that allows you to reset the date and time as required.

Selecting a Time Format

To choose between AM/PM and 24-hour time format, you also need to use the Windows control panel. Solar Fire lets you enter time in virtually any format - the time format you select here determines how times are written in Solar Fire displays and printouts. Your computer will probably already be preset to whatever time format is usually used in your country.

>> To reset the time format

From the Windows Control Panel, select the "Regional Settings" icon. In the "Time" tab or area of the screen, you can select various time format options, including whether a 12hr or 24hr clock is used, and how AM/PM is displayed.

Selecting a Date Format

In most cases the computer will already be preset to show dates using the normal convention for your country. Solar Fire displays dates in its own format, but decides on whether to show the International order (Day, Month, Year) or the American order (Month, Day, Year) according to the format that you select with in the Control Panel.

>> To reset the date format

From the Windows Control Panel, select the "Regional Settings" icon. In the "Date" tab or area of the screen, you can select various date format options, including the order in which the day and month appear.

Setting the Default Place

On its Main Screen, Solar Fire has a constantly updated display of the current Ascendant and Midheaven for whatever location is currently selected as the default place. When you first install Solar Fire, this default place will probably not be set to the place where you currently live. It is recommended that you set the default place to the location where you are currently living, so that the displayed Ascendant and Midheaven will be correct for you own location. Solar Fire also uses the default place that you set as a "first guess" whenever you choose to relocate a chart to a new location. If this is set to your current location, then this guess will probably often be correct, and this will save you from having to enter new location details needlessly.

>> To set the default place

1.   Click on the Place panel of the Date and Place status bar.

2.   If your current location is one that is already listed in the list of Favorite Places, then select it with the mouse.

3.   Otherwise click on the **Add...** button to open the Atlas and either find your location or enter it a new location. See Using Place Databases for full instructions on choosing a place from the Atlas.

4.   Once your location appears on the list of favorite places, then select it with the mouse and select the **Set as Default** button.

5.   You can then click on the **Save** button to return to the Main Screen.

The location shown in the status bar at the top of the Main Screen will now show the newly saved location, and the Ascendant and Midheaven will be correct for this location.

You will need to update the default place details in the same way whenever you move with your computer to a new place.

Pre-Setting Calculation Options

Solar Fire is shipped to you with the most commonly used chart options already selected for you. Choices like house system, coordinate system and zodiac are easy to find, as they appear on the "New Chart Data Entry" screen itself. However, there are some less frequently used options that can be set in the "Preferences" dialog of Solar Fire, and you may like to set them before you start calculating charts.

- Geocentric Latitude Correction

- Lunar Parallax Correction

- Lunar Node Type

- Zodiac

- Angle Progressions

- Progression Day Type

- User Progression Rate

- Primary Direction Rate

- Vulcan Calculation

- Part of Fortune

These options are described in detail in Changing Preferences.

Customizing the Compliments Text

Most chart and grid pages printed from Solar Fire contain some text placed on a corner of the page that gives the name and address of your software supplier. You can alter this text to display your own name and address (or any customized message) if you wish.

>> To change the compliments text

1.   Select the **Edit Settings...** item from the **Preferences** menu on the Main Screen.

2.   Select the Compliments tab.

3.   This will display six lines of text that you can freely edit.

4.   When you click on the **Save** button, any charts subsequently printed will display the newly edited compliments text, and this text will also be permanently retained by Solar Fire for future sessions.

Chapter 4: Finding Your Way Around Solar Fire

We have designed the Solar Fire program to be flexible and easy to use. There are often several different ways of achieving the same objective, and it is up to each individual user to decide the manner in which they prefer to proceed.

Most operations, such as casting a new chart, will be very easy to learn for those who are experienced astrologers, and the intuitive manner of operation of the program should enable inexperienced astrologers to proceed almost as quickly.

To facilitate data entry and selection, most dialog boxes have default values, so that it is not necessary to enter new data every time the screen is used. Generally, whenever a dialog box is called up, it will initially contain all the values that were entered into that box the last time it was used. For example, when a new chart is cast, the chart's name, date, time, location, house type etc. are all retained. The next time that a new chart is cast, it will only be necessary to update the items that need to be changed. This makes it very quick and easy to generate the same chart with a different house system, or with a slightly different birth time, for example.

Starting Solar Fire

>> To start Solar Fire

• Activate the Solar Fire icon on your desktop, or

• From the **Start** button menu select Programs / Solar Fire / Solar Fire Gold, or

• Find and open the Solar Fire folder, and then double-click the Solar Fire Gold program icon.

When the program loads, an initial screen will be displayed showing an end-user license message. The first time the program is run after installation, you must click on the OK button to acknowledge the license agreement. On subsequent occasions, this screen will disappear automatically after a few seconds.

Using Solar Fire

When you start Solar Fire, the main screen appears, ready for you to create
charts. To use the program, you will need to be able to select menu items
and command buttons, enter information into dialog boxes, and use scroll
bars and list boxes. If you are unfamiliar with using menus, dialog boxes,
list boxes and scroll bars, then it is desirable that you read your Windows
documentation to familiarize yourself with these concepts.

Solar Fire's Main Screen

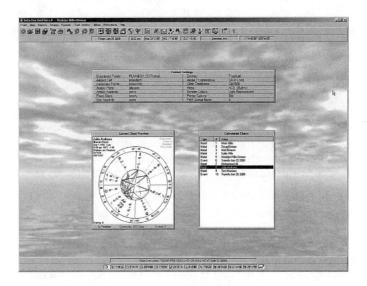

Solar Fire's main screen consists of the following components.

- Menu

- Toolbar

- Date and Place

- Current Settings

- Current Chart Preview

- Calculated Charts

- Solar Live Latest Link

- Planet Bar

- Background

Each of these is described in more detail in the following sections. Note that you can switch off some of these components by using options under the **Preferences** menu.

Menu

The menu provides access to all the available functions and actions that Solar Fire can perform. Some menu items can be activated by shortcuts – either particular key combinations, or via toolbar buttons or the current settings panel, for example.

Toolbar

The toolbar contains a range of graphical buttons that provide shortcuts to various items within Solar Fire. It may be customized by changing the selection or ordering of the buttons it contains, and can also be switched off altogether if you prefer. See Editing the Toolbar Buttons for instructions on customizing the toolbar.

Date and Place

The Date and Place bar contains the current system date and time, the current Ascendant and Midheaven positions, and the current place name and timezone details. If the details shown are incorrect then you can change them as follows.

>> To change the date

Click on the date box in this panel. This will display the control panel utility that allows you to adjust the date on your computer system.

>> To change the time

Click on the time box in this panel. This will display the control panel utility that allows you to adjust the date on your computer system.

>> To change the place

Click on the place box in this panel. This will display the Preferences dialog for editing and selecting your current location from an atlas. See Current Default Place for more details. Changing the place will usually result in the correct timezone being displayed as well.

>> To change the timezone

Click on the timezone box in this panel. This will display a timezone selection panel from which you can select the correct timezone.

Note: The Ascendant and Midheaven positions are calculated according to the date, time and place details as displayed in the other boxes on this panel. However, other options that affect these positions are

• The Geocentric Latitude Correction – See Apply Geocentric Correction to Latitude for further information.

• The Default Zodiac type – See Default Zodiac for further information.

Current Settings

The current setting panel displays a range of items that reflect how various options have been set. For example, the name of the currently selected displayed points file, aspect set, default zodiac and screen colors are all shown here.

As well as allowing you to see what options are in effect, this panel provides a shortcut to altering these options, simply by clicking on the option you wish to change. For example, clicking on the Displayed Points area will cause the File Manager to appear with a list of displayed point selections, allowing you to select an alternative file or perform various other functions.

Current Chart Preview

The current chart preview panel displays a preview style wheel (see Wheel Styles and Dial Styles) and chart details of whichever calculated chart is currently selected – or optionally the wheel may be switched off and just chart details and comments displayed. The chart's astrological settings, such as its coordinates, house system and zodiac are shown at the upper right of the preview window. Any such settings that differ from Solar Fire's current defaults for those settings are highlighted to draw your attention to them.

>> To change the chart preview display type

Use a right hand mouse click while the mouse is over the Chart Preview panel.

This will display a pop-up menu with the following options.

- **Chart Wheel** – Display a preview chart wheel with small captions

- **Chart Details** – Display larger chart captions

- **Chart Details & Comments** – Display chart captions and chart comments (if any)

- **Preview Wheel Style** – Allowing you to select an alternative wheel style to display

The following information is also displayed just below the preview window.

- **Save Status** – This is a caption that indicates whether or not this chart is already saved in a chart file. The text can be "Not Saved", "Saved", "Retained" or "Cannot be Saved". If the current chart was opened from a file, or was saved to a file, then hovering the mouse over this item causes a pop-up hint to appear showing the filename and record number of the chart, and clicking on this item will cause the **Chart Open** dialog to appear, displaying this file and highlighting this chart entry in it.

- **Comments** – This is text that indicates whether or not any comments have been added to this chart, and if so how many characters of text. Clicking on this item will open up the comments editing dialog in which you can see the comments and edit them if you wish.

- **Events** – This is text that indicates whether or not any life events have been added to this chart, and if so how many events. Clicking on this item will open up the events editing dialog in which you can see the events and add, delete or edit them if you wish.

Calculated Charts

The calculated charts panel contains a list of all the charts that are currently available in Solar Fire.

You can add to this list by casting new charts, opening saved charts, or generating subsidiary charts using various options in the **Chart** menu.

You can select any number of charts in this list by using the mouse and Ctrl or Shift keys. (The Current Chart Preview panel will always display the details of the most recently selected chart.) Some function in Solar Fire will allow all your selected charts to be processed, whilst others can work only with the single current chart. For example, when you choose View / Current Chart or Chart / Save to File, all the selected charts will be processed. However, when you choose Interps / View, only the current chart is used.

You can also delete charts from this list if you wish.

Planet Bar

The planet bar panel contains the current positions of the ten main chart bodies, as well as information on lunar phases and eclipses. Planets that are currently in retrograde motion are shown in red, and those that are direct are shown in black. These positions are automatically updated on a regular basis.

You can get further information about each planet or item by moving the mouse over its box. This will cause a "hint" type message to appear, giving the following information.

• The Moon and the Sun – Sign, date and time of last sign ingress, and of next sign ingress.

• Other Planets – Date and time and position of last and next planetary station.

• Lunar Phases - Date and time of the last and next new or full moon.

• Eclipses - Date, time and eclipse type of the last and next eclipses.

Background

The background of the main screen may be customized to show either a uniform color or a user-selected graphic.

>> To set the main screen background options

Click the right-hand mouse button anywhere over the background area of the main screen.

This will bring up a pop-up menu with the following options.

• **Background Graphic...** - This will display a file selection dialog allowing you to browse for a graphic file that you wish to display. This must be a file of type *.bmp, *.rle, *.gif, *.jpg, *.jpeg, *.wmf, *.emf, *.ico.

Once selected the graphic will be either tiled or stretched according to the option selected below.

• **Background Color...** - This will display a color selection dialog allowing you to select any desired color. Note that you must clear any existing graphic file before this change will take effect.

• **Clear Graphic** – This will clear any graphic file that has been previously selected, in which case the current background color will be applied.

• **Tile** – If a graphic file is being displayed, this will tile the graphic to fill the entire background area.

• **Stretch** - If a graphic file is being displayed, this will stretch the graphic to fill the entire background area.

Exiting from Solar Fire

>> To exit from the program

Select the **Exit** option from the **Chart** menu. If you have cast any new charts during your session that have not been saved, then the program will prompt you to save them as part of the exit procedure.

Using On-line Help

Solar Fire has comprehensive on-line help, which can be invoked from anywhere within the program.

>> To invoke help from any screen

Press the **F1** key. This will call up a Windows help screen containing information about whichever screen or control currently has the focus. This is known as *context sensitive* help.

>> To invoke help from the menu

Select the **Contents** option from the **Help** Menu -This will display the contents page of the on-line help file.

Once the help screen is displayed, it is possible to navigate through the text and topics as desired, and to select any of the options that are available in Windows help files.

Using the Keyboard

Although Windows is most easily used with a mouse, use of the keyboard is compulsory for certain data entry items, and it is possible to perform almost all operations from the keyboard instead of the mouse if this is desired.

Additionally, there are various "short-cut" keys that enable some tasks to be invoked more quickly from the keyboard then by using a mouse.

Dialog Boxes

Movement and editing within a dialog box may be carried out according to the key definitions as described in your Windows manual. A brief reminder of some of these keys follows.

TAB	Move from option to option
SHIFT+TAB	Move from option to option in reverse order
ALT+character	Move to option whose letter matches character
Arrow key	Move cursor within a data box
HOME	Move cursor to start of data within a data box
END	Move cursor to end of data within a data box
INSERT	Toggle between type over and insert modes
DELETE	Delete the next character or the selected text
BACKSPACE	Delete the previous character
ENTER	Activate the dialog box's default

	command button
SHIFT+cursor	Select text across which cursor moves

When the text in a dialog box is selected (highlighted), then typing any text will cause the existing text to be deleted. To avoid this, use the END or cursor keys to switch off the selection of text before typing any characters.

Short-Cut Keys

A variety of short-cut keys have been defined within Solar Fire to facilitate the activation of certain frequently used menu options without having to use the mouse. Each short-cut key combination activates an item from the menu. A list of these keys follows.

F1	Context sensitive help
F2	New chart
F3	Open chart
F4	Progressed chart
F5	Return chart
F6	Harmonic chart
F7	Combined chart
F8	Prenatal chart
F9	Rising/Setting chart
F11	Lunar Phase chart
F12	Save chart to file
CTRL+F1	Dual Wheels

CTRL+F2	BiWheel
CTRL+F3	TriWheel
CTRL+F4	QuadriWheel
CTRL+F5	Synastry grid
CTRL+F6	User defined page
CTRL+F7	Planetarium
CTRL+F8	Solar Maps
CTRL+A	Aspect set
CTRL+C	View current chart
CTRL+D	Displayed points
CTRL+E	Edit current chart
CTRL+G	View current chart+grid
CTRL+H	View current grid
CTRL+I	View Interpretations
CTRL+L	Toggle lunar node type
CTRL+N	Edit chart events
CTRL+P	Print chart/s
CTRL+R	Restore settings
CTRL+S	Save settings
CTRL+T	Aspected Points
CTRL+V	View last image

CTRL+Z	Toggle chart zodiac
SHIFT+F1	Reports for current chart
SHIFT+F2	Synastry reports
SHIFT+F3	Dynamic report
SHIFT+F4	Graphic Ephemeris
SHIFT+F5	Eclipse Search
SHIFT+F6	Electional Search
SHIFT+F1 2	Locality chart
SHIFT+INS	Edit chart comments
DEL	Delete current chart
CTRL+INS	Copy&edit current chart

When you are viewing interpretations in the interpretations window, the following short-cut keys apply

F2	Previous information type
F3	Next information type
CTRL+C	Current Chart Mode
CTRL+G	General Mode

Chart Calculation and Storage

When the Solar Fire program saves and reads charts to and from chart databases, only the chart details are stored eg. name, date, time, location, etc.. Planetary positions and house cusp positions are not stored in a chart database file.

However, once a new chart is cast in the program or opened from a chart database, all planetary positions and house cusps are calculated and stored until the user exits from the program. These are known as "Calculated Charts", and the main screen displays a list of all such charts in a list box.

It is only possible to display a chart, aspect grid, report, or to generate any subsidiary charts, after that chart has been calculated and is listed in the "Calculated Charts" list box on the main screen.

Calculated charts can be of any type - natal, progressed, return, composite, harmonic, etc.

The following table summarizes which chart types may be used in each type of operation. The ☼ symbol denotes that it is possible to perform the operation in the left hand column on the chart type at the top of that column.

The chart operations are as follows.

Open	To retrieve chart details from a chart file and calculate the chart
Save	To store the details of a chart to a chart database file
Edit	To copy and edit an existing calculated chart
Delete	To delete a chart from the list of calculated charts
Retain	To retain calculated charts for use in future sessions
Progress	To calculate a progressed or directed chart from a base chart
Return	To calculate a planet or asteroid return chart from a base chart
Combine	To calculate a combined chart from two or more base charts
Harmonic	To calculate an harmonic or arc transform chart from a base

	chart
Antiscia	To calculate an antiscia or contra-antiscia chart from a base chart
Locality	To calculate a relocated or locality chart from a base chart
View	To view a calculated chart or aspect grid on the screen or to print it
Report	To generate a report from a base chart
Dynamic	To generate a transits/progressions report or graphic ephemeris from a base chart

Charts which are equivalent to Natal are - Return, Ingress, Transit, Davison, Lunar Phase, Lunar Phase Return, Rise/Set, Prenatal, Relocated

	Calculated Chart Type				
Operation	Natal or Equivalent	Progressed/ Directed	Composite/ Coalescent	Harmonic	Antiscia/ Contra-antiscia
Open	✪	✪	✪	✪	✪
Save	✪	✪	✪	✪	✪
Edit	✪	-	-	-	-
Delete	✪	✪	✪	✪	✪
Retain	✪	✪	✪	✪	✪
Progress	✪	-	-	-	-
Return	✪	-	-	-	-
Combine	✪	✪	-	✪	✪
Harmonic	✪	✪	✪	-	✪

	Calculated Chart Type				
Operation	Natal or Equivalent	Progressed/ Directed	Composite/ Coalescent	Harmonic	Antiscia/ Contra-antiscia
Antiscia	✺	✺	✺	✺	-
Locality	✺	✺	✺	✺	✺
View	✺	✺	✺	✺	✺
Report	✺	✺	✺	✺	✺
Dynamic	✺	✺	✺	✺	✺

Chapter 5: A Guided Tour of Solar Fire

Once you've carried out a few simple tasks in Solar Fire, you'll probably be able to run most of the program without reference to the manual. This section takes you through the basic tasks and gives you an idea of the many things that Solar Fire can do.

If you have never used any version of Solar Fire before, then the easiest way to learn the program is to go through this chapter and try out each operation that is described. If you are eager to plunge in on your own, we recommend that you start with the tasks labeled with an asterisk (*), below.

If you have already used earlier versions of Solar Fire, then you can skip most of this section, simply noting the parts that are new.

- Starting Solar Fire (*)
- Casting a natal chart (*)
- Casting a solar return chart (*)
- Viewing and printing a biwheel
- Viewing and printing a synastry grid
- Changing the aspect set and redrawing a chart

Casting a Natal Chart

The steps involved in calculating and displaying or printing a new natal chart are as follows.

1.   Select the **New...** option from the **Chart** menu on the main screen.

2.   Enter all the natal details, including name, date, time, place and timezone. (It is possible to use the **Place...** or **Zone...** buttons to choose an existing location or timezone.)

3.   Select a house system, coordinate system and zodiac type from the available choices on the screen. (Normally, western astrologers use Placidus or Koch houses, geocentric coordinates and the tropical zodiac.)

4.   Optionally select a chart type, chart ratings and source comment.

5.   Click on the **OK** button. The program will then calculate all the planetary positions and house cusps, and add the chart to the list of Calculated Charts on the main screen.

6.   Select the **Current Chart** option from the **View** menu on the main screen.

7.   To print the chart on your printer, select the **Print...** button from the "View Chart" screen, or select the **Print Chart...** option from the **View** menu on the main screen.

Casting a Solar Return Chart

The steps involved in calculating and displaying or printing a solar return chart are as follows.

1.   Either cast a new chart or open the existing chart for which you wish to generate a solar return chart.

2.   Select the **Return & Ingress...** option from the **Chart** menu on the main screen.

3.   Select the chart that you wish to use by clicking on the charts list, and ensure that the selected calculation method is "Solar Return".

4.   Optionally enter a date and select which solar return you require, and the details of the place for which you wish the solar return to be calculated. (It is possible to use the "Location" option buttons or the **Place...** or **Zone...** buttons to choose an existing location or timezone.)

5.   Click on the **OK** button - The program will then calculate all the planetary positions and house cusps, and add the chart to the list of Calculated Charts on the main screen.

6.   Select the **Current Chart** option from the **View** menu on the main screen.

7.   To print the chart on your printer, select the **Print...** button from the "View Chart" screen, or select the **Print Chart...** option from the **View** menu on the main screen.

Displaying or Printing a BiWheel

The steps involved in displaying or printing a biwheel chart are as follows.

1.   Either cast new charts or open the existing charts that you wish to use in the biwheel.

2.   Select the **BiWheel...** option from the **View** menu on the main screen.

3.   Select the charts that you wish to place on the inner and outer wheels by clicking on the charts list and the positions list.

4.   Click on the **View** button - The biwheel will then be drawn on the "View Chart" screen.

5.   To print the biwheel on your printer, select the **Print...** button from the "View Chart" screen, or repeat the first 3 steps above and then select **Print...** button from the "BiWheel Selection" dialog box.

Displaying or Printing a Synastry Grid

The steps involved in displaying or printing a synastry grid are as follows.

1.   Either cast new charts or open the existing charts that you wish to use in the grid.

2.   Select the **Synastry Grid...** option from the **View** menu on the main screen.

3.   Select the charts that you wish to place across and down the grid by clicking on the charts list and the positions list.

4.   Click on the **View** button - The grid will then be drawn on the "View Chart" screen.

5.   To print the grid on your printer, select the **Print...** button from the "View Chart" screen, or repeat the first 3 steps above and then select **Print...** button from the "Synastry Grid Selection" dialog box.

Changing Aspects

The usual steps involved in changing the aspect set and viewing a chart with the new aspect set are as follows.

1.   Select the **Aspect Set...** option from the **Chart Options** menu on the main screen.

2.   Select the name of an alternative aspect set from the list, and click on the **Select** button. (It is possible to first create or edit the contents of an existing aspect set by clicking on the **Create...** or **Edit...** buttons.)

3.   Select the **Last Image** option from the **View** menu on the main screen - The last image that you created will then appear on the "View Chart" screen. In order to redraw any of the existing chart images with new aspect set:

4. Click on the required entry in the list of images.

5. Select the **ReDraw** button from the "View Chart" screen.

Help and Web Support

In order to use any of the automated email options in Solar Fire, you must have a MAPI compliant email program. See About MAPI for further information.

However, note that if your email program cannot be configured for MAPI, you can still create your own email and paste the email data created by Solar Fire into the body of the email.

In order to run any of the internet related functions of Solar Fire, you need either to be already connected to the internet when you run them, or to have the possibility of connecting when prompted to do so.

Register by Email

Registration is desirable, but not obligatory, in order to keep us informed of your current contact details.

It is helpful to re-register whenever you change your street or email address.

\>> **To register by email**

Select the **Register by Email** menu item from the **Help** menu

This will display the **Confirm Current Details** dialog box.

Once you have entered or updated your details, click on the "Proceed" button to open your default email program with a new email containing your registration details, and addressed to us. You can then preview the email and send it at your leisure.

Find Program Updates on Web

>> **To find program updates on the web**

Select the **Check for Updates on the Web** menu item from the **Help** menu

If your computer is not already connected to the internet, then you will be prompted to connect, or connection will start automatically, depending on the internet connection options in your operating system.

When a connection is established, your current program version number will be automatically compared with the latest available version number over the internet, and if an update is available, you will be asked whether you wish to proceed with the update.

If so then your default web browser will open and display a web page containing links to download and install the latest software updates.

Note: Using this option does not send any information about you over the internet apart from your current program version information, and that information is not retained.

Get Technical Support by Email

It is possible to get technical support by letter, phone, fax or email. However, the most efficient means of contact for us is by email, and if you use this built-in option, it increases the likelihood of a rapid resolution because of the detailed information that it automatically provides us about your program setup.

>> **To get technical support by email**

Select the **Get Technical Support by Email** menu item from the **Help** menu

Firstly, you will be prompted to enter your contact registration details.

Once you have entered or updated your details, click on the "Proceed" button to open your default email program with a new email containing your registration details, program setup information, some computer configuration information, and addressed to us.

You can then preview the email, insert a description of your problem or query, and send it at your leisure.

Submit Suggestions by Email

Our philosophy of software design is to create software that addresses the needs and desires of the users. Consequently we welcome any feedback and suggestions that you might feel inspired to send us.

>> To submit suggestions by email

Select the **Submit Suggestions by Email** menu item from the **Help** menu

Firstly, you will be prompted to enter your contact registration details.

Once you have entered or updated your details, click on the "Proceed" button to open your default email program with a new email containing your registration details.

You can then preview the email, insert your feedback or suggestion, and send it at your leisure.

Encyclopedia

>> To open the on-line Encyclopedia

Select the **Encyclopedia** menu item from the **Help** menu

This encyclopedia contains definitions and articles from Nicholas deVore's original 'Encyclopedia of Astrology' with edits and updates by Esoteric Technologies Pty Ltd, 2007. Nicholas deVore, 1882-1960, was President of the New York based Astrological Research Society.

Importing Charts, Files and Settings

If you have owned an earlier version of Solar Fire, and it is still installed on your computer, or if you have a copy of Solar Fire on another disk which is accessible to your computer (via a network or other link), then it may be possible to import copies of charts files, other files and Solar Fire settings and Preferences from those other copies of Solar Fire.

The main benefits of this utility are

• Upon first installation, to allow you to automatically set up Solar Fire Gold v7 in the same way as your previous version of Solar Fire.

• At any later time, to import chart files from Solar Fire on another computer.

Note: Due to the flexibility of Solar Fire in allowing a variety of user-created files and settings and the fact that there are many differences in design of different versions of Solar Fire, this import process may not always be 100% successful in setting up Solar Fire exactly as you would like. You may find after importing settings that you still need to make several adjustments to settings manually.

>> To open the import dialog

Select **Import Charts and Settings** from the **Utilities** menu.

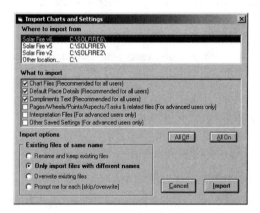

Where to Import From

When this dialog opens, it searches for earlier versions of Solar Fire on your computer, and if any are found, adds them to the list titled **Where to import from**, including their folder paths.

The final entry in the list is **Other Location...**, which will be a blank entry initially, or otherwise points to the last location your specified here.

>> To set or change the Other Location

Click on the **Other Location...** list item.

This will display a file open dialog, allowing you to navigate to the desired location (which may also be on another disk or another computer on a network). You must locate and select the file **solfire.exe** in the Solar Fire folder that you require. Once you have done so, the newly selected folder path of the selected location will be displayed in the list.

What to Import

You can choose what items to import by clicking in their checkboxes individually, or by using the **All On** or **All Off** buttons.

The items that may be selected for importing are as follows.

- **Chart Files** – All Solar Fire type chart files and chart comments files (with file extensions *.SFcht, *.cht and *.chm).

- **Pages/Wheels/Points/Aspects/Tasks & related files** – All Solar Fire type files of these various types, including color schemes. This will include any user created files of these types that you may have stored with the other copy of Solar Fire. *Note:* If you also select Other Saved Settings, then all settings relating to these files such as your default displayed point set, aspect set and color scheme setting will also be set for you.

- **Interpretation Files** – All Solar Fire interpretation files (with file extensions *.int). *Note:* If you also select Other Saved Settings, then the default interpretation file settings will also be set for you.

- **Default Place Details** – The location and timezone that is set within the other copy of Solar Fire.

- **Compliments Text** - The compliments text that is set within the other copy of Solar Fire.

- **Other Saved Settings** – Most other settings and preferences.

Note: If you are using **Other location...**, then any files types can be imported, but place, compliments and other settings cannot, and will be omitted from the list.

Import Options

•   **Rename and keep existing files** – Use this option to ensure that all existing files are kept and remain available in addition to any newly imported files. Any existing files in your current copy of Solar Fire that have the same name as files you are importing are simply renamed first, by appending a number to the end of the existing file name (eg. Main.cht is renamed to Main_2.cht).

•   **Only import Files with different names** – Use this option to keep all existing files, and import only those files that have different names from existing files.

•   **Overwrite existing files** – Use this option to adopt all imported files, keeping only those existing files that have a different name from any of those being imported.

•   **Prompt me for each (skip/overwrite)** – Use this option to decide on a file by file basis whether to import any existing file which has the same name as an existing file.

Note: that you can use different import options with different import items. To do so, just choose one item on the **What to Import** list to import at a time, and set the require import option separately for each one before importing.

Chapter 6: Casting a New Chart

This chapter describes how to enter data to cast a new natal or event chart.
The same conventions apply to entering data for subsidiary charts,
dynamic report and all other places where you would enter dates, times or
places.

Pre-Setting Calculation Options

There are several options in Solar Fire that affect the calculation of the
chart. If you wish to alter them, then you must do so before the chart is
cast, as you cannot set them on the "New Chart Data Entry" screen. These
options are

Geocentric Latitudes - Whether or not the entered latitude is converted to
a geocentric latitude. Most astrologers do not use geocentric latitude.

Lunar Parallax - Whether or not a correction is made to the moon's
position due to location. Most astrologers do not correct the moon for
parallax.

Lunar Node Type - Whether the true node or mean node is calculated.
Astrologers today are fairly evenly divided on this issue.

Vulcan Calculation - Which method of calculating Vulcan's position is
used. This option is only relevant if you intend to display Vulcan in your
chart. Most astrologers do not display Vulcan.

Part of Fortune - Which formula is used to calculate the position of the
Part of Fortune in the chart, ie. whether to use Asc+Moon-Sun for both day
and night births, or to change it to Asc+Sun-Moon for night births.

MC in Polar Regions – Which formula is used to calculate the position of
the MC for charts cast in locations when the Sun does not rise across the
horizon during the day.

>> To alter any of the above options

1.   Select the **Edit Settings...** item from the **Preferences** menu on the
Main Screen.

2.   Select the Calculations tab.

3.   Alter any settings as required

See Changing Preferences for more information on these options.

The New Chart Data Entry Dialog Box

>> To begin casting a new chart

Choose **New...** from the **Charts** menu. This will display the "New Chart Data Entry" dialog box into which natal details and chart options may be entered.

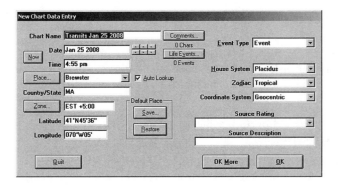

When this dialog box is displayed it will already contain data. If you have not yet cast or opened a chart since the program was started, then the data displayed is whatever has last been saved as default values. (See Saving and Restoring Settings for details of how to alter default values.) Otherwise it will contain the data from the last chart that was cast or opened.

Casting an Instant Chart for Here and Now

To cast a quick chart for the current time and place, you can use the default time and place values that you have already set. This is handy for casting a quick horary or event chart.

>> To calculate a chart for the current moment

Select the **Now** button. The Chart Name box will appear as "Transits of [date]", and the Date and Time fields will be updated to correspond to the computer's internal clock.

>> To calculate a chart for the default place

Select the **Restore** button. The boxes **Place** through to **Longitude** will fill with whatever values were selected for the default place. (You will probably have set the default place to be your current location.)

Entering the Chart Name

Up to 30 characters of text may be entered to describe the chart. Typically this will be the name of the person for whom a birth chart is being cast (eg. "John Smith"), but could also be a description of an event (eg. "President's Inauguration"), or a horary question (eg. "Where are my keys?"). You must enter at least 1 character in the Chart Name box.

Note: If the name you enter contains the string "transit" anywhere, then the event type is automatically set to "Event". If the name you enter ends with a "?", then the event type is automatically set to "Horary". However, you can subsequently alter this automatic event type selection if you wish.

Note: For chart list indexing and when combined charts are being produced, the last item on the line is assumed to be a "last name" (except in the case of Event and Horary charts). Therefore, when entering chart names for a person's natal chart, we recommend that names always be entered with the first name first, and the last name last.

Entering a Date

You can enter the date in almost any format you like, and when you leave the date box, the date will be converted into Solar Fire's standard format. If you enter an impossible date such as February 30 or a month number greater than 12, or use a format that the program does not understand, then you will get an error message and be given a chance to try again.

There is also a group of three spin buttons to the right of the date entry box. These buttons allow you increment the individual parts of the date upwards or downwards without having to retype the entire date. For example, the rightmost spin button allows you to change the year number up or down by one year at a time.

Following are some examples of valid dates, and the manner in which they are displayed by the program.

User Entered Date	International Display Format	US Display Format
1 Dec 1992	1 Dec 1992	Dec 1 1992
1 Dec 92	1 Dec 1992	Dec 1 1992
1 Dec 02	1 Dec 2002	Dec 1 2002
Dec 1 1992	1 Dec 1992	Dec 1 1992
1 December 1992	1 Dec 1992	Dec 1 1992
1st December 1992	1 Dec 1992	Dec 1 1992
1 Dec 1992 AD	1 Dec 1992	Dec 1 1992
1 Dec 1992 BC	1 Dec 1992 BC	Dec 1 1992 BC
1 Dec 0092	1 Dec 0092	Dec 1 0092
1/12/92	1 Dec 1992	Jan 12 1992
12.1.92	12 Jan 1992	Dec 1 1992

The display format that Solar Fire uses is based on the date order settings within Windows, which may be set by using the **Regional Settings** icon on the Windows **Control Panel**.

Description of Format

You must enter a day, month and year, separated by any of the following characters: blank( ); slash(/); period(.); colon(:); semi-colon(;) or comma(,). If you use a month name or abbreviation instead of a month number, then you do not need to use any separators. You may also enter just a day number, in which case the last entered month and year are assumed, or just a day and month in which case the last entered year is assumed. You may also enter just a 4 digit year number, in which the day and month are automatically set as 1st January.

• A day number (eg. 1, 2, 3, ..., 31). You may also use any of the following suffixes: "st", "nd", "rd" or "th".

• A month name, abbreviation or number (eg. Jan, Feb, Mar, ..., Dec, or 1, 2, 3, ..., 12). These must be English month names, but may be in upper, lower or mixed case. Abbreviations must contain at least the first three letters of the month name. If you use a month name or abbreviation, then it does not matter whether you put the day or the month first. However, if you use a month number, then you must ensure that you enter the date in whatever order has been set in Windows. See Selecting a Date Format for instructions on settings the Windows date order.

- A year number (eg. 57, 1957, 2005, -6). You may also use any of the following epoch indicators: "AD", "A.D.", "BC", "B.C.", "CE", "C.E.", "BCE", "B.C.E". If you only enter two digits, then the year is assumed to be within the time window specified in the Preference settings. To enter dates in the 1st century, you must use a 00 prefix (eg. 0059 for year 59).

Optionally there may also be any of the following items:

- A calendar style indicator (ie. OS, O.S., NS, N.S.)

The epoch is assumed to be AD unless BC or BCE has been entered, or if the year is negative. If the year is negative, then Solar Fire will automatically convert the year into a BC year, and remove the minus sign. (Note that there is a difference of 1 year between BC years and negative (astronomical) years eg. the year -6 is converted into 7 BC. This is due to the absence of a year 0 in the BC format.)

Modern and Old Calendars

Unless you specify otherwise (by entering an OS or NS suffix), Solar Fire assumes that the dates that you enter

- on or before 14th October 1582 are in the old style (Julian) calendar.

- on or after 15th October 1582 are in the new style (Gregorian) calendar.

The Gregorian calendar was not adopted everywhere at the same time. Sometimes dates after 15th October 1582 are given in terms of the old style calendar (often followed by the initials O.S.). Also, some sources convert pre 1582 dates to new style dates (often followed by the initials N.S.).

If you wish to enter a date on or after the 15th October 1582 which is expressed as an old style date, then add the suffix "OS" or "O.S." to the entered date (eg. 17 Dec 1723 OS).

If you wish to enter a date before the 15th October 1582 which is expressed as a new style date, then add the suffix "NS" or "N.S." to the entered date (eg. 7 Jan 1503 NS).

The way in which these dates are displayed in Solar Fire depends on user-modifiable preferences. You can determine whether or not Solar Fire will automatically convert any entered dates into the default calendar for that date, or alternatively whether any dates that you enter with an OS or NS suffix will always be displayed exactly as they were entered. Additionally, you can specify a range of years between which the OS or NS indicator is displayed with all dates. See Changing Preferences for more details.

The following table shows the adjustment that Solar Fire makes in order to convert from old style to new style dates:-

15 Oct 1582 to 28 Feb 1700	Add 10 days
29 Feb 1700 to 28 Feb 1800	Add 11 days
29 Feb 1800 to 28 Feb 1900	Add 12 days
29 Feb 1900 to 28 Feb 2100	Add 13 days

Entering a Time

The time that you enter should be ordinary clock time of the locality, or "Universal Time". If you enter a Universal Time or Greenwich Mean Time, be sure to change the initials in the **Zone...** box to "UT" or "GMT". If necessary you can also enter a Local Mean Time or a Local Apparent Time which were the prevalent time standards prior to the late 19th century. If you enter time as Local Mean Time or Local Apparent Time then you should enter "LMT" or "LAT" in the **Zone...** box.

There is no need to convert a time to Ephemeris Time (ET), as Solar Fire does this internally whenever it is necessary.

You may enter a time in any of the most commonly used formats. Any characters within the time may be in upper, lower or mixed case. Entered times are always immediately transformed into a standard display format if they are recognized. If they are not recognized as valid times then an error dialog box appears, after which a further attempt may be made.

The display format that Solar Fire uses is based on the time format settings within Windows, which may be set by using the **Regional Settings** icon on the Windows **Control Panel**. See Selecting a Time Format for further details.

Following are some examples of valid times, and the manner in which they are displayed by the program:

User Entry	AM/PM Format	24Hr Format
Noon	12:00 PM	12:00
12	12:00 PM	12:00
12 PM	12:00 PM	12:00
12 AM	0:00 AM	0:00
12:00	12:00 PM	12:00
12:00:00	12:00 PM	12:00
6	6:00 AM	6:00
13:00	1:00 PM	13:00
13:25	1:25 PM	13:25
13:25:49	1:25:49 PM	13:25:49
1:25:49 AM	1:25:49 AM	1:25:49
1:25:49 PM	1:25:49 PM	13:25:49

Description of Format

You must enter at least an hour; minutes and seconds are optional. You can separate hours, minutes and seconds with a blank( ), slash(/), period(.), colon(:),semi-colon(;) or comma(,).

You can enter time in the 24 hour format (with an hour from 0 to 23), or you can use an AM/PM format by typing either AM or PM after the time. If the hour number is less than 12, then there is no need to type AM.

You can also enter any of the following words: "Noon", "Midday" or "Midnight".

Entering Location Details

The location details are: the place name, the country or state, the timezone, the latitude and the longitude. It is possible to enter each of these items manually onto the "New Chart Data Entry" screen, but there are also shortcuts to finding and entering the location details that you need.

>> To restore the default location details

You would normally already have set the default location to be where you live. To retrieve all the details and insert them automatically into the required text boxes, simply select the **Restore** button.

To recall a place that you have used recently, or is on your list of favorite places

Click on the down arrow on the **Place...** drop-down box and select the required place from the list

>> To perform an automatic atlas lookup

1.   Ensure that the **Auto Lookup** check box is checked

2.   Enter the name of the required place into the **Place...** box. You can enter up to 20 characters to describe the location name. Typically this would be city name or city name and state (eg. "London" or "New York NY").

3.   Enter the country or state into the **Country/State** box. You can enter up to 20 characters to describe the country or state (eg. Canada, USA, Australia, NY, MA, NSW, VIC).

4.   As soon as you move the cursor out of the **Country/State** box (or press the Enter key whilst the cursor is still in the **Country/State** box), an atlas lookup will be performed invisibly to you, and if the place is found, then the remaining zone latitude and longitude boxes will be updated with the details stored in the atlas for this place.

5.   If the place is not found in the atlas, then you will see a dialog box informing you of this, and you will be taken into the database dialogs in order to try to find the required place.

>> To perform a manual atlas lookup

Select the **Place...** button. This will display a dialog box that allows the selection or entry of a place from a database of locations. This is described in detail in Using Place Databases. Using this button will cause data to be automatically entered into all the boxes relating to location, including time zone, longitude and latitude. Note that if you are using Solar Fire's own place database, then it may still be necessary to alter the time zone if the current time zone in use is non-standard. (Eg. the place database may enter "GMT +0:00" into the time zone box when London is selected. However, if summer time is in effect then this should be altered to "BST -1:00" by using the **Zone...** button or by entering "BST" into the Zone box.). If you are using the ACS Atlas, then the time zone will be adjusted automatically, if necessary.

If you have already obtained all the location details from the atlas, then you can skip the following sections that describe how to enter timezones, latitudes and longitudes.

Entering a Time Zone

Time zones may be selected either by using the **Zone...** button to display the "Time Zone Selection" screen, or by entering a time zone mnemonic or a time directly into the **Zone...** box.

You can enter standard time zones, Local Mean Time or Local Apparent Time.

• **Standard Time Zones** – These are standards that were adopted by various authorities in order to ensure that all people living in the same region used the same time standard.

• **Local Mean Time (LMT)** – This is the standard time of the longitude of a location. This was used in most places prior to the adoption of standard time zones. Using this standard, the mean position of the Sun is on the meridian at noon, but note that the true Sun varies from this position by up to about 15 minutes either way.

• **Local Apparent Time (LAT)** – This is the time according to the true position of the Sun in its diurnal arc, which is equivalent to sundial time. By this standard, noon occurs on each day when the Sun is exactly on the meridian. This is the standard that was generally used prior to LMT.

>> To enter a time zone using its mnemonic abbreviation

Enter one of the standard 3 or 4 letter time zone abbreviations (eg. "EST", "AEST", "BST", "CWT", etc.). For the program to recognize the abbreviation, it must be in Solar Fire's internal time zone database. If the abbreviation is not recognized, you will see an error dialog box, and you can try again. If it is recognized, then the corresponding zone time will be automatically appended after the abbreviation in the **Zone...** box.

>> To enter a time zone using its time offset

Enter the number of hours (and optionally minutes and seconds) from Universal Time or Greenwich Mean Time eg. +8 or 8 for Pacific Standard Time, or -10:30 for Australian Central Daylight Time. For zones west of Greenwich, use a plus (+) sign or no sign. For zones east of Greenwich, use a minus (-) sign. You must use a colon(:) to separate hours minutes and seconds.

>> To enter Local Mean Time

Type "LMT" into the **Zone...** box. The correct zone time for the current longitude will be appended after the abbreviation in the **Zone...** box, and if you subsequently alter the longitude, this zone time will be amended automatically.

>> To enter Local Apparent Time (Sundial Time)

Type "LAT" into the **Zone...** box. The correct zone time for the current date and location will be appended after the abbreviation in the **Zone...** box, and if you subsequently alter the longitude or date, this zone time will be amended automatically.

>> To choose a time zone from the database of time zones

Select the **Zone...** button. This will display the "Time Zone Selection" dialog box from which a time zone may be selected.

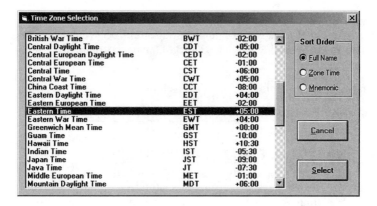

You can alter the order in which entries are shown by selecting the **Sort Order** as follows

- **Full Name** - the records will be sorted into ascending alphabetical order of their full descriptive name.

- **Zone Time** - the records will be sorted into numerical order by their hours from GMT. (Note that the ordering is from 0 to 12 positive numbers followed by 0 to 12 negative numbers).

- **Mnemonic** - the records will be sorted into ascending alphabetical order of their mnemonic abbreviation.

>> To retrieve time zone details to the screen from which the Zone... button was selected

Select the desired time zone entry from the list box

Click on the **Select** button.

Entering Longitudes and Latitudes

Longitudes and latitudes must be entered either in degrees and minutes with a letter indicator of which hemisphere they are in, or as a decimal degree number with its sign indicating which hemisphere (-ve for East or South).

Longitudes and latitude must have at least a degree number (ie. 0 to 180 for longitude, 0 to 90 for latitude) and a hemisphere code (ie. E or W for longitude, N or S for latitude). They may also have a minutes number (ie. 0, 1, 2, 3, ..., 59) and a seconds number. Separators between the numbers may be any of the following: blank( ); slash(/); period(.); colon(:); semi-colon(;) or comma(,).

Some examples of valid longitudes are as follows.

0W 0W0 149e38 78W23 E 167 52 -167.8667

Some examples of valid latitudes are as follows.

0S 0N0 17S58 62n17 S 45 23 -45.3833

Enter ordinary geographic latitudes, even if you want to use the geocentric latitude. (Atlases always give geographic latitudes). If you wish to use geocentric latitudes in chart calculations then you should switch the **Geocentric Lats** option on. See Optional Correction Factors for instructions on how to do this.

Selecting an Event Type

By default, any new chart is labeled as an "Unspecified" chart, which is a catchall name to cover any kind of astrological chart. However, you are also able to select some alternative labels that describe more exactly what type of event the chart describes. Some of these labels are used in other parts of Solar Fire to help display chart information in its most appropriate format.

If the event type that you wish to select is not already highlighted in the **Event Type** list box, then simply find the required event type from the drop-down list and highlight it.

The event types available in Solar Fire are as follows.

• **Unspecified** – This is used for charts which were created in older versions of Solar Fire, or alterative astrology programs when imported into Solar Fire.

• **Male** – use this label for the birth chart of a male. This label is used in synastry reports to apply the correct gender language to the interpretations.

• **Female** – use this label for the birth chart of a female. This label is used in synastry reports to apply the correct gender language to the interpretations.

• **Event** – use this label for any non-natal chart, such as a transit chart or mundane event.

- **Horary** – use this label for any chart which is cast for the purpose of asking an horary question. In this case, the Chart Name can contain the text of the question.

Selecting a House System

If the house system that you wish to use is not already highlighted in the **House System** drop-down list box, then simply find the required house system from the list and highlight it.

You can reset the default house system that is selected whenever you start Solar Fire by altering a preferences setting. See Houses for instructions on selecting the default house system, and a description of what they mean.

Selecting a Zodiac

You can select any of the available zodiac types by highlighting the desired option on the drop-down list of zodiac types.

Most Western astrologers normally use the Tropical zodiac, whereas Sidereal astrologers normally use one of the other (sidereal) zodiacs. Most Western astrologers who practice sidereal astrology use the Fagan-Allen zodiac.

The initial default value of the zodiac selection is set according to your choice of zodiac in the **Preferences** menu. See Zodiac for instructions on changing the default zodiac.

Selecting a Coordinate System

You can select either **geocentric** or **heliocentric** coordinates from the drop-down list of coordinate types.

Most astrologers use the geocentric coordinate system. If you select the heliocentric coordinate system, then the chart will be calculated with heliocentric planetary positions on geocentric houses.

If you do not want to display geocentric houses on a heliocentric chart, then you could select "0 Deg Aries" as your house system, as this is a "neutral" house system which is independent of the chart's location on earth.

Entering a Source Rating

The source rating is an optional code that indicates how accurate or reliable the chart's date and time are. This is very useful when charts are exchanged with other astrologers, because it can help avoid misunderstandings about how accurately a chart's time is known. For example, a chart's time may be given as "10:43 am", implying that it was timed to the nearest minute, but if the source rating is given as "D – Conflicting/Unverified", then an astrologer would be very cautious about drawing firm conclusions from the chart.

>> To enter a source rating

Either

- Select a pre-defined rating category from the drop-down list box, or

- Enter any rating code up to 2 characters long

The predefined rating codes are known as "Rodden Rating" codes as devised and promoted by Lois Rodden. These codes are:

- **AA** - From birth record, eg. directly from a birth certificate or hospital record, or quoted from such a record

- **A** - From memory or from a news report

- **B** - From a biography or auto-biography

- **C** – Original source unknown or rectified from an approximate time

- **DD** – Conflicting with other sources or otherwise unverified

- **X** - Time unknown eg. only the date is known or has been rectified without an approximate starting time

- **XX** – Date in question or otherwise undetermined

Entering a Source Description

In addition to entering a source rating code, you can optionally also enter a brief source description to elucidate the rating code. The purpose of this field is to provide more information about the chart rating than can be conveyed by the two-character source rating code.

Some examples of possible source descriptions are

- AA - "Birth certificate" or "Quoted from hospital record"
- A – "The Times 3 Nov 1992" or "Mother's memory"
- B – "from 'A Good Life' by C.Cook"
- C – "Rectified from 10am by John Smith"
- DD – "Alternative time 11:15pm" or "Several alternatives known"
- X – "Time unknown"
- XX – "Calendar type uncertain"

Entering Chart Comments

It is possible to enter up to about 30,000 characters (many pages) of free text which is stored and saved along with the chart details. This can be used to store, for example, biographical information, a description of the chart event, records of what astrological analysis has been done on the chart, notes on the chart's rectification etc.

>> To enter or edit chart comments

Click on the **Comments** button

This will open up the comments editing window, which allows you to browse, enter or edit any comments text. Any text that you enter will remain associated with the chart when you use it in Solar Fire, so that when you save the chart to a file, the comments that you enter here will also be saved with it.

Note that you can also easily edit any comments that you enter here after you have calculated the chart, and also after you have saved the chart, if you wish to, from other places in the program.

However, if you do not save this chart to a file or retain it before exiting from Solar Fire, then any comments that you enter here will be discarded along with the chart that you create here.

Entering Life Events

It is possible to enter an indefinite number of life events relating to a chart, which are stored and saved along with the chart details. These events can be accessed in other parts of Solar Fire, making it easy to cast subsidiary charts (such as progressions or directions) for such life events, or view the chart animation screen for these life events, without having to re-enter the event details again.

Each life event can also have an unlimited amount of free text stored with it. This can be used, for example, to store a description or detailed account of the event and circumstances surrounding it.

>> To enter or edit life events

Click on the **Life Events...** button

This will open up the Life Events editing window, which allows you to browse, enter or edit any life events. Any events that you enter will remain associated with the chart when you use it in Solar Fire, so that when you save it to a file, the life events that you enter here will also be saved with it. See 50 for an explanation of how to use the Life Events editing window.

Note that you can also easily edit any life events that you enter here after you have calculated the chart, and also after you have saved the chart, if you wish to, from other places in the program.

However, if you do not save this chart to a file or retain it before exiting from Solar Fire, then any life events that you enter here will be discarded along with the chart that you create here.

Calculating the New Chart

When all the required data items have been entered and preferred options chosen, select either the **OK** or the **OK More** button.

- **OK** - The chart is then calculated and added to the list of Calculated Charts on the Main Screen, and the New Chart Data Entry screen closes.

- **OK More** - The chart is then calculated and added to the list of Calculated Charts on the Main Screen, and the New Chart Data Entry screen remains open ready for you to enter details for another chart.

It is possible to view, print, report on, or cast subsidiary charts from any such chart on the list of calculated charts by selecting the appropriate options from the menu.

Chapter 7: Working with Life Events

Solar Fire allows you save an unlimited number of life event records for any natal type chart. These life events are saved with the natal chart (provided that the chart file to which they are being saved is a SFv6 format chart file), and the events remain permanently linked with it.

The advantage of storing life events along with a natal chart is that it makes it very quick and easy to cast subsidiary charts (such as transits, progressions and others) for these events without ever having to re-enter any of the event data, as well as being able to select these events from a pop-up list when working with the natal chart in the animation module, again without having to re-enter any of the event data.

It is possible to import life events from the individual natal charts in a chart file, and also to export life events into natal charts in a chart file. Thus, if you already have a chart file that contains an ordinary natal chart for each life event of someone's life, you can automatically copy those into life events records.

Note – you cannot save life events to any older format Solar Fire charts (such as SFv1/2, SFv3/4 or SFv5). If you try saving a chart that includes life events into one of these chart files, then you will be given a warning message telling you that the life events will not be saved if you save the chart into that chart file. If you do not already have a new format (SFv6) chart file, then you must first create a new chart file (by using the **Create** button in the File Manager), and choose the option to create it with the new chart file format when prompted.

Editing Life Events

It is possible to open the life events dialog from various places in Solar Fire, including the Main Screen, the New Chart Data Entry screen, various Subsidiary Chart Data Entry screens, the Animation screen etc.

>> To Open the Life Events dialog box from the Main Screen

Choose **Edit / Edit Chart Events...** from the **Chart** menu or

Click on the Events caption at the bottom of the Current Chart box

>> To Open the Life Events dialog box from the New Chart Data Entry Screen or from any subsidiary chart data entry screen

Click on the **Events** button

This will display the Life Events dialog box.

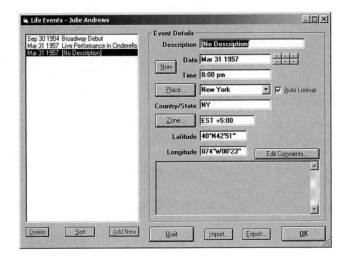

>> To add a new event

Click on the **Add New** button.

This will create a new entry ready for you to edit.

>> To delete an event

Highlight the event you wish to delete.

Click on the **Delete** button.

>> To edit an event

Use the fields and buttons in the Event Details frame to edit the various event details as required.

Note that the various fields and buttons in this frame work identically to those of similar appearance in the New Chart Date Entry dialog. See The

"New Chart Data Entry" Dialog Box for a full explanation of how to use these items.

>> To sort events into date order

Click on the **Sort** button.

>> To import events from a chart file

Click on the **Import** button.

If necessary, navigate to the folder in which the required chart file resides.

Select the required chart file and click **OK**.

This will import all the charts from the selected chart file, add them to any events that are already present, and then sort them all into date order.

Note: You cannot overwrite any existing events. If you wish to discard any existing events, then you must delete them first.

Note: If you do not wish to use all the charts in the selected chart file as life events, then you will have to delete any unrequired events after importing them all.

>> To export events to a chart file

Click on the Export button.

If necessary, navigate to the required folder.

Either select an existing chart file, or enter a name for a new chart file.

Select the required chart file and click **OK**.

This will export all the life events records and save them as natal charts in the selected chart file.

Note: If there are any existing charts already in the selected chart file, then the life event records will be appended to those existing charts.

Note: All life events in the list are exported. If you do not wish to use all the life events as charts, then after exporting, you will need to open the chart file and delete the unwanted charts.

Chapter 8: Using Place Databases

This chapter describes how to select a place for use in chart casting, and how to manage the place database and atlas data.

There are up to three different sources of place data

- Built-in ACS Atlas – provided within Solar Fire.

- Standalone ACS Atlas – may be purchased as a separate product.

- Solar Fire Place Database – provided within Solar Fire.

If you are using Solar Fire's own place database, then this chapter explains how to add, edit or delete entries from a place database file, or copy entries between two different place database files. If you have a standalone ACS Atlas installed on your computer, then you can choose whether you wish to use this Atlas in preference to Solar Fire's own place database or built-in ACS Atlas. See Atlas to Use for instructions on how to select which Atlas you wish to use.

It is possible to invoke the ACS Atlas or Solar Fire place database from any screen on which a location must be entered, for example in the New Chart Data Entry screen, the Subsidiary Chart Data Entry Screens and the Dynamic Reports screen.

Using the Solar Fire Place Database

>> To open the Place Database dialog box

Select the **Place...** button.

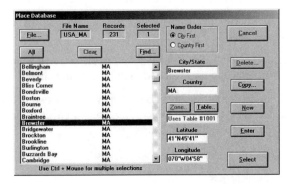

The list box on the left of the screen contains a list of all the place and country or state names that are stored in the currently selected place database file. The name of the currently selected place database file is displayed in the box titled "File Name". The number of place records stored in this file is shown in the box titled "Records". If there are no records in this file then the number of records will be zero, and no place names will appear in the list box. The number of places that have been selected for deletion or copying is shown in the box titled "Selected".

Finding a Place

>> To find a place in the list box

Do any of the following

• Select the **File...** button - This will display the "File Manager" dialog box with a list of place database files, from which it is possible to select an existing place database file or create a new one. Refer to Using the File Manager for instructions on using the File Manager.

• Select a **Name Order** - The **City First** option will list the places in ascending alphabetical order according to the place name. The **Country First** option will list the places in ascending alphabetical order according to the country or state name, and by place name within each country or state.

• Click on any place on the list and type any alphabetic key on the keyboard - This will move the list pointer to the first place name starting with that alphabetic character. Repeated use of the same key will cause the pointer to jump to subsequent entries starting with the same character.

• Select the **Find...** button - This will display a dialog box allowing a character or series of characters to be entered. Subsequently selecting the OK button from this box will move the list pointer to the first place name beginning with the entered character or series of characters.

• Browse the list by using the scroll bars on the right hand side of the list box.

Selecting a Place

>> To retrieve a place from the list for use within the program

Do either of the following

- Select the required place and use the **Select** button.

- Double click on the required place.

The place database screen will disappear and you will be returned to whichever screen was previously displayed, and the selected place details will be copied automatically onto that screen.

Adding a New Place

>> **To add a new place record**

Select the **New** button - This will clear all the data from the individual place data entry boxes, and it is possible to enter data for a new place record. It is possible to cancel the entry of this new record by selecting the **Cancel** button at any time. See the next section for details on how to enter data.

Editing Place Details

>> **To edit the details of an existing place record**

1.   Select the required place from the list box

2.   Edit Place Name - Up to 20 characters may be entered to describe the location name. Typically this would be city name (eg. "Adelaide" or "New York".).

3.   Edit Country - Up to 20 characters may be entered to describe the country or State (eg. "Australia" or "NY").

4.   Select either the **Zone...** button or the **Table...** button - Selecting the **Zone...** button will display a dialog box which allows the selection of a fixed time zone from a database. This is described in detail on Entering a Time Zone. Using this button will cause data to be entered automatically into the time zone box. Selecting the **Table...** button will display the "Timezone Table" dialog that allows a time zone table to be selected or edited for the current location. See Using Solar Fire Timezone Tables for instructions on using the timezone tables. If a table is selected, then Solar Fire will use that table to find the correct timezone applicable to any location that you look up in the database.

5.   Enter a Time Zone - Time zone may be entered as a standard mnemonic or as a time. If the format is not acceptable then an error dialog box will be displayed. See Entering a Time Zone for details on acceptable formats.

6.　Enter a Latitude - Enter the location latitude in an acceptable format. If the format is not acceptable then an error dialog box will be displayed. Acceptable formats are described in detail on Entering Longitudes and Latitudes.

7.　Enter a Longitude - Enter the location longitude in an acceptable format. If the format is not acceptable then an error dialog box will be displayed. Acceptable formats are described in detail on Entering Longitudes and Latitudes.

8.　Finally, select the **Enter** button - This will display a dialog box asking if you wish to save the changes that you have just made to this record. You are still able to cancel any changes that you have made to this record by selecting the **Cancel** button from this dialog box. If you select the **OK** button then the changes will become permanent, and the record will be moved to its appropriate place in the database file according to the currently selected sort order.

Selecting Places to Copy or Delete

You can select any number of places to copy or delete in a single operation, by holding down the **Ctrl** key whilst clicking on subsequent places in the list. The number of places selected is displayed in the "Selected" box.

>> To select all the places in the current database

Select the **All** button.

>> To unselect any selected places

Select the **Clear** button.

Copying Places

>> To copy one or more places from the current place database into another existing place database file

Select the required places and use the **Copy...** button - This will display a dialog box with a list of target place databases, from which you must select one. If the **Select** button is chosen then a "Copy Places" dialog box will be displayed, giving the options of copying all of the selected places without confirmation, of being asked for confirmation of the copying of each individual place, or of canceling the deletion process. If the **Yes** button is selected then, for each selected place in sequence, a dialog box will be displayed asking whether or not that individual place should be copied. If the **No** button is selected then all of the selected places will be copied immediately. If the **Cancel** button is selected then no further places are copied.

If you wish to copy places into a new place database, it is necessary to create the new database file before using this copying procedure. See Using the File Manager for instructions on how to create a new database file.

Deleting Places

>> To permanently delete places from the current place file

Select all the required places and use the **Delete...** button.

This will display a "Delete Places" dialog box, giving the options of deleting all of the selected place records without confirmation, of being asked for confirmation of the deletion of each individual place record, or of canceling the deletion process. If the **Yes** button is selected then, for each selected place in sequence, a dialog box will be displayed asking whether or not that individual place should be permanently removed. If the **No** button is selected then all of the selected places will be removed immediately. If the **Cancel** button is selected then no further places are deleted.

Using Solar Fire Timezone Tables

Any place that is stored in a Solar Fire place database file may be linked to a lookup table of time zone changes, so that Solar Fire can automatically find the appropriate time zone for any date.

The timezone table is fully editable, so that you have the option of entering your own data, or if necessary making corrections to any timezone data which is out-of-date.

>> To access the timezone table selections

1.   Enter Solar Fire's place database screen by clicking on the **Place...** button in any screen.

2. Select a place for which you wish to view, edit or select timezone tables.

3. Click on the **Table...** button. This will display the "Timezone Table" dialog box.

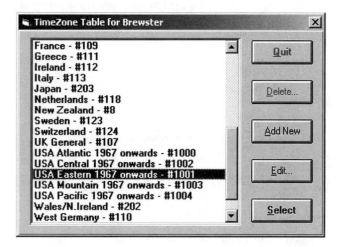

From this screen, you can create new zone tables, edit existing tables, delete them, or select a table for use with the currently selected location.

>> To create a new zone table

1. Click on the **Add New...** button. This will display the "Edit Time Zone Table" dialog for a new table with no entries.

2. Follow the instructions below for editing a zone table.

>> To delete a zone table

1. Select the required entry on the list of available zone tables

2. Click on the **Delete...** button.

>> To select a zone table for the currently selected location

1. Select the required entry on the list of available zone tables

2.   Click on the **Select** button.

>> To select a zone table for many locations at once

1.   From the Place Database screen, select all the required locations by clicking on them individually with the **Ctrl** key held down, or by clicking on the **All** button.

2.   Select the **Table...** button.

3.   Select a table from the list of available time zone tables.

4.   Click on the **Select** button.

>> To unselect a zone table for one or more locations

1.   From the Place Database screen, select all the required locations by clicking on them individually with the **Ctrl** key held down, or by clicking on the **All** button.

2.   Select the **Table...** button.

3.   Select the **!No Table!** entry from the list.

4.   Click on the **Select** button - All the selected locations will revert to using a fixed time zone instead of a zone table.

Editing a Time Zone Table

>> To edit a zone table or view zone table data

1.   Select the required entry on the list of available zone tables

2.   Click on the **Edit...** button. This will display the "Edit Time Zone Table" dialog displaying the data for the current zone table.

>> To set the title and other options

1.   Enter a **Table Name** - preferably a name that is descriptive of the locations to which this table applies.

2.   Optionally select the **Next Table** - From the **Next Table** drop-down list, select any other existing table that should be used for dates following the last date in the current table. In most cases you will want to leave this set to "None".

3.   Set the verification message option - If the time zones in this table are likely to continue changing regularly after the last entry in the table, then you may choose to have Solar Fire issue a warning message for charts with dates beyond the last entry in this table. If you want to see such messages, ensure that this option is checked.

>> To add an entry to the table

1.   Click on the **Add Entry** button.

2.   Edit the **Start Date** - the date on which the new time zone takes effect

3.   Edit the **Start Time** - the time at which the new time zone takes effect

4.   Edit the **Time Zone** abbreviation or longitude standard - You can enter any of Solar Fire's standard time zone abbreviations, or click on the ... button next to the Time Zone box to choose a zone from the list of available zones. You can also enter any longitude in Solar Fire's usual longitude format (eg. 135E00) to apply a fixed zone standard. Each 15 degrees of longitude corresponds to 1 hour of time, so 135E00 corresponds to -9 hours from GMT.

Note that when you add a new entry, the date of the new entry is automatically set to be the same day of week in the same week of the month as the second most recent entry in the table, but one year later. For example, if the second to last entry was the last Sunday in March of 2000 (26 March 2000), then the new entry will be set to the last Sunday in March 2001 (25 March 2001). This feature will save you much effort if all you want to do is to extend the date range of the table based on the continuation of the current pattern of daylight savings. All you need to do is to click on the **Add Entry** button repeatedly until the table reaches the required year.

>> To delete an entry

1.   Select the required entry in the table

2.   Click on the **Delete Entry** button.

>> To sort all entries into correct order of date

Click on the **Sort Table** button. This will put the earliest entry at the top of the list down to the latest entry at the bottom.

>> To save any changes you have made

Click on the **Save** button. This will sort the list, and return you to the previous screen.

Using the ACS Atlas

>> To activate the ACS Atlas dialog box:

Select the **Place...** button.

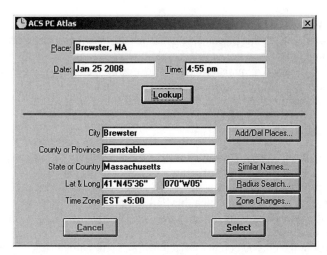

When the ACS PC Atlas dialog appears, the place, date and time boxes will contain the information that was held on the previous screen. You have the option of changing any of these if you wish to, and then clicking on any of the four main command buttons, which are described below. When you have found the place that you require, then clicking on the **OK** button will return you to the previous screen, and the displayed place details will be copied automatically onto that screen.

Atlas Lookup

You may enter the place to look up using any of the following formats:

• PlaceName

• PlaceName, CountryOrStateName

• PlaceName, CountyOrAdminDivisionName, CountryOrStateName

When you click on the Lookup button, one of the following will occur,

• **A Place name with a country name or US State name** – (eg. "Athens, Greece") If this place name exists as a unique name in the given country or state, then the lookup is performed immediately, and the results shown in this dialog. If there is more than one such place with this name, then you will be presented with a list of these places, from which you can select one. If the place name does not exist, then you will be presented with a list of places in that country or state whose names are closest, alphabetically, to the one you entered.

•   **A Place name with country name as "US" or "USA"** – (eg. "Athens, USA") If this place name exists in a US state within the atlas, then you will be presented with a list of all places found with that state name and the local administrative division in which they fall. If the place name does not exist within the atlas, then you will be presented with a list of US state names from which to choose, after which you will be presented with a list of places in the chosen state whose names are closest, alphabetically, to the one you entered.

•   **A Place name (without country or state name)** – (eg. "Athens") If this place name exists in the atlas, then you will be presented with a list of all places found with their country or US state name and the local administrative division in which they fall. If the place name does not exist within the atlas, then you will be presented with a list of country or state names from which to choose, after which you will be presented with a list of places in the chosen country or state whose names are closest, alphabetically, to the one you entered.

Similar Names

If you click on the **Similar Names** button, or if the place you are looking for was not found, then you will be presented with the City dialog box.

>> **To select the required city**

Click on the required entry and select the **OK** button, or double-click on the required entry - If you select the **Cancel** button, then you will return to the ACS Atlas screen after seeing a message indicating that the lookup was not successful.

Radius Search

If you click on the **Radius Search** Button, then the selection box appears.

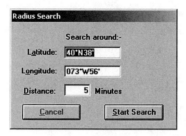

The initial settings of the longitude and latitude will be the same as the most recent entry that was found in the atlas. You have the option of altering these if you wish, and of specifying the radius of the search in minutes of arc by editing the Distance box. By default it is set to 1 minute of arc.

>> To start the search

Select the **Start Search** button - You will be prompted for the country or state in which you wish to search, and the results will be presented in the City dialog box, from which you may select any entry. If no entries are found within the given radius, then you will be returned to the ACS Atlas screen without any result.

Zone Changes

>> To see a list of dates and times at which the time zone changes occur

Select the **Zone Changes** button - You may be prompted for the country or state, and for the city for which you wish to see the zone changes and the results will be presented in a dialog box.

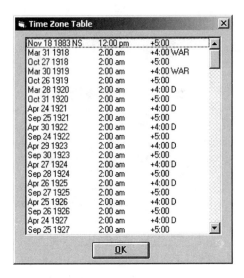

Selecting the **OK** button will simply return you to the ACS Atlas screen.

Adding or Deleting Place

The ACS Atlas comes with an extensive range of locations from around the world. However, from time to time you may like to add your own places to the atlas, thus allowing them to be looked up with the correct timezone changes automatically applied.

>> To add or delete a place to the ACS Atlas:

Click on the **Add/Del Places...** button.

This will display the Personal Atlas Locations Dialog

This dialog lists any personal locations that you have already added previously, but will be blank the first time you use it.

>> To add or a place to the ACS Atlas:

Click on the **Add New...** button.

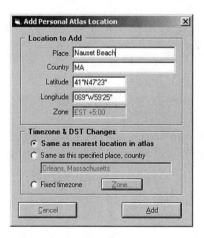

This displays a dialog into which you can enter the required new place details.

The items you need to supply are:

- **Place** - Enter the name of the place you wish to add

- **Country** - Enter the Country or US State name in which this place is located. Normally this will be a country or US State name which already exists in the ACS Atlas, but it is possible to enter a new country name if you wish.

- **Latitude** - Enter the latitude of the place. See Entering Longitudes and Latitudes

- **Longitude** - Enter the latitude of the place.

- **Zone** - If the timezone option is set to "Fixed timezone", then you can enter a timezone yourself. See Entering a Time Zone

- **Specified Place, Country** - If the timezone option allows it, you can enter a location which exists as a valid location within the ACS Atlas. See Using the ACS Atlas

- **Timezone & DST Changes** - This has three possible settings, as follows.

- **Same as nearest location in atlas** - If you select this option then the timezone and DST changes for your newly added place will automatically be the same as that for the nearest place in the atlas. This is normally the best option, unless your new location is near a border, for example, in which case the nearest place may not be in the same timezone region, and you may then want to specify a place which you know is in the correct region, instead.

- **Same as this specified place, country** - Allows you to specify an existing place in the ACS Atlas from which the timezone settings will be copied.

- **Fixed timezone** - If you don't want your place to have automatic daylight savings adjustments applied, you can either enter a fixed timezone, or use the **Zone...** button to select one from the list.

>> To delete a place from the ACS Atlas:

Highlight the place you wish to delete, and then use the **Delete** button.

Note - you can only delete places that you have previously added as personal places yourself. It is not possible to delete any of the locations that form part of the ACS Atlas as supplied.

Chapter 9: Retrieving Charts From a File

This chapter describes how to find and select charts from your Solar Fire chart files, so that you can view, work with, edit and print them.

Whenever you retrieve a chart from a file, you do so from the "Chart Database" dialog box. This dialog box is also a gateway to editing and manipulating chart files.

>> To display the Chart Database dialog box

Select **Open...** from the **Chart** menu.

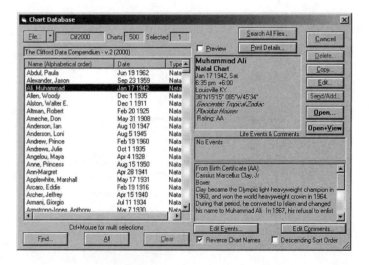

Whenever this screen is displayed, the list box on the left of the screen contains a list of all the chart names that are stored in the currently selected chart database file. The name of the currently selected chart database file is displayed in the box to the right of the **File...** button, and its descriptive title (if it has one) is displayed below this. The number of charts stored in this file is shown in the **Charts** box. If there are no charts in this file then the number of records will be zero, and no chart names will appear in the list box. The number of charts that have been selected for copying, deleting or opening is shown in the box titled **Selected**.

Choosing Chart Data Columns to Display

It is possible to select a range of different columns to display in the chart list, to rearrange the order of the columns and to resize them. Any column rearrangement you make is remembered for future sessions.

>> To resize the width of a column

Use the mouse to drag the column border between any two column headers, or

Double-click on a column border to make the column automatically resize to fit the largest item of data that is displayed in that column.

>> To edit the column selection and order

Use a right hand mouse click when the cursor is over the column headers.

This will display the Choose Columns dialog.

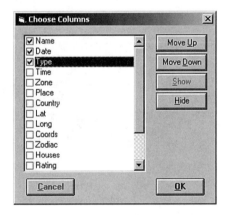

You can select or unselect any of the available columns by either clicking in the checkbox to the left of the column name, or by using the **Show** or **Hide** buttons.

You can change the order of a column by highlighting it and then using the **Move Up** or **Move Down** buttons to re-order it relative to the other columns.

Note: The **Name** column must always be the first, and it is not possible to change its order.

Note: If the selected columns' widths are cumulatively wider than the displayed width of the list, a horizontal scroll bar will appear at the bottom of the list, allowing you to scroll to see the extra columns. Alternatively you can increase the displayed width of the list by resizing the width of the entire dialog.

Selecting the Required Chart File

If the chart that you want is not in the current chart file, then you can select another file to look in.

>> To select a recently used chart file

Click on the **down arrow** button to the right of the **File...** button. This will display a pop-up menu with a list of the ten most recently used chart files, sorted in order of access with the most recent at the top. Select an entry from this list to re-open that chart file.

Note: If any chart files in this list are in different folders to the folder of your current chart file, then their folder paths will be displayed on the menu. Any chart files on the list that are in the same folder as your current chart file will not have any folder path displayed.

>> To select a different chart file

Select the **File...** button. This will display the "File Manager" dialog box with a list of chart database files from which it is possible to select an existing chart file or create a new one. See Using the File Manager for instruction on using the File Manager.

Searching All Chart Files

Solar Fire can also search through all your chart files at once for any chart or charts with the same string of characters in the chart name.

>> To search through all chart files in a directory or folder

1.   Select the **Search All Files...** button.

2.   In the displayed dialog box, type in the series of characters that you wish to find (eg. type in "kennedy" to find all charts with Kennedy in their name), and select the **OK** button. Alternatively, to re-access a recently used search string, click on the down arrows of the drop down box and select an item from the presented list.

3.   All of the valid chart files in Solar Fire's current chart directory (ie. the directory or folder in which the currently selected chart file resides) will be searched, and the results are displayed in the **Chart Search Results** dialog.

4.   You can double-click any chart in the list to open it (ie. to add it to the list of calculated charts on the main screen). There are various other options available here – see Working with the Results of a Chart Search for a full explanation of all the options available to you in the **Chart Search Results** dialog.

Note: If you wish to search all chart files in a different directory or folder, then you can do so by first selecting a chart file that resides in that directory or folder. Alternatively, you can control precisely which chart files are searched by using the **Chart Search** facility from Solar Fire's main screen, instead. (See Chart Search)

Finding a Chart in the Current Chart File

The **Stored Charts** list box displays a list of all the chart names that are in the current chart file. You can use any of the following ways to help find the required chart or charts.

•   Scroll the list by using the scroll bar on the right hand side of the list box.

•   Jump to the beginning entry for any letter of the alphabet by selecting any chart on the list and then pressing the key for the letter you want. Hit the same key to move through each successive entry beginning with the same letter.

•   Use the **Find...** button to find charts with any character string in their name or in their chart comments, or to find charts with certain planetary placements or aspects.

•   Sort the list in various ways to make finding charts easier, by clicking on the Name, Date or other column headers and using the Reverse Chart Names and Descending Sort Order check boxes.

The sort options have the following effects:

Name will list charts in either alphabetical order of their listed names, or in the order in which the charts are stored in the file. Subsequent selection of this option will toggle between these sort modes.

Date will list charts in order of their date and time.

Other column headers will list charts in the order of the value of that columns. For example, the Zodiac column sorts the charts into alphabetical order of the zodiac type name.

Reverse Chart Names will display the listed chart names starting with the last distinct character string (ie. preceded by at least one blank) in each chart name as it was entered. eg. an entered name of "Bill Clinton" is displayed as "Clinton, Bill". If this option is not checked, then the chart names are shown exactly as they were entered. (Note that the titles of charts that are marked as Horary or Event charts are not affected by this option – they are always displayed exactly as they were entered.)

Descending Sort Order will list the charts starting from the highest value to the lowest value ie. from Z to A, from last date to earliest date, from last chart entered to first chart entered. If this option is not checked, then the charts will be listed in ascending order of the current sort option, instead.

Searching for Character Strings

>> To find charts containing certain character strings in their names or comments

1. Select the **Find...** button.

2. From the drop-down menu, select one of the following options

2.1. **Next Chart Name with...** - to select the next chart on the list (after the currently highlighted chart) which contains a specified character string in its name

2.2. **All Chart Names with...** - to select all the charts on the list which contain a specified character string in their name

2.3. **Next Chart Comment with...** - to select the next chart on the list (after the currently highlighted chart) which contains a specified character string in its comments

2.4. **All Chart Comments with...** - to select all the charts on the list which contain a specified character string in their comments

3.   In the displayed dialog box, type in the series of characters that you wish to find (eg. type in "kennedy" to find all charts with Kennedy in their name, or "athlete" to find all charts with the word athlete in their comments), and select the **OK** button.

4.   If any chart or charts are found with the specified string, then they will be selected (highlighted) on the list. It is then possible to open, copy or delete all of these charts using the appropriate buttons.

Performing an Advanced Search for Chart Details or Astrological Criteria

You can search for charts in the current chart file or other chart files using a variety of advanced criteria.

>> To enter the "Chart Search" dialog box

1.   Select the **Find...** button.

2.   From the drop-down menu, select the **Chart Search...** option

This displays the Chart Search dialog. See Chart Search for a full explanation of this feature.

Selecting Charts Manually

A chart is selected by clicking the mouse onto its name in the **Stored Charts** list box. A selected chart is shown in the list box with a reverse video, highlighted entry. It is possible to select any number of charts to open, copy, delete or print a summary, by holding down the **Ctrl** key whilst clicking on subsequent charts in the list. Any selected chart may also be deselected by clicking on it again whilst holding down the **Ctrl** key.

>> To select all the charts in the current file

Click on the **Select All** button.

>> To deselect all selected charts

Click on the **Clear** button.

Note: The chart edit button is only enabled if a single chart has been selected, because it is not possible to edit multiple charts simultaneously.

Opening Charts

Any number of selected charts from the current chart file may be opened and added to the list of calculated charts in the Main Screen. If opening a single chart, you can also automatically view it in a wheel as well.

>> To open a single chart from the list of Stored Charts

Select the required chart and then click on the **Open** button, or double-click on the required chart.

>> To open multiple charts at once

Select all the required charts and then click on the **Open** button.

>> To open a single chart, and immediately view it as a wheel

Select the required chart and then click on the **Open+View** button.

This is simply equivalent to opening the chart, and then choosing **Current Chart** from the **View** menu.

Chapter 10: Manipulating Charts in Files

This section gives you the tools to keep your chart files up-to-date and organized. It shows how to correct a chart that has been incorrectly cast; how to add comments to a stored chart, such as notes on the source of the data, biographical notes or other client notes; how to copy, delete and move charts from one file to another; how to add a descriptive title to a chart file, making it easier to tell what the file contains; how to print a summary of charts contained in a file.

The instructions in this section assume a basic knowledge of how to find, select and open charts as described in the previous section. See Retrieving Charts From a File for further information.

Editing Chart Details

Instead of opening a chart exactly as it is stored in the chart file, you may wish to change some of the chart's details, for example to correct an incorrect birth time, or to specify a different location, house system, zodiac or event type for the chart.

>> To edit a chart

Select a single chart, and then click on the **Edit** button. This will display the "New Chart Data Entry" dialog box with the data from the selected chart. Type any new data over the existing data. Before selecting the **OK** button:

>> To replace the stored chart with the newly edited chart

Select the **Replace Chart in File** option by ensuring that it is checked. The original chart will be overwritten with the newly edited details, and you will be returned to the "Chart Database" screen.

>> To create a separate copy of the edited chart

Do not select the **Replace Chart in File** option (ensure that it is unchecked). The original chart will remain in the chart file, and a new chart will be opened with the newly edited details. To keep a permanent copy of this new chart you will need to save it to a file yourself. See Saving Charts to a File for further instructions on saving files.

>> To alter one or more chart's event type

Select one or more charts by highlighting them, and then use the shortcut keys shown below to set the selected chart/s event type.

- **Ctrl+F1** - Unspecified

- **Ctrl+F2** - Male

- **Ctrl+F3** - Female

- **Ctrl+F4** - Event

- **Ctrl+F5** - Horary

Copying Charts

You can copy any number of charts from the current chart file into any other chart file, either existing or new.

>> To copy charts into another file

1.   Select the required charts

2.   Click on the **Copy...** button. This will display the File Manager with a list of target chart files.

3.   Either select one of the files on the list, or select the **Create** button to create a new empty chart file to copy the charts into.

4.   A "Copy Charts" dialog box will be displayed, giving the options of copying all of the selected charts without confirmation, of being asked for confirmation of the copying of each individual chart, or of canceling the copying process. If the **Yes** button is selected then, for each selected chart in sequence, a dialog box will be displayed asking whether or not that individual chart should be copied. If the **No** button is selected then all of the selected charts will be copied immediately. If the **Cancel** button is selected then no charts are copied.

Note: When charts are copied to another chart file, any chart comments that are associated with the charts are copied as well.

Deleting Charts

>> To delete charts from the current chart file

1.   Select the required charts

2.   Click on the **Delete...** button, and choose the **Selected Charts...** item from the drop-down menu

3.   This will display a "Delete Charts" dialog box, giving the options of deleting all of the selected charts without confirmation, of being asked for confirmation of the deletion of each individual chart, or of canceling the deletion process. If the **Yes** button is selected then, for each selected chart in sequence, a dialog box will be displayed asking whether or not that individual chart should be deleted. If the **No** button is selected then all of the selected charts will be deleted immediately. If the **Cancel** button is selected then no further charts are deleted.

In certain situations you may find that you have stored more than one copy of a chart in a chart file. This might occur if you are copying various charts from one file to another, for example, and accidentally copy the charts more than once. Fortunately there is an easy way to get rid of any duplicate charts without having to find them all manually.

>> To remove duplicate copies of charts from the current chart file

The process is the same as above, except instead of choosing the **Selected Charts...** item, choose the **Duplicate Charts...** item from the drop-down menu.

Note: Charts are considered to be duplicates if they have the same basic chart details (Name, date, time, location, house system, zodiac etc.). However, special conditions apply if the comments associated with each of the duplicate charts are different: If comments are present on only one of the charts, then those comments are retained. However, if comments are present on both charts, but are different, then only the comments from the chart that is stored later in the file will be kept.

Moving Charts

>> To move charts from the current chart file to another chart file

First copy the charts to the new file, and then delete them.

Adding or Editing Chart Comments

You can add permanently saved comments to any chart. These comments are displayed in the **Chart Comments** box whenever the chart is highlighted in the list of **Stored Charts**.

>> To add or enter comments for a chart

1.   Select the required chart from the list of Stored Charts

2.   Click inside the **Charts Comments** box, or select the **Comments...** button

This will display the comments editing dialog where you can type in whatever text you wish

Any changes that you make are permanently saved as soon when you select the **Save** button. You can enter up to about 30,000 characters of text (which is equivalent to about 10 pages of typewritten text).

Changing the Chart File Description

To aid in identifying and selecting chart files, you can give any Solar Fire chart file a description of up to 80 characters. This description is displayed in the File Manager, as well as on the "Chart Database" screen. However, note that you cannot enter a description for Solar Fire chart files which are v2 (Standard Edition) format or earlier.

>> To add or edit a chart file description

Click inside the chart description box above the list of chart names, and type in whatever you want. Any changes that you make are permanently saved as soon as the cursor leaves the description box.

Printing a Summary of Charts in a File

You can print out a summary listing of any or all charts contained within a single chart file. The summary may be printed at three different levels of detail:

Brief Listing - Each chart occupies a single line of output, and contains only the essential details that would be required to recast the chart: Name, date, time, timezone, latitude and longitude.

Full Listing - Each chart occupies two lines of output, and contains the same information as the brief listing plus the coordinate system (geocentric/heliocentric), zodiac type, house system, place name and country/state.

Full with Comments - The details of each chart occupy two lines of output, containing the same information as the full listing, and any chart comments that are associated with the chart occupy additional text lines below the chart details.

>> To print a summary of all charts in the current chart file

1.   Select the **Print Details...** button and from the drop-down menu select the **All Charts** option.

2.   Select the **Print Details...** button and from the drop-down menu select one of the listing options **Brief Listing...**, **Full Listing...** or **Full with Comments...**.

3.   The "Print" dialog box will appear, from which you can alter printer settings, add this job to the print queue, or print it immediately. See Printing from Solar Fire for further information on printing.

>> To print a summary of only the selected charts in the current chart file

1.   Select the **Print Details...** button and from the drop-down menu select the **Selected Charts Only** option.

2.   Proceed as in steps 2 to 3 above.

Chart File Limitations

The number of charts which can be stored in a single chart file is about 64,000.

As a general recommendation, it is suggested that you save no more than several thousand charts in any one chart file. This will ensure that Solar Fire's performance remains good, and avoids the likelihood of the chart file limitations ever being reached.

Chapter 11: Casting Subsidiary Charts

This chapter describes how to select, enter data for and cast Solar Fire's subsidiary chart types. These types include

- Transit charts

- Progressed charts - secondary, tertiary, minor, user-defined rate

- Directed charts - solar arc, ascendant arc, vertex arc, user-defined arc

- Return charts - any planet or asteroid, any harmonic, plus Wynn-Key and progressed solar returns

- Ingress charts - any planet or asteroid

- Harmonic charts - any harmonic or age harmonic

- Arc Transform charts - any pair of chart points

- Antiscia or Contra-Antiscia charts

- Zodiacal Analogue charts

- Relationship charts - from 2 charts

- Composite charts - from up to 15 charts

- Coalescent charts - from 2 charts

- Prenatal charts - 19 types

- Rising/Setting charts - rising, setting, culminating or anti-culminating of any planet or asteroid

- Lunar phase and eclipse charts - any of the main transiting phases or progressed phases plus lunar phase return charts

- Locality charts - relocated, Johndro or Geodetic

- Vedic charts – various Vedic divisional charts

Selecting a Base Chart

Nearly all of the above chart types require a base chart, which is usually a natal chart. If you have not already cast the natal chart see Casting a Natal

Chart for instructions on creating a new chart, or Retrieving Charts From a File for instructions on opening an existing chart.

You can cast most subsidiary chart types for any natal chart. Whether or not you can use other types of charts as base charts depends on the type of subsidiary chart you are casting. If the base chart that you select is inappropriate, then the data in the **Base Chart Details** box will become grayed, and the **OK** button will become grayed and disabled. In this case you cannot proceed until you choose another base chart which is of an appropriate type.

Selecting or Entering Event Details

If the base chart you are using has any stored life events associated with it, then you have the option of selecting one and automatically filling in the event details instead of entering them all manually.

If you would like to re-use any new event details that you are about to enter, then you can create a new life event to be stored with the base chart instead of making a one-off data entry here.

>> To create a new stored Life Event for this base chart

1.   Click on the **Events** button, which opens the **Event Selection** dialog.

2.   Click on the **Edit** button, which opens the **Life Events** dialog, ready for you to add a new life event.

Once you have created the new Life Event, you can select it by highlighting it in the Event Selection dialog and clicking the OK button.

>> To select a previously stored Life Event

1.   Click on the down arrow at the right of the **Event Description** box, and select one of the events from that drop-down list, OR

2.   Click on the **Events** button, and select one of the events from the **Event Selection** dialog box.

Whether or not you are using stored Life Event details here, you have the option of entering an event description. This description becomes the main title of the subsidiary chart to be calculated, with the base chart name as a secondary title.

If you omit an event description, then the subsidiary chart title is simply the same as that of the base chart (as was always the case in earlier versions of Solar Fire).

Entering Subsidiary Date, Time and Place Data

If you have not selected a stored Life Event, then you must enter the event details in this dialog manually.

The **Date**, **Time**, **Place**, **Country**, **Zone**, **Latitude** and **Longitude** fields in the subsidiary charts data entry screens follow the same data-entry conventions as those in the **New Chart Data Entry** screen, and you can use the Solar Fire place database and ACS Atlases in the same way. Most forms of data entry will work, and Solar Fire will give you a message if the data that you enter is not acceptable. See Casting a New Chart for further information.

Casting a Transiting, Progressed or Directed Chart

You can create a progressed or directed chart from any natal type chart. You can progress geocentric, heliocentric, Tropical and Sidereal charts. The resulting coordinate system and zodiac type of the progressed chart are always of the same as those of the natal type chart that you are progressing.

Whilst it is also possible to cast a transits chart as if it was an ordinary natal chart independent of any other chart by using the **Chart** / **New** menu item, casting it is as a subsidiary chart instead has the following advantages.

•　　It is possible to retrieve stored Life Events details instead of having to re-enter them as you cast the chart

•　　The transits chart can include an event description

•　　It is possible to apply precession correction or a converse transits option

The progression rate may be:-

•　　Secondary - a day for a year

•　　Mean tertiary - a day for a mean lunar month

•　　True tertiary - a day for each true lunar month

- Minor - a mean lunar month for a year

- User-defined - a rate that can be set in the **Preferences** dialog

The direction arc may be:-

- Solar Arc - the longitudinal distance moved by the secondary progressed sun

- Ascendant Arc - the longitudinal distance moved by the secondary progressed ascendant

- Vertex Arc - the longitudinal distance moved by the secondary progressed vertex

- User Rate - a rate that can be set in the **Preferences** dialog

- User Arc – a fixed angle that can be set each time this option is used

- Profection Annual – an annual rate of 30 degrees, corresponding to a direction of one sign (or house) per year.

Progressed charts are calculated according to certain options that are set in the Preferences dialog.

>> To pre-set basic progression options

From the **Preferences** menu of the main screen, select **Edit Settings...**, and click on the **Progs/Dirns** tab.

- **Chart Angle Progressions Type** - to determine how to progress the Midheaven (which also determines the Ascendant, house cusps and other chart angles). See Chart Angle Progression Type.

- **Progression Day Type** - to determine the type of daily cycle on which the progression rate is based. See Progression Day Type.

- **User Progression Rate...** - to determine what progression rate is used when the User-Defined progression rate option is chosen. See Rate for User Defined Progs.

- **User Direction Rate...** - to determine what annual direction rate is used when the User-Defined direction arc option is chosen. See Rate for User Defined Directions.

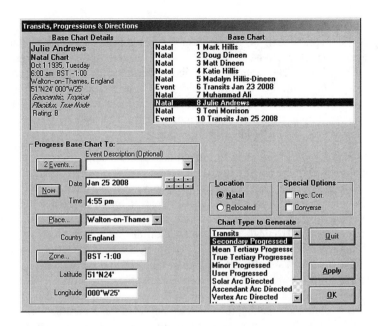

>> **To cast the transiting, progressed or directed chart**

1. Ensure that the required natal type chart that you want to progress or direct is already calculated.

2. Choose the **Tran/Prog/Dirn...** menu item from the **Chart** menu

3. Select a chart type from the **Chart Type to Generate** list box.

4. Select a chart from the **Base Chart** list box.

5. Enter the **Date** to which you wish to progress or direct the base chart.

6. (Optional) Enter the **Time** to which you wish to progress or direct the base chart. The time is not important for secondary progressed chart (and most directed charts), unless the Mean Quotidian rate is being used for angle progressions.

7. Select the **Location** type. Normally the location of a progressed or directed chart would be the same as the natal chart location. However, if the natal chart is that of a person who moved during the first few months of their life, it may be appropriate to relocate the secondary progressed chart. If the **Natal** option is selected then all the boxes relating to location, including time zone, longitude and latitude will contain the location details from the selected base chart. Note that although it may be technically

correct to alter the time zone if the current time zone is different from the natal one, in practice this is not necessary, as the difference in the resultant progressed chart would be negligible. If the **Relocated** option is selected then all the boxes relating to location, including time zone, longitude and latitude will contain the current default values. (See Saving and Restoring Settings for details on default values.) Any of these values may be altered in the same manner as when creating a new chart. See Casting a New Chart for instructions on how to alter location values.

8.   (Optional) Select **Special Options**. It is possible to apply two types of special options to the calculation of the progressed or directed chart. If the **Prec. Corr.** option is checked, then the calculation of the chart will be done according to how far the planets have moved on the Sidereal zodiac, rather than the Tropical zodiac. However, the resulting chart will be still be calculated for the Tropical Zodiac. Note that if the base chart which you are progressing or directing already has a Sidereal zodiac, then this option will have no effect, and the resulting chart will have a Sidereal zodiac. Note that for most progressed or directed charts, the effect of precession is negligibly small, and this option is included for completeness. If the **Converse** option is checked, then the calculation of the progressed or directed chart will be done backwards in time from the time of the base chart instead of forwards. An additional arc multiplier button (**Mult**) is visible whenever Solar Arc, Ascendant Arc or Vertex Arc directions have been selected as the method to calculate. Clicking on this button produce a drop-down menu with the possible arc multipliers - x1 (Normal), x2 (Double Arc), x0.5 (Half Arc), x-1 (Negative Arc), x-2 (Negative Double Arc), x-0.5 (Negative Half Arc).

9.   Select either the **Apply** or **OK** button. The subsidiary chart will be calculated and added to the list of calculated charts in the list box on the main screen of the program. Use the **OK** button to close this dialog after the calculation. Use the **Apply** button to leave this dialog open to calculate further charts. After this dialog closes, you can view, print, report on, and otherwise manipulate the newly calculated charts.

Casting a Return, Ingress or Transit Chart

You can cast solar, lunar, planetary or asteroid returns, ingresses into any zodiac sign, or transits to any planet in a base chart or to any user-defined zodiac point. You can also produce multiple returns from one starting date, including demi, quarti and other partial or harmonic returns. You can also calculate two types of progressed solar returns.

You can cast returns for geocentric, heliocentric, Tropical and Sidereal charts. The resulting coordinate system and zodiac type of the progressed chart are always of the same as those of the natal type chart that you are progressing.

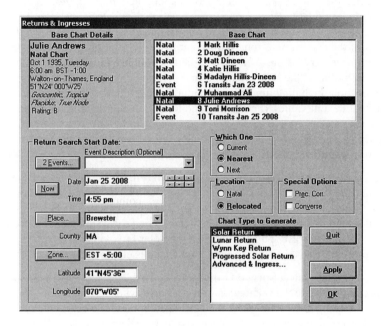

>> **To cast a single Solar or Lunar return or Wynn-Key or Progressed Solar Return**

1. Ensure that the natal type chart that you want the return for is already calculated.

2. Choose the **Return...** menu item from the **Chart** menu

3. Select the required chart type from the **Chart Type to Generate** list box.

4. Select a chart from the **Base Chart** list box.

5. Enter the **Date** from which you wish to search, or for Wynn-Key or Progressed Solar Returns enter the exact date for which you wish to calculate the return chart.

6. The **Time** is not needed for ordinary solar or lunar returns, as the program will find the exact time of the return. However you should enter a

time for Wynn-Key or Progressed Solar Returns, as this is used as the time for which the return is calculated.

7. Select the **Location** type. Normally the return chart is relocated to wherever the person is living at the time of the return. If the **Natal** option is selected then all the boxes relating to location, including time zone, longitude and latitude will contain the location details from the selected base chart. Note that although it may be technically correct to alter the time zone if the current time zone is different from the natal one, in practice this is not necessary, as the difference in the resultant progressed chart would be negligible. If the **Relocated** option is selected then all the boxes relating to location, including time zone, longitude and latitude will contain the current default values. (See Saving and Restoring Settings for details on default values.) Any of these values may be altered in the same manner as when creating a new chart. See Casting a New Chart for instructions on how to alter location values.

8. Select a **Which Return** option. If the **Current** option is selected, then Solar Fire will search backwards from the entered date to find the return that occurred most recently. If the **Next** option is selected, then Solar Fire will search forwards from the entered date to find the return that will occur next. If the **Nearest** option is selected, the Solar Fire will find either the current or the next return, depending on which is closer to the entered date.

9. (Optional) Select **Special Options**. It is possible to apply two types of special options to the calculation of the progressed or directed chart. If the **Prec. Corr.** option is checked, then the calculation of the chart will be done according to how far the planets have moved on the Sidereal zodiac, rather than the Tropical zodiac. However, the resulting chart will be still be calculated for the Tropical Zodiac. Note that if the base chart which you are using already has a Sidereal zodiac, then this option will have no effect, and the resulting chart will have a Sidereal zodiac. For each year of life, about 50 seconds of arc will be added to the return planet's longitude, thus allowing for the precession of the equinoxes. If the **Converse** option is checked, then the calculation of the progressed or directed chart will be done backwards in time from the time of the base chart instead of forwards.

10. Select either the **Apply** or **OK** button. The subsidiary chart will be calculated and added to the list of calculated charts in the list box on the main screen of the program. Use the **OK** button to close this dialog after the calculation. Use the **Apply** button to leave this dialog open to calculate further charts. After this dialog closes, you can view, print, report on, and otherwise manipulate the newly calculated charts.

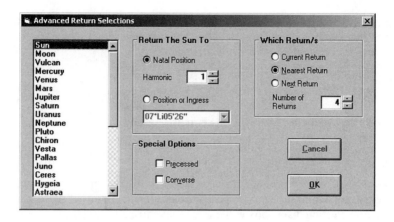

>> To cast multiple solar, lunar or other returns

1. Follow the steps 1 to 7 above, under "To cast a single solar or lunar return".

2. In the **Chart Type to Generate** box, select **Advanced & Ingress**, and then click on the **Options...** button. This will display the "Advanced Return Selections" dialog box.

3. From the list of chart points on the left of the screen, select the body for which you wish to find a return.

4. Select the options in the **Which Return/s** and **Special Options** as in steps 8 and 9 above.

5. Next to **Number of Returns**, type in the number of successive returns that you want, or click on the spin button to increase or decrease the number of returns.

6. Select the **OK** button. Solar Fire will calculate the first return just as it would for a single return chart, and then each successive return after that up to the number that you specified. When you return to the Main Screen, you will find that all these returns have been added to the **Calculated Charts** listbox.

>> To cast demi, quarti or other harmonic returns

1. Follow the steps 1 to 5 above, under "To cast multiple solar, lunar or other returns".

2. In the **Return...To** area, select **Natal Position**, and next to **Harmonic**, type in a number or use the spin button to change the number. You would enter 2 for demi returns, 4 for a quarti returns, etc.

3. Select the **OK** button.

>> To cast planetary or asteroid returns

1.   Proceed as you would for casting multiple returns, choosing a planet or asteroid instead of the Sun or Moon, and then select the **OK** button.

If you are casting geocentric planet/asteroid returns, then it is possible that there may be three or even five possible dates for that return. If so, then a Return Selection dialog box will appear containing a list of all the dates, showing whether each return is direct or retrograde.

If only one return date is found, then the chart for that date is calculated automatically, and the temporary dialog box will disappear. If more than one return is found then you may choose one or more of the return charts to be calculated. Use the **Ctrl** key whilst clicking on each required chart in order to make multiple selections. (Note that if you have specified a number of returns greater than 1, then selecting the **Cancel** button will prevent any further returns from being calculated.)

Note: Even with the most accurate astronomical calculations, the slower a planet is moving, the harder it is to pinpoint the exact time of its return. For outer planets in general, and for inner planets when they are near a station point, it is best to treat the chart angles and house positions as approximate. In the chart details of the return chart, an estimated accuracy of the return time is given, so that you can judge how accurate the chart angles and house cusps really are, in each case.

>> To cast a chart for a sign ingress or for a transit to any planet or user-defined point

1. Follow the steps 1 to 5 under "To cast multiple solar, lunar or other returns".

2. In the **Return...To** area, select **Position or Ingress**, and in the drop-down box below this, either select one of the existing longitudes for sign ingresses, or type in you own value. If you are finding a return to a planet's position, then you can automatically insert that planet's position into this box by double-clicking on that planet in the listbox on the left of the screen. (However, don't forget to subsequently reselect the required return planet by highlighting it with a single click.)

3. Select the **OK** button.

Casting an Harmonic, Transform, Antiscia or Analogue Chart

You can create an harmonic, arc transform, antiscia or contra-antiscia or zodiacal analogue chart from any other type of chart.

These chart types are calculated as follows:

Harmonic - The longitude of each point in the chart is multiplied by the specified harmonic value.

Harmonic Age - The longitude of each point in the chart is multiplied by the exact age (in decimal years) of the base chart's subject at the time of the event. (The harmonic value is zero at time of birth.)

Harmonic Age+1 - The longitude of each point in the chart is multiplied by the exact age of the base chart's subject at the time of the event plus one year. (The harmonic value is one at time of birth.)

Arc Transform - The longitude of each point in the chart is multiplied by an harmonic value calculated from the longitudinal separation between a pair of points in the chart. This has the effect of bringing that planetary pair into exact conjunction in the Arc Transform chart.

Antiscia - The longitude of each point is reflected in the 0 Cancer/0 Capricorn axis.

Contra-antiscia - The longitude of each point is reflected in the 0 Aries/ 0 Libra axis.

Long Equiv Decl – The declination of each point is converted into longitude equivalent (keeping it in the same quadrant of the circle as its original longitude).

Long Equiv Decl (Ant) – The declination of each point is converted into longitude equivalent and then reflected in the 0 Cancer/0 Capricorn axis.

Z-Analogue Latitude – Zodiacal analogue of latitude. The latitude of each point is expressed as a longitude. Latitudes from 0 to +90 degree correspond to 0 Aries to 0 Cancer, whereas latitudes from 0 to –90 degrees correspond to 0 Aries to 0 Capricorn.

Z-Analogue RA – Zodiacal analogue of right ascension. The right ascension of each point is expressed as a longitude.

Z-Analogue Decl - Zodiacal analogue of declination. The declination of each point is expressed as a longitude. Declinations from 0 to 90 degree North correspond to 0 Aries to 0 Cancer, whereas declinations from 0 to 90 degrees South correspond to 0 Aries to 0 Capricorn.

Z-Analogue Azi - Zodiacal analogue of azimuth. The azimuth of each point is expressed as a longitude. Due east corresponds to 0 Aries, and due north corresponds to 0 Cancer. Although this is the traditional way of displaying azimuth as a zodiacal analogue, in contrast with the local horizon coordinate chart, it produces a rotated image of the true compass directions (rotated by 180 degrees), so cannot easily be used as a map overlay.

Z-Analogue Loc Horz - Zodiacal analogue of local horizon coordinate. The local horizon coordinate of each point is expressed as a longitude. Due west corresponds to 0 Aries, and due north corresponds to 0 Capricorn. This produces a chart which corresponds to planetary compass directions for the chart's location, and is similar to the Local Horizon chart generated by Solar Maps.

Z-Analogue Altitude - Zodiacal analogue of altitude. The altitude of each point is expressed as a longitude. Altitudes from 0 to +90 degree correspond to 0 Aries to 0 Cancer, whereas altitudes from 0 to –90 degrees correspond to 0 Aries to 0 Capricorn.

Z-Analogue Prime Vert - Zodiacal analogue of prime vertical. The prime vertical of each point is expressed as a longitude. This chart is also known as a Campanus Mundoscope.

Z-Analogue PV Amp - Zodiacal analogue of prime vertical amplitude. The prime vertical amplitude of each point is expressed as a longitude. Prime vertical amplitudes from 0 to +90 degree correspond to 0 Aries to 0

Cancer, whereas prime vertical amplitudes from 0 to –90 degrees correspond to 0 Aries to 0 Capricorn.

Z-Analogue Diurn Arc - Zodiacal analogue of diurnal arc. The diurnal arc of each point is expressed as a longitude. Points which do not cross the horizon during their diurnal rotation are omitted and are not displayed. 0 Aries corresponds to rising across the horizon, 0 Capricorn to culminating, 0 Libra to setting across the horizon, and 0 Cancer to anti-culminating. This chart is also known as a Placidus Mundoscope.

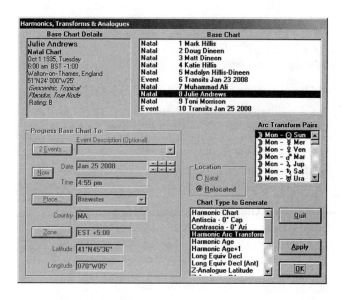

>> To cast an harmonic, antiscia, contra-antiscia, longitude equivalent or zodiacal analogue chart

1. Ensure that the natal type chart that you want to use is already calculated.

2. Choose the **Harmonic/Transform...** menu item from the **Chart** menu

3. Select the required chart type from the **Chart Type to Generate** list box.

4. Select a chart from the **Base Chart** list box.

5. [Harmonic Only] Type a numerical value into the **Harmonic** box, or use the spin button to set an integer value. The harmonic value may be any positive number, either integer or real (ie. it may contain decimal places).

6. [Arc Transform Only] Select a planetary pair from the **Arc Transform Pairs** list.

7. Select either the **Apply** or **OK** button. The subsidiary chart will be calculated and added to the list of calculated charts in the list box on the main screen of the program. Use the **OK** button to close this dialog after the calculation. Use the **Apply** button to leave this dialog open to calculate further charts. After this dialog closes, you can view, print, report on, and otherwise manipulate the newly calculated charts.

>> To cast an age or age+1 harmonic chart

1. Ensure that the natal type chart that you want to use is already calculated.

2. Choose the **Harmonic...** menu item from the **Chart** menu

3. Select the required chart type from the **Chart Type to Generate** list box.

4. Select a chart from the **Base Chart** list box.

5. Either select a stored life event or enter the event details into the appropriate edit boxes.

6. Select either the **Apply** or **OK** button. The subsidiary chart will be calculated and added to the list of calculated charts in the list box on the main screen of the program. Use the **OK** button to close this dialog after the calculation. Use the **Apply** button to leave this dialog open to calculate further charts. After this dialog closes, you can view, print, report on, and otherwise manipulate the newly calculated charts.

Casting a Combined Chart

This section describes how to create a composite, relationship or coalescent chart by combining two charts, or a group composite chart composed of up to 15 base charts.

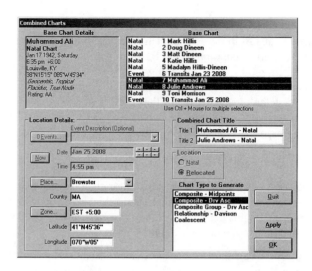

>> To cast a composite, Davison relationship or coalescent chart

1. Ensure that the natal type charts that you wish to combine are already calculated.

2. Choose the **Combined...** menu item from the **Chart** menu

3. Select the required chart type from the **Chart Type to Generate** list box.

4. Select two or more charts from the **Base Chart** list box. Holding down the **Ctrl** key allows multiple charts to be selected at once. You should only select two charts, unless you have selected the "Composite Group" chart type, in which case you may select up to 15 charts.

5. (Optional) Edit the **Title1** and **Title2** boxes. As charts are selected, these title boxes are automatically updated. When either one or two charts are selected, the title list boxes contain the chart name of each chart suffixed with its chart type. When more than two charts are selected then the **Title1** box contains the last names of each selected chart, separated by slashes (/), and the **Title2** box contains the chart type of the first selected chart on the list of base charts. These titles will appear whenever the chart is displayed or printed. These may be edited if you wish.

6. Select the **Location** type. If have selected the "Composite - Midpoints" or "Relationship - Davison" then this option will be disabled, and you can pass to the next step. Normally the combined chart is relocated to wherever the relationship exists. If the **Natal** option is selected then all the boxes

relating to location, including time zone, longitude and latitude will contain the location details from the selected base chart, although only the latitude is used in the chart calculation. If the **Relocated** option is selected then all the boxes relating to location, including time zone, longitude and latitude will contain the current default values. (See Saving and Restoring Settings for details on default values.) Any of these values may be altered in the same manner as when creating a new chart. See Casting a New Chart for instructions on how to alter location values.

7. Select either the **Apply** or **OK** button. The subsidiary chart will be calculated and added to the list of calculated charts in the list box on the main screen of the program. Use the **OK** button to close this dialog after the calculation. Use the **Apply** button to leave this dialog open to calculate further charts. After this dialog closes, you can view, print, report on, and otherwise manipulate the newly calculated charts.

Note - You cannot calculate a composite chart based on other composite charts. The mathematical basis on which composite charts are calculated does not work if composite charts are combined. The only way of combining more than two natal charts is to use the "Group Composite" method.

Casting a Prenatal Chart

This section describes how to create a prenatal chart for an individual whose natal chart has already been cast. The most commonly used type of prenatal chart is the conception chart, for which two different methods of calculation are available. However, there are many other types of prenatal chart type available, plus the ability to derive a natal chart from the date of conception or quickening, if they are known. See Prenatal Charts for a full discussion of the different types of prenatal charts that can be calculated.

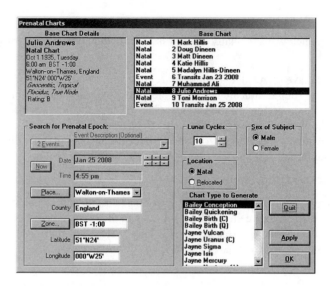

>> **To cast a prenatal chart**

1. Ensure that the base chart that you wish to use is already calculated.

2. Choose the **Prenatal...** menu item from the **Chart** menu

3. Select the required chart type from the **Chart Type to Generate** list box.

4. Select a chart from the **Base Chart** list box.

5. Select the **Location** type. Normally, a prenatal chart should be located where the individual was at the time of the prenatal chart. For example, a conception chart should be located to where the conception took place. However, for some of the other prenatal chart types you cannot know a definite location. In these cases it is recommended that the natal location is used. If the **Natal** option is selected then all the boxes relating to location will contain the details from the selected base chart. If the **Relocated** option is selected then all the boxes relating to location, will contain the current default values, and any of these values may be altered in the same manner as when creating a new chart. See Casting a New Chart for instructions on how to alter location values.

6. If the prenatal chart type is one for which the calculation is based on a number of lunar cycles, then you can specify the number of cycles in the **Lunar Cycles** box. The number of lunar cycles is automatically preset to a suggested value eg. for the conception charts it is set to 10 lunar cycles

(about 273 days) which is the normal term of pregnancy. If you know that the pregnancy was especially short or long term, then this number may be changed.

7. If you have selected a "Bailey Conception" or "Bailey Birth (C)" charts, you should indicate the sex of the individual using the Sex of Subject option buttons. If the sex is not known, then the best alternative is to use the Jayne Uranus (C) or Jayne Birth (C) chart types instead, as these are equivalent to the Bailey Conception and Birth charts but ignore the sex of the subject.

8. Select the **OK** or **Apply** button

A dialog box may appear listing details of the possible prenatal charts. You can select one or more entries from the list and then select the **OK** button in order to calculate the selected charts. These calculated charts will be added to the list of Calculated Charts on the Main Screen.

Casting a Rising/Setting Chart

This section describes how to create a chart for the moment of rising, setting, culmination or anti-culmination of any planet or asteroid on any given day. For rising and setting charts it is possible to choose whether to calculate the chart for the time at which the planet or asteroid would appear to cross the horizon visually, or alternatively to calculate the chart for the time at which its centre crosses the true astronomical horizon.

You can create these types of charts without a base chart. However, if you wish to base them on the date of an existing chart, you should have already cast or opened the chart that you wish to use.

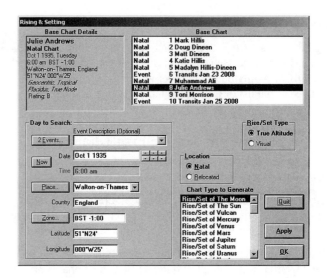

1. Choose **Rising/Setting...** from the **Chart** menu.

2. Select the chart type you want from the **Chart Type to Generate** list box.

>>> To base the rising/setting chart on the date and location of an existing chart:

Select a chart from the **Base Chart** list box.

>>> To do a rising/setting chart for some other date or place:

1. Fill in the required **Date**, or click on the **Now** button for today's date. Select the **Relocated** option button and fill in the required location details.

2. If you are doing a rising or setting chart (as opposed to a culmination or anti-culmination chart), select one of the following **Rise/Set Type** options

True Altitude - the rising or setting time is that for which the centre of the body crosses the astronomical horizon. This ignores atmospheric refraction, the size of the body and parallax effects.

Visual - the rising or setting time is that for which the leading edge of the body rises or the trailing edge would set visually on an idealized flat horizon. This takes account of atmospheric refraction and the size of the body. In the case of the moon, the lunar parallax is also taken into account.

3. Select the **OK** button.

A dialog box will appear listing the times of rise, set, culmination and anti-culmination were found. Select one or more entries on the list and then select the **OK** or **Apply** button in order to generate the charts. These charts will be added to the list of Calculated Charts on the Main Screen.

Casting a Lunar Phase or Eclipse Chart

This section describes how to create a chart for

Progressed Lunar Phases - Any of 8 main progressed lunar phases (new moon, crescent, first quarter, gibbous, full moon, disseminating, third quarter, balsamic), starting 2 phases prior to the search date.

Transiting Lunar Phases - Any of the 4 main transiting lunar phases (new moon, first quarter, full moon, last quarter), starting 4 phases prior to the search date.

Phase Returns - Any lunar phase return (a chart in which the phase angle between the sun and the moon returns to its natal phase angle), starting one lunar month prior to the search date.

Phase Family - Any lunar phase belonging to a "moon phase family", connected to the other members in the family either past or present. The Lunar Gestation Cycle divides the "Moon phase family" by 9 month intervals beginning the series at any New Moon and locates the next or nearest "family related" Moon phase being a First Quarter, Full Moon and finally Last Quarter Moon, all occurring at similar positions in the zodiac. (For a detailed explanation, please see the book "Lunar Shadows, The Lost Key to the Timing of Eclipses" by Dietrich Pessin, who originated this concept.)

Eclipses (List) - Any total or partial solar or lunar eclipse, selectable from a list, starting one year prior to the search date. *Note:* The calculated eclipse times may be either times of maximum eclipse or times of exact lunar phase depending on the eclipse settings in Preferences.

Eclipse (Solar or Lunar) - The most recent or next eclipse of any type.

Eclipse (Solar only) - The most recent or next solar eclipse.

Eclipse (Lunar only) - The most recent or next lunar eclipse.

New Moon - The most recent or next new moon.

Full Moon - The most recent or next full moon.

New or Full Moon (Syzygy) - The most recent or next syzygy moon.

You can create a transiting lunar phase chart without a base chart. However, before creating any other type of lunar phase or eclipse chart, it is necessary to have either cast or opened the base chart that you wish to use.

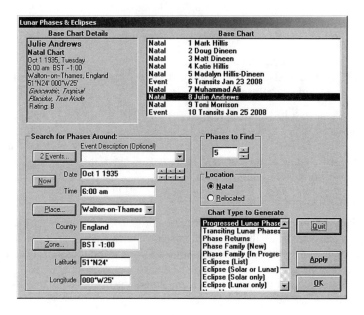

>> **To cast a transiting, progressed or lunar phase return or family chart**

1. Choose **Lunar Phase...** from the **Chart** menu.

2. Select the chart type you want from the **Chart Type to Generate.**

3. If you want to base the lunar phase chart on an existing chart, then select a chart from the **Base Chart** list box. This is optional for transiting lunar phase or family charts, but obligatory for progressed phases.

4. Optionally enter or select event details (including **Date** and **Time** around which to search for the charts). As the program will find the exact time of the lunar phases around the entered date, there is often no need to enter or alter the time.

5. If you have selected "Progressed Lunar Phases" or "Lunar Phase Returns", then you will probably want to select a current date. You can do

this by either manually entering a new date, or by selecting the **Now** button. For all other chart types to generate, selecting a base chart will automatically set the date and time from the base chart. This makes it quick and easy to find the prenatal lunar phases and eclipses.

6. Select **Location** type. If you select the **Natal** option, then all the boxes relating to location will contain the location details from the base chart. If you select the **Relocated** option, then all the boxes relating to location will contain the current default values, and you can enter new location data if you wish to.

7. If you have selected a chart type to generate that produces a list of possible events to choose from, then you can set the number to find in the **Phases to Find** or **Eclipses to Find** box.

8. If you have selected a chart type to generate which results in a single chart, then you can choose whether to find the chart prior to (**Current**), nearest to (**Nearest**), or after (**Next**) the search date in the **Which One** box. If your search date is the date of your base natal chart, then the **Current** option will find a pre-natal chart, and **Next** will find a post-natal chart.

9. Select the **OK** or **Apply** button.

10. For those chart types to generate which produce selection lists, a dialog box will appear listing the lunar phases that were found and their dates and times. You can select one or more entries on the list and then select the **OK** button in order to generate the charts for the chosen lunar phases. Any charts calculated from this procedure are automatically added to the list of Calculated Charts on the Main Screen.

Casting a Locality or Relocated Chart

This section describes how to relocate a chart or to cast a chart for a locality.

The types of locality charts that may be calculated are

Relocated - calculated for the exact same time as the base chart, but for a different latitude and longitude.

Geodetic - using either right ascension or longitude, and optionally allowing a user-defined geographic longitude base point. This technique involves adjusting the MC of the base chart according to a projection of the zodiac onto the earth's surface.

Johndro - using either right ascension or longitude. This technique is similar to the geodetic technique, but incorporates a zodiacal precession adjustment in fixing the base point longitude.

You can create a locality chart based on any geocentric natal type chart. The house system and zodiac type of the resulting chart are always the same as that of the base chart that you have selected.

>> To relocate a chart

1. Choose **Locality...** from the **Chart** menu.

2. Select the "Relocated" chart type from the **Chart Type to Generate.**

3. Enter the details of the location to which you wish to relocate the chart.

4. Select the **OK** button.

The relocated chart will be added to the list of Calculated Charts on the Main Screen.

>> To cast a Geodetic or Johndro type chart

1. Choose **Locality...** from the **Chart** menu.

2. Select the required chart type from the **Chart Type to Generate**.

3. Enter the details of the location for which you wish the chart to be calculated.

4. Select the **OK** button.

If you have selected a User Geodetic chart type, then you will be prompted to enter the terrestrial longitude at which you wish the zodiac to start. In standard Geodetic charts, this longitude is 000W00 (ie. the Greenwich meridian). The Geodetic or Johndro chart will be added to the list of Calculated Charts on the Main Screen.

Casting a Vedic Chart

This section describes how to cast a Vedic or Vedic divisional chart.

A Vedic Natal chart is identical to any other natal chart in Solar Fire except that it must use a sidereal zodiac rather then the tropical zodiac as conventionally used in Western astrology. (The most commonly used sidereal zodiac is "Lahiri", which is the officially nominated zodiac in India.)

It is possible to calculate any Vedic divisional chart using a tropical chart as the base chart. However, conventionally, they are only calculated using base charts that have a sidereal zodiac. Therefore, if you try to calculate a Vedic divisional chart using a base chart that does not have a sidereal zodiac, then Solar Fire will prompt you with a warning message. (This warning may be switched off if you wish).

If you wish to work with Vedic charts in the conventional way, then it is recommended that you ensure that you have all your required base charts already calculated in a sidereal zodiac. You can do this in a variety of ways, as follows.

• Create a new natal chart using **Chart / New**, and ensure the selected zodiac is a sidereal one.

• Use **Chart / Edit / Edit Chart** or **Copy and Edit Chart** and change the selected zodiac to a sidereal one.

• Use **Chart / Edit / Toggle Chart Zodiac** to change the zodiac (and optionally also house system) of an existing base chart. See Default Zodiac and Default House System for information on changing your preferred zodiac and house system for vedic (sidereal) charts.

• Use **Chart / Vedic** (ie. this dialog) and choose the "Vedic Natal" method to create a new base chart using the default sidereal zodiac.

>> To cast a Vedic or Vedic divisional chart

1. Choose **Vedic...** from the **Chart** menu.

2. Select the required chart type from the **Chart Type to Generate.**

3. Select the **OK** or **Apply** button.

The chart will be added to the list of Calculated Charts on the Main Screen.

Chapter 12: Saving Charts to a File

This chapter describes how to save a calculated chart to a chart database file, so that it may be opened again in subsequent sessions with the Solar Fire program.

You can save charts of all types created in Solar Fire apart from multiple composite charts. Although these types of charts cannot be saved to a chart database file, you may still **retain** them for use in subsequent sessions of Solar Fire. See Retaining Charts for details on how to retain charts.

The **Chart Details** display box on the Main Screen indicates whether or not the chart can be saved, and if it can be saved, whether it has already been saved or retained.

It is possible to save as many copies of a chart as you wish, either to the same chart file or to a different one. (See Using the File Manager for information about how to create new chart files.)

Note that if the Auto Chart Save option is switched on, then all new or edited charts will be saved automatically to the currently selected chart file as soon as they are cast. See Auto Chart Save for more information about this option.

>> To save one or more charts from the Main Screen

1. Select the required chart or charts from the list of Calculated Charts

2. Select the **Save to File...** item from the **Chart** menu

3. If you are saving a single selected chart, and that chart is already saved, then a dialog box will appear asking you to confirm whether you wish to save another copy of the chart. If you are have selected more than one chart to save, then you will not be asked to confirm whether to resave any saved charts - all selected charts will be saved to the selected chart file regardless of whether or not they have been previously saved.

4. The File Manager will appear, listing all of the available chart database files. Select the required chart file from this list, or click on the **Create** button to create a new empty chart file, and then click on the **OK** button.

>> To save the currently displayed chart in the "View Chart" screen

Select the Save button and then follow step 4 above.

>> To save any unsaved charts before exiting from Solar Fire

When you exit from Solar Fire you will be asked whether you want to save any charts that have not yet been saved. If you choose not to, then the program will close immediately. Otherwise the Unsaved Charts dialog will appear.

>> To save one or more charts to the displayed chart file

1.   Highlight the charts you wish to save to this file.

2.   Click on the **Save** button.

Once the charts are saved they will disappear from the list, leaving only any other unsaved charts. If no unsaved charts remain, then the program will close.

>> To select a different chart file to save charts into

Click on the **File** button

This will display the File Manager, from which you can select another chart file or create a new one.

>> To exit without saving any more charts

Click on the **Discard All** button.

The program will close without saving any remaining charts.

>> To go back to Solar Fire without closing

Click on the **Cancel** button.

Chapter 13: Manipulating Calculated Charts

As soon as you calculate a chart or retrieve a chart from a chart file, the name of the chart is added to the "Calculated Charts" list on the Main Screen. A calculated chart is open and ready to view, see reports on, cast subsidiary charts from, and print. Calculated charts may or may not have been saved to a file.

This section describes certain file-type manipulations that you can do with calculated charts, even though they may not yet have been saved to a file.

If a calculated chart has not already been saved, it can be saved after being edited or retained. Once an unsaved chart is removed from the list of "Calculated Charts", it cannot be saved or retrieved.

Editing a Calculated Chart

This section describes how to copy and edit, or edit and replace, a natal or event chart that appears on the list of "Calculated Charts" on the main screen. It is not possible to edit any type of chart other than a natal or event chart or its equivalent. If you wish to alter any other type of chart you will have to use one of the subsidiary chart options such as Progressed, Return, Harmonic, etc.

It is also possible to copy and edit, or to edit and replace a chart that is already stored in a chart file. For instructions on how to do this, see Retrieving Charts From a File.

>> To copy and edit a natal type calculated chart

1.   From the main screen, select the required chart in the list of "Calculated Charts".

2.   Select the **Edit / Copy and Edit...** item from the **Chart** menu. (If the selected chart is not editable, then this option is disabled).

3.   The "New Chart Data Entry" dialog box will appear, displaying the details of the selected chart.

4.   Type over whatever details you wish to change.

5.   Select the **OK** button. An edited copy of the original chart will be created and added to the list of calculated charts. The original chart will remain in the list.

>> To edit and replace a natal type calculated chart

1.   From the main screen, select the required chart in the list of "Calculated Charts".

2.   Select the **Edit / Edit Chart...** item from the **Chart** menu. (If the selected chart is not editable, then this option is disabled).

3.   The "New Chart Data Entry" dialog box will appear, displaying the details of the selected chart.

4.   Type over whatever details you wish to change.

5.   Select the **OK** button. An edited copy of the original chart will replace the original chart on the list of calculated charts.

Toggling Zodiac or Node Type

If you wish to change the zodiac or lunar node type of a chart that appears on the list of "Calculated Charts" on the main screen, then you can do so via a shortcut, without having to edit the chart details.

>> To toggle the zodiac (and optionally also house system) of a chart

1.   From the main screen, select the required chart/s in the list of "Calculated Charts".

2.   Select the **Edit / Toggle Chart Zodiac** from the **Chart** menu.

The change is instantly applied to the selected chart/s. See Default Zodiac and Default House System for information on changing your preferred zodiac and house system for vedic (sidereal) charts.

>> To toggle the node type of a chart between true and mean

1.   From the main screen, select the required chart/s in the list of "Calculated Charts".

2.   Select the **Edit / Toggle Node Type** from the **Chart** menu.

The change is instantly applied to the selected chart/s. However, any new charts you cast or open will still use the default lunar node type. To change the default lunar node type, see the Calculations section in Editing Settings.

Deleting Charts from the List of Calculated Charts

This section describes how to remove one or more charts from the list of "Calculated Charts". You might wish to do this if you already have a large number of charts calculated, and wish to reduce the list of charts to a more manageable size. Any type of chart may be deleted.

>> To remove one or more charts from the list of "Calculated Charts"

Select the required chart(s) from the list of "Calculated Charts"

1.　　Select the **Delete...** item from the **Chart** menu

2.　　A dialog box will appear, asking you to confirm whether or not you wish to delete the selected charts. If you select the **OK** button, then the charts will be removed.

Retaining Charts

This section describes how to retain or remove a selection of calculated charts to appear automatically in the list of Calculated Charts in subsequent Solar Fire sessions.

Retained charts are different from saved charts in that any types of calculated charts may be retained, whereas multiple composite charts may not be saved to file. Also, retained charts are stored with all the planetary positions pre-calculated, whereas charts saved to file must have their planetary positions re-calculated each time that the chart is opened. Retained charts use much more disk storage than saved charts - about 3000 bytes for each chart, whereas saved charts use only about 300 bytes. Typically it is useful to retain only a small number of charts that you like to work with frequently. Retaining a large number of charts uses a lot of space and clutters up the list of calculated charts. For example, if you frequently work with your own and your partner's charts, then you might like to retain both of your natal charts plus your composite chart, and perhaps also your current solar return charts.

>> To retain one or more charts for subsequent sessions of Solar Fire

Select the required charts from the list of "Calculated Charts"

Select the **Retain Chart/s...** option from the **Chart** menu

This will display a dialog box asking you to confirm whether or not you wish to retain the selected charts. If you select the **OK** button, then these charts will be added to the list of retained charts for subsequent sessions

>> To clear the retained charts

Select the **Clear Retained...** option from the **Chart** menu

This will display a dialog box asking you to confirm whether or not you wish to clear the selection of currently retained charts. If you select the **OK** button, then no charts will be retained for subsequent sessions.

Note that these options have no effect on the list of calculated charts during the current session. They only take effect when Solar Fire is next started up.

Chapter 14: Emailing Charts

This chapter explains how to send chart files and chart data by email, either from Solar Fire's main screen, or from the "Chart Open" dialog.

You can send data directly from within Solar Fire provided that you have a MAPI compliant email program.

If you do not have a MAPI compliant email program, then Solar Fire will generate files that you can attach to your emails manually, instead.

About MAPI

MAPI is a mail automation protocol that allows third party programs to automate the generation of email.

In order to use these automated email options, you must have a MAPI compliant email program. All Microsoft email programs (eg. Outlook and Outlook Express) and Eudora are MAPI compliant, for example.

You may also need to ensure that the MAPI options are activated in some email programs, for example in Eudora Pro v3, you may need to go into the Tools / Options menu item, find the MAPI category, and ensure that "Use Eudora MAPI server" is switched to either "When Eudora is Running" or "Always". If you are unsure about any of these options, you should consult the documentation of your email program (eg. search for "MAPI"), or contact the manufacturer of your email program.

Sending Charts By Email

>> To send a chart file from the main screen

1.   Select the required chart/s from the list of calculated charts

2.   Select the **Send Charts by Email...** item from the Chart menu.

3.   Select any required chart email options (as described in the following section)

>> To send a chart file from the Chart Open dialog

1.   Optionally, select the required chart/s from the list of charts in the current chart file

2.   Optionally, click on the **Send/Add...** button to choose between the **Selected Chart Only** or **All Charts** items.

3.   Click on the **Send/Add...** button and select the **Send Charts by Email** item.

4.   Select any required chart email options (as described in the following section)

These methods will create any optionally required temporary chart files containing the selected charts (and optionally also a chart comments file containing any comments associated with these charts), and start up your email program with these files already attached to an outgoing email, and optionally also with chart details already listed within the body of the email.

You will need to address the email, and optionally edit it or append text to the body of the message as required before sending it.

Selecting Chart Email Options

You have various options available to you regarding the format in which the chart data will be sent. For example, you can send it as an attached chart file, or alternatively with the chart details appearing as written text within the body of your message. If it is sent as an attached file, then you can choose whether this will be a Solar Fire chart file (readable only by others who own Solar Fire), or whether it will be a text file containing written chart details.

Whenever you invoke any chart email command in Solar Fire, you will be presented with the **Email Charts** dialog, which allows you to select from the various options.

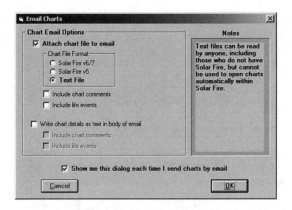

If you uncheck the "Show me" option at the bottom of the dialog, then your current settings will be remembered and applied to all future chart emailing, without you being re-prompted with this dialog. However, you can re-enable this, or edit any of the settings in this dialog at any time by choosing **Preferences / Edit Settings / Charts / Chart Data Email Options** from the main screen.

Attach chart file to email

This option is recommended if you have a large number of charts to send, because there are limits to how many chart details may be sent in the body of the email.

You must also choose this option if you wish to make the charts available to the recipients to open within their own copies of Solar Fire.

• **Chart File Format** – If all recipients own Solar Fire Deluxe or Gold, then choose Solar Fire v6/v7 format. If all recipients own Solar Fire v5, but not all own Deluxe or Gold, then choose Solar Fire v5 format. If any recipients might not own Solar Fire, then you have a choice of either using the Text File format instead of a Solar Fire chart file, or alternatively of attaching a Solar Fire chart file anyway (for the benefit of all those recipients who do own a copy), but additionally including chart details as text in the body of the email for those recipients who do not own Solar Fire.

• **Include Chart Comments** – This is only relevant if any of the charts you are emailing contains any comments text. If so, you can choose to include or omit it with this option.

- **Include Life Events** – This is only relevant if any of the charts you are emailing contains any stored life events. If so, you can choose to include or omit them with this option. Note that this option is not available if you have chosen the Solar Fire v4/v5 chart file format, because this format cannot store life events.

Write chart details as text in body of email

This option is recommended only if you don't have a large number of charts to send, because there are limits to how many chart details may be sent in the body of the email.

This option may be chosen *in addition* to the chart file option if you wish – thus providing the chart information to your recipients both as an attached file and within your email.

- **Include Chart Comments** – This is only relevant if any of the charts you are emailing contains any comments text. If so, you can choose to include or omit them with this option.

- **Include Life Events** – This is only relevant if any of the charts you are emailing contains any stored life events. If so, you can choose to include or omit them with this option.

Following is an example of chart details as text, as it would appear both in the body of the email, or as an attached text file. This example includes comments text, but no life events.

Mary Decker - Natal Chart
4 Aug 1958, 2:59 am, EDT +4:00
Raritan New Jersey, 40N34'10", 074W38'
Geocentric Tropical Zodiac
Rating: AA
Comments: From Birth Certificate (Mary Frances Wood, AA)
Mary Theresa Decker
Athlete
Decker (later Slaney) was an outstanding athlete and winner in major competitions during the Eighties. At the Olympics, this world-class runner never fulfilled her potential. During the 1984 Olympics she was accidentally tripped up by Zola Budd, ruining both athletes' chances for medals.

Chapter 15: Viewing Charts, Grids and Pages

This chapter describes how to view charts, aspect grids or other page displays for charts that appears on the list of "Calculated Charts" on the main screen.

Before viewing a chart or its grid, it is necessary to have either cast or opened the charts that you wish to use. If you have not yet done so, see Casting a Natal Chart for instructions on casting a new chart, or Retrieving Charts From a File for instructions on opening an existing chart.

Viewing a Single Chart or Grid

Any type of chart that Solar Fire calculates can be viewed in wheel form or in an aspect grid as follows.

>> To view a chart from the main screen

Select a chart on the list of "Calculated Charts".

Choose **Current Chart...** from the **View** menu, or Double click the mouse on a chart on the list of "Calculated Charts".

>> To view an aspect grid from the main screen

Select a chart on the list of "Calculated Charts".

Choose **Current Grid...** from the **View** menu.

>> To view a chart and aspect grid on the same page, from the main screen

Select a chart on the list of "Calculated Charts".

Choose **Current Chart+Grid...** from the **View** menu.

>> To view a chart or grid whose image was the last one to be displayed

Choose **Last Image...** from the **View** menu.

Viewing MultiWheels and Synastry Grids

There are a variety of wheel and grid displays that show more than one chart eg. biwheels, synastry grids, dual wheels etc.

>> To view any displays which require more than one chart

Select the required option from the **View** menu. These options are

- **Dual Wheels** - Two separate charts

- **BiWheel** - Two concentric charts

- **TriWheel** - Three concentric charts

- **QuadriWheel** - Four concentric charts

- **QuinquiWheel** - Five concentric charts

- **Synastry Grid** - An aspect grid showing inter-chart aspects

Selecting any of these options will display the "Chart Selection" screen, which allows two or more charts to be selected for viewing, printing or reporting.

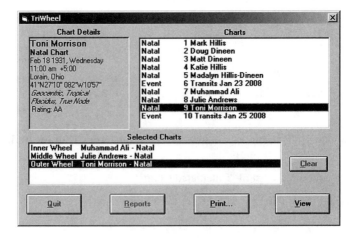

>> To select the positions of charts on the multiwheels (or on the synastry grid)

Select a wheel (or grid) position on the **Selected Charts** list box

Select a chart for this position from the **Charts** list box

Repeat above steps for each chart position

When a chart is selected, its name and type is written into the **Selected Charts** list box. If there are further selections to be made, then the highlight bar will move to the next wheel (or grid) position on the **Selected Charts** list, ready for the next chart to be selected from the **Charts** list box. It is possible to change the selection of any chart by repeating the above procedure as often as required. Whilst all the chart selections have not yet been made, the **View**, **Report** and **Print...** buttons are disabled, and cannot be used.

>> To clear all the selections that have been made so far

Select the **Clear** button. This will return the state of the screen to how it appeared before any selections were made.

When all required charts have been selected, then the following options are available.

>> To view the chart, grid or page

Select the **View** button. If this image has not already been created, then it will create the image. Otherwise it will locate the old image, and in both cases it will then display the desired image on the "View Chart" screen.

>> To print the chart, grid or page

Select the **Print...** button. This displays the "Print Chart" dialog box, allowing the user to cancel printing, add the print job to the batch print queue, to alter printer settings, or to print immediately. See Casting a Natal Chart for more details on these options.

For dual wheels, biwheels, synastry grids and page displays which contain 2 charts only, a further option is available.

>> To view a report using the two selected charts

Select the **Reports...** button. This will display the "Report View" screen, which allows a variety of synastry reports for the selected charts to be browsed, edited or printed. See Synastry Reports for further details about synastry reports. The same set of synastry reports is generated regardless of whether the user has selected the biwheel, synastry grid or other user defined page option.

Reports are not available for triwheels or quadriwheels or other pages that contain more than two charts. (It is possible, however, to generate reports on the individual charts in a multiwheel by selecting the appropriate options from the main screen menu.)

Viewing Pages

There are a variety of supplied and customizable pages that may show one or more charts and other astrological data in ways that are not possible from any of the other display options in Solar Fire. For example, a page may display a single wheel in a non-standard scaling and positioning, or may display multiple wheels, grids or tabulations on a single page.

>> To view any page

From the main screen:-

Select the **Page Topic Index...** option from the **View** menu. This will display the Page Selection by Topic dialog box, listing all available page layout files categorized by topic. If you select a page layout file that displays the same number of charts as are already selected in the list of calculated charts, then it will display that page immediately, using the currently selected charts. Otherwise the "Chart Selection" screen will be displayed, which allows the charts to be selected prior to viewing the page.

From the View Chart screen:-

Select the **Pages...** button (or make a right hand mouse button click over the list of images at the top right of the screen). This will display the "Page Selection by Topic" dialog box, listing all page layout files that use the same number of charts as the currently displayed page type. When you have chosen a page, you have the option of selecting the **View** button to preview the new page without creating a new image, or selecting the **OK** button to create a new image and close the Page Selection dialog.

>> To view any of the four most recently viewed page types

From the main screen, select the name of the required page from the list in the **View** menu underneath the **User Defined Page...** option. This list is empty the first time you run Solar Fire, but is updated each time you view a user-defined page, and is retained from one session on Solar Fire to the next.

The user may change the appearance of any existing pages, and new pages may be created from scratch. See Editing a Page Design File for more information.

Using the Page Topic Index

The Page Topic Index is a dialog that contains a list of displayable wheels and pages, categorized into various topics, in a collapsible/expandable list. You have the ability to select pages from this list to view or preview, and to re-organize the arrangement and names of topic categories as you wish.

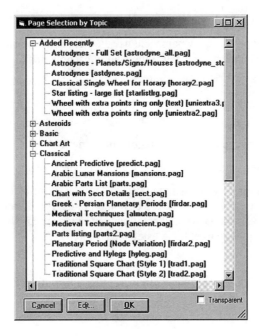

- **Cancel** – closes this dialog without selecting a page.

- **Edit...** – opens the highlighted page for editing in the Page Designer.

- **OK** - selects the highlighted page and closes the dialog.

- **Apply** - selects the highlighted page but leaves the dialog open. This is useful in order to preview multiple pages before selecting a final one.

- **Transparent** – (only available in Windows 2000, XP or later) allows the dialog to be made semi-transparent. This is useful in helping you to see otherwise hidden parts of pages when you are using the Apply button to preview pages without closing this dialog.

>> To add a new topic category

Click on any topic category name and use the right hand mouse button to display a pop-up menu, and select the **Add Topic** item.

This will display a dialog allowing you to enter the new category name

>> To rename a topic category

Click on the topic category name and use the right hand mouse button to display a pop-up menu, and select the **Rename Topic** item.

This will put a focus box around the topic category name and allow you to edit it.

>> To move a page from one category into another

Simply drag the page description onto another topic category name.

If the topic category you wish to move to is off the top or bottom of the page, then drag the page off the top or bottom of the list. This will cause the list of pages to collapse, and scroll up or down respectively, thus making the required target topic category visible.

>> To refresh the list of pages after creating a new page or editing a page title

Use the F5 key.

This is the standard Windows key for refreshing lists of files.

Shortcuts for Viewing Multiple Wheels or Charts

It is possible to expedite the process of viewing wheels, grids and pages by selecting multiple charts from the list of Calculate Charts before selecting the required viewing option.

>> To create chart wheel images for several charts at once

1.   Select all of the required charts from the list of Calculated Charts on the Main Screen.

2.   Select the **Current Chart** menu option from the **View** menu.

An image will be created for each of the selected charts without any further action on your part.

>> To view a biwheel without using the Multiwheel selection screen

1.   Select all of the required charts from the list of Calculated Charts on the Main Screen.

2.   Select the **BiWheel** menu option from the **View** menu.

An image of the biwheel will be displayed immediately. The first chart on the list of calculated charts will be on the inner wheel. If you want to reverse the order of charts, then you can select the **Swap** button.

>> To create images for several biwheels at once

1.   Select all of the required charts from the list of Calculated Charts on the Main Screen.

2.   Select the **BiWheel** menu option from the **View** menu.

An image will be created for each pair of selected charts. The first chart of each pair will be on the inner wheel. If you want to reverse the order of charts, then you can select the **Swap** button.

The same principle applies for any selectable page as well. For example, if you have an eight-wheel page, then you can select the eight charts from the list of Calculated Charts in order to avoid having to select them later in the Multiwheel selection screen. The main limitation of this shortcut is that the charts are always taken in the order in which they appear in the list of Calculated Charts.

Chapter 16: Using the View Screen Features

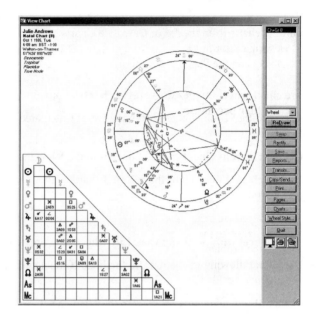

The View Chart dialog is sizeable down to minimum dimensions of 640x480 pixels.

If you are viewing a chart or page for the first time, then its image will be drawn according to the currently selected chart options, and the chart's reference number will be added to the list box on the top right hand side of the screen.

If you are viewing a chart or grid whose image has already been created previously, then its existing image will simply be redisplayed.

>> To change any of the display options

Place the mouse over any part of the displayed chart or page image and click on the right-hand mouse button. This will display a pop-up menu containing the same items as the main screen's **Chart Options** (such as displayed points, aspect set, color schemes etc.) from which you may select any items to change with the left-hand mouse button, as usual. See Changing Chart Options for instructions on altering chart options. After you have changed any display options, select the **ReDraw** button in order to regenerate the image using the current set of chart options.

If you invoke this menu while the mouse is hovering over an object on the page (such as a wheel, grid of tabulation), then the pop-up menu also has an option allowing you to edit properties of that object. See Editing Properties of Objects on the Page for further information.

>> To view any other previously created image

Select the desired chart or page item from the list box. The image of the selected chart, grid or page will be displayed in place of the last image.

It is possible, during computation of a chart or grid image, that the computer may run out of video memory. In this case an error dialog box will appear, notifying the user of the problem. If this happens, you can take several different corrective steps. The first time that this happens, it might still be possible to generate the image despite the error. To try to generate the image despite the problem, select the **ReDraw** button. If the error recurs, then use the following procedure. Firstly, print all the chart images that you wish to keep (or add them to the batch print queue), and then from the main screen. Then select the **Clear Images...** option from the **View** menu. This will delete all the chart, grid and page images that have been created so far, and free up all associated memory. You can then proceed normally again.

Whilst viewing a chart, there are a number of buttons and controls that may be used for various purposes. Some of these, such as the **Rectify** button or the **Save** button may be used when a single chart is being viewed, and others, such as the **Swap** button, when multiple charts are being viewed.

Using View Screen Buttons

There are three page viewing mode buttons underneath the Quit button. These are:-

Normal view - this displays the page as optimized for normal viewing on the screen

Printer Preview (Full) - this displays the full page as it would be printed

Printer Preview (Zoomed) - this displays the page as it would be printed, but zoomed enough to allow its full width or height to fit in to the available space, and allowing the rest of the page to be viewed by scrolling

Note: Page designs may contain multiple page sizes. If the page design you are using contains different information in its page sizes for screen as opposed to its printer page sizes, then you will see this difference reflected when you change viewing modes.

Note: If the page design you are displaying contains only printer sized pages, then the **Normal view** button will be hidden.

The other buttons are:-

ReDraw - This option causes the displayed page to be redrawn according to the current settings and display options.

Swap - This option is only available for page displays involving two or more charts. It causes the displayed charts to be swapped or cycled. For example, if you are displaying a biwheel, then the inner and outer charts are swapped. If you are viewing a quadriwheel, then each time you use this option, the innermost chart moves to the outermost position, and the others charts are moved inwards correspondingly.

Rectify - This allows you to easily and interactively edit the date, time, Ascendant, Midheaven, latitude or longitude of the chart (or of the first or innermost chart on the page if there are multiple charts). It is described fully in Adjusting a Chart to a new Time or Date.

Save - This allows the displayed chart to be saved to a file. It is fully described in Saving Charts to a File.

Reports - This invokes the **Reports** screen, which is fully described in Generating Chart Reports**.**

Transits - This invokes the **Dynamic Report Selection** screen, which is fully described in Using Dynamic Reports and Time Maps.

Copy/Send - This invokes a "Copy Image To" dialog that allows you to select whether to send the currently displayed image to the clipboard, to a file, or to an email attachment, with various selectable options. See Copying, Publishing and Sending Graphics.

Print - This allows the displayed image to be sent to your printer, or to the print queue for printing later. You can also alter printer settings before printing, if desired.

Pages – This displays the "Page Selection by Topic" dialog, allowing you to select other page types to preview or display.

Charts – This displays the chart selection dialog, allowing you to select alternative charts to be displayed with the currently displayed page type. *Note:* You can also edit the charts events or comments from this dialog, by using a right hand mouse click to bring up a pop-up menu when hovering over any chart in the list.

Wheel Style – If the currently displayed page has only one wheel type displayed, then this will display the File Manager with a list of wheel style files that you can select for this wheel type. If there is more than one wheel type displayed on the current page (eg. a uniwheel and a biwheel), then this will display the Chart Options menu, from which you can choose one of the wheel style types.

Adjusting a Chart to a new Time or Date

This section describes how to use a rectification-assisting tool to adjust the date, time or angles of a natal or event chart. (If the chart that you are displaying is not a natal or event type chart, then the **Rectify...** button will be disabled.)

>> To adjust a chart

1.   Display the chart that you wish to rectify in the "View Chart" window. (If you are viewing a multiwheel, then make sure that the chart you wish to rectify is the first charts listed, which is usually the innermost chart.)

2.   Click on the **Rectify...** button

3.   This will display the "Rectify Assist" dialog box.

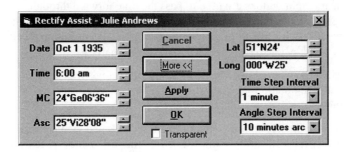

>> To adjust the chart's date

Click on the spin button next to the **Date** box to change the date by 1 day at a time, or type a new date directly into the box.

>> To adjust the chart's time

Click on the spin button next to the **Time** box to change the time by whatever interval is selected in the **Time Step Interval** box, or type a new time directly into the box. (You can make the **Time Step Interval** box visible by clicking on the **More** button.)

>> To adjust the chart's MC or Asc

Click on the spin button next to the **MC** or **Asc** box to change the angle by whatever interval is selected in the **Angle Step Interval** box, or type a new time directly into the box. (You can make the **Angle Step Interval** box visible by clicking on the **More** button.)

>> To adjust the chart's latitude or longitude

1.   Click on the **More** button to make the **Lat** and **Long** boxes visible.

2.   Click on the spin button next to the **Lat** or **Long** box to change the angle by whatever interval is selected in the **Angle Step Interval** box, or type a new latitude or longitude into the box.

Whenever you adjust any of the values, then the data displayed in each of the other boxes is updated automatically to ensure inter-consistency between them. For example, adjusting the MC by 1 degree will cause the time to shift by 15 seconds.

Note that if spin buttons are used to pass the time forward through midnight, then the date is automatically incremented by one day. If the time passes backwards through midnight, then the date is automatically decremented by one day.

Angles can be entered in degrees, minutes and seconds (eg. "133 24 20") or in zodiacal annotation (eg. "13 Cn 24 20"). For more information on entering angles see Entering Angles.

Time can be entered in hours, minutes and seconds and include an am/pm indicator (eg. "7:30" or "2:23pm"). See Entering a Time for more details.

>> To preview the effect of the changes on the chart image

Click on the **Apply** button. This will create a new calculated chart, and replace the chart image with an image using the new chart, but leave the "Rectify Assist" dialog box where it is for further adjustments to be made.

You can check the **Transparent** box to make this dialog semi-transparent. This allows you to see otherwise hidden parts of the chart when you are applying changes and leaving this dialog open.

>> To apply the changes and return to the Chart View screen

Click on the **OK** button. This will create a new calculated chart, and replace the chart image with an image using the new chart, and The "Rectify Assist" dialog box will disappear.

You may repeat these procedures as many times as you wish with the same chart image. When you display the first adjusted image, a new chart is created. When subsequent adjustments are made, this new chart is edited, and no further new charts are created. Note that the new chart calculated this way will be unsaved (unless you have switched on the Autosave option), so you may wish to save it before proceeding by clicking on the **Save** button.

Using Dials and Pointers

It is usually possible to alternate between displaying a chart wheel and a dial display of the same chart or charts by simply selecting the desired option with the mouse from the **Wheel/Dial** drop-down list. The style of wheel or dial that is displayed depends on whatever is selected as the default style under the **Wheel Styles...** and **Dial Styles...** of the **Chart Options** menu.

This option has no effect if the displayed page is one that uses a specifically named wheel or dial style. However, if you are using any of Solar Fire's pre-defined displays from the **View** menu, such as the **Biwheel** or **Wheel+Grid** options, or if you are using an ordinary page layout which uses default display styles, then this option will work as expected.

Whenever a dial is displayed, a pointer is displayed in the middle of the innermost chart in the dial. Initially this pointer will be pointing to the zero point on the dial scale. You can move the pointer in a variety of ways, set an orb for the display of midpoints, and select which chart the pointer is associated with. Before any of these things can be done, you must first switch on the pointer options box.

>> To switch on the pointer options box

Click anywhere inside the innermost chart of the dial that you want to use. If the page you are viewing has more than one dial on it, then the pointer options box will only appear inside one dial at a time. Clicking on another dial will switch it off in the previous dial, and switch it on in the newly selected dial.

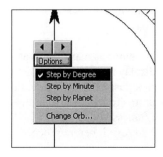

>> To step the pointer around the dial

1.   Click on the **Options** button in the pointer options box to see the drop-down menu

2.   Select one of the following Step options

o   **Step by Degree** - Step by one degree on the dial scale at a time

o   **Step by Minute** - Step by one minute of a degree on the dial scale at a time

o   **Step by Planet** - Step to the next planet position on the dial

3.   Click on the left or right arrows on the spin button above the options button. Each click will step the pointer to the next degree, minute or planet position on the dial, depending on which step option was chosen.

If the dial is a multiwheel, then the pointer will always initially be associated with the innermost chart in the dial. However, you can select another chart to use the pointer with, as follows.

>> To select which chart to use the pointer with

1.   Click on the **Options** button in the pointer options box to see the drop-down menu.

2.   Select one of the charts listed at the bottom of the menu.

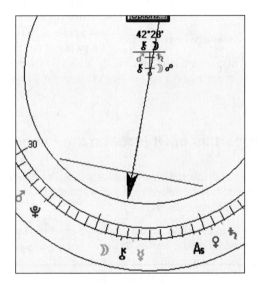

When the pointer reaches a position where it is at the midpoint of two planets, then a solid red line is drawn between those two planets. If those two planets also happen to form an aspect in the chart, then a dashed line is drawn from each planet to the centre of the dial. The dashed line takes on the same color as the color of the aspect is formed, according to the current selected aspect colors.

In addition to the lines which appear, a midpoint tree is displayed underneath the options box indicating which planets are forming the midpoint to the pointer position, and if an aspect is formed, then the aspect symbol is also displayed.

In the example shown, the pointer is pointing to 42°28', and this is the midpoint of the Mars and Saturn, and also of Chiron and the Moon. Additionally, Chiron and the Moon are in opposition (180°) aspect.

Initially the orb for midpoints and aspects is set to 1°00'. However, you can change this orb. The orb is measured in terms of a 360 degree circle, regardless of the modulus of the dial, so a 1 degree orb corresponds to 1/4 degree on the dial scale of a 90 degree dial, and to 1/8 degree on the dial scale of a 45 degree dial, for example.

>> To change the orb of the midpoint tree in the dial

1.   Click on the **Options** button in the pointer options box to see the drop-down menu.

2.   Select the **Change Orb...** option.

3.   This will display a dialog box which allows you to enter the orb that you require, in decimal degrees or degrees and minutes, separated by a space.

Editing Properties of Objects on the Page

Some objects on the displayed page (such as wheels, grids and tabulations) have properties that may be edited in place, without the need to first open the page design in the page designer.

Place the mouse over an object on the displayed chart or page image and click on the right-hand mouse button. If the object has any editable properties, then the first item on the menu will be "Properties of <ObjectType>...", and selecting it will display a small pop-up dialog which allows you to edit these properties.

When this dialog appears, it contains a list of properties that may be edited in the selected page object, and the values to which they are currently set.

Properties that have no predefined value are shown as "Default", followed by the name of the current Solar Fire default value that applies in the absence of a specifically selected value. For example, the Points File value is "Default (PLAN&CH)", which means that this object has no Points File value, and therefore Solar Fire's current default points file will be applied when this object is displayed, and that the current default points file happens to be "PLAN&CH.PTS".

The types of properties that may be edited are as follows:

- Frame Type – for any object that has a rectangular frame.

- Points File – for any object that requires a point file selection.

- Aspect File – for any object that requires an aspect file selection.

- Rulership Level – for any object that uses a rulership level.

- Weighted Scores – for any object that has an option of weighted versus unweighted scores.

- Zodiac Type – for any object that requires a zodiac type setting.

- Modulus – for any object that uses a modulus value (such as a sort strip).

- Maximum Orb – for any object that uses a maximum orb (such as an aspects list).

- Graphic File – for the graphic object only.

- Dignity/Almuten File – for objects that use dignity/almuten definitions.

- Star File – for objects that require a star file selection.

- Parts File – for objects that require an Arabic Parts file selection.

- Asteroid File – for objects that require an asteroid file selection.

- Extra Bodies File – for objects that require a extra bodies file selection.

- Extra Ring Points File – for objects that require an extra ring points file selection.

- Wheel File – for wheel objects (uniwheel, biwheel, triwheel, quadriwheel).

>> To edit a property

Click on the property name on the list of available properties.

If the current value of this property is not a "Default" value, then the edit box below the list will be set to that value, ready for you to edit.

If the current value of this property is a "Default" value, then the edit box below the list will remain empty, ready for you to enter a value if you wish.

There are three ways of choosing a value.

•   For properties which are file names – click on the > button to open a file selection dialog.

•   For properties which have a pre-set list of possible values - click on the down-arrow to scroll through the list of values and select one.

•   For other properties – type the new value directly into the edit box.

After you have edited each property, its new value will be displayed in the list.

>> To reset a property to its default value

Move the cursor into the edit box, delete any text in it, and then press the Enter key.

>> To apply and view your changes

Click on the **Save** button.

This will close the dialog and redraw the page.

Note: **Only the currently displayed page size is affected by any changes you make in this way.** Page designs may contain multiple page sizes. If you wish to alter properties of objects in any other page sizes (such as the page size which is used when printing the page), then you must open the page file in the Page Designer and edit the objects in each page size individually, as required.

Chapter 17: Copying, Publishing and Sending Graphics

You can copy any of Solar Fire's chart displays and graphic ephemerides to the Windows clipboard (to be pasted into another program), to a file anywhere on your computer or network, or to a file that is automatically attached to an email ready to be addressed and sent. Various graphic file formats may be used, as well as some other options governing the appearance of the output.

>> To copy, publish or send a graphic

- From the Chart View screen, select the Copy button

- From the Graphic Ephemeris screen, select the Copy menu item after using the right hand mouse button over the ephemeris area

This will display the "Copy Image To..." dialog, allowing various selections to be made.

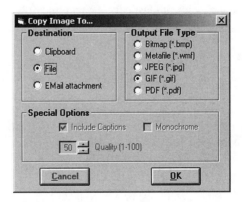

Destination

- **Clipboard** – This will send the graphic to the Windows clipboard, from where it can be pasted into any other program that recognizes the graphic type. For example, you can paste it into a word processor or desktop publishing program.

- **File** – This will send the graphic to a file of your choice. You will be prompted to specify a file name and location.

- **Email attachment** – This will generate a graphic file that is automatically attached to an outgoing email, ready to send, provided that you have a MAPI compliant email program. See About MAPI for further details.

Graphic Type

- **Bitmap** – This will create a bitmap file, which is a fixed resolution graphics file used in many Windows applications. This type of graphic may be placed and scaled in some other application, but as it has a fixed resolution, doing so may cause some loss of image quality. Typically this type of file is rather large (often over 1Mbyte), and is therefore not usually suitable for sending over the internet, unless it is first zipped or compressed in some way.

- **Metafile** - This will create a Windows metafile, which is a scalable graphics file used in many Windows applications. It is possible to place and scale the graphic to your requirements without loss of image quality, using the commands of the application that you are using. Hence this format is good for high quality desktop publishing. This type of file is usually very small in size, but it has the disadvantage that if you send it over the internet, the recipient must have the required Solar Fire fonts installed on their machine, or else they will see incorrect symbols in place of any astrological glyphs. (See PDF as a possible better alternative).

- **JPEG** – This will create a JPEG file, which is a somewhat like a compressed bitmap file. This type of graphic may be placed and scaled in some other application, but as it has a fixed resolution, doing so may cause some loss of image quality. Generally the JPEG format is preferred when your images contain photographic or artistic elements. (Otherwise the GIF format is usually much better).

- **GIF** – This will create a GIF file, which is a compressed bitmap file (without loss of clarity) allowing a maximum of 256 colors. Typically this type of file is very small, and is especially well suited to sending over the internet and via email. The main exception is if the image you are sending contains a very large range of colors (such as you would find in a photographic image). In such cases, there would be a significant loss of color depth, and the JPEG format may be preferable.

- **PDF** – This will create a PDF file containing the graphic on a single page, the size of which is dictated by your default printer page size settings. This format is fully scaleable, so is well suited for desktop publishing type requirements. This option automatically includes embedded astrological font glyphs inside the PDF file, to ensure full portability to other computers over the internet, for example.

Special Options

•   **Include Captions** - When copying to a Metafile or PDF format, it is possible to select whether or not the chart details and compliments text are included in the output. Sometimes, for desk-top-publishing requirements, it is preferable to have the chart on its own without any text, and for any captions to be added separately to the document.

•   **Monochrome** - When copying to a Metafile or PDF format, it is possible to select whether or not the generated graphic should be in the currently displayed color scheme, or in monochrome (black lines and text only). As many publications are only in monochrome, this option makes it easy to ensure that the graphic is in an appropriate format.

•   **Quality** – When copying to a JPEG format, it is possible to choose the level of trade-off between quality and size of the graphic. The range is 1 (lowest quality, smallest storage size) to 100 (highest quality, largest storage size). Typically, a value of 50 provides an adequate level of quality without using too much storage. If you are sending graphics that have a lot of detail and small text, you may wish to increase the quality, whereas if the graphic does not have much fine detail, and only has large glyphs, then you might be able to economies by decreasing the quality.

Chapter 18: Viewing Interpretations

Solar Fire contains text on a large variety of astrological topics, including the meanings of certain astrological archetypes, plus interpretations of planets in signs, houses, in aspect to one another etc. You may view any of the text by opening the interpretations window. This can be done from the main screen of Solar Fire, or from the "View Chart" or "Animation" screens.

Solar Fire is supplied with three separate sets of interpretations – for natal charts, for synastry between two charts, and for transits to a natal chart.

Solar Fire allows you to create or use sets of interpretations of the following types

- Natal - Supplied with Solar Fire

- Progressed

- Return

- Combined

- Prenatal

- Synastry (Natal to Natal) - Supplied with Solar Fire

- Transits to Natal - Supplied with Solar Fire

- Progressions to Natal

- Directions to Natal

- Transits to Natal (Calendar)

- Firdaria

When you open the interpretations window, Solar Fire automatically detects which category of interpretations is required in the current circumstances, and opens that interpretations file. For example, if you are viewing a Solar Return chart when you open the interpretations window, then Solar Fire will open the interpretations file that has been selected to apply to Return charts.

When Solar Fire is first installed, most of the categories are set to use the standard natal interpretation set. Only the Synastry and Transits to Natal category use a different set. In order to change which set of interpretations Solar Fire will use for each of the above categories, you must change the appropriate settings on the **Interpretations Files** option of the **Interps** menu. See Changing the Interpretations File for instructions on how to do this.

You can use any set of interpretations with any type of chart if you wish to, for example using the natal interpretations for a progressed chart, return chart or composite chart. However, if you do so, then you will need to bear in mind that some of the interpretations will not apply in the same way as they would to a natal chart. It is also possible, in the future, that you will be able to purchase alternative sets of interpretations which are written in different styles, or which apply to different chart types.

You can edit the existing text or create you own new set of interpretations by using a separate utility program which is supplied with Solar Fire. For instructions on how to use this, see Compiling Interpretations.

The interpretations window has two modes of operation:

General Mode - In this mode, you can browse through every possible combination of interpretation and definition text.

Current Chart Mode - In this mode, you are limited to browsing through interpretation relating solely to the current chart. (The current chart is whichever chart was last selected from Solar Fire's main screen, or the chart which you were displaying in the "View Chart" screen immediately before opening the interpretations window.

Opening the Interpretations Window

>> To open the interpretations window from the main screen

Choose the **View...** item from the **Interps** menu

If there are any calculated charts in the main screen's list of calculated charts, then the interpretations window will open in Current Chart Mode and initially contain text relating to the current chart. If there are no charts calculated yet, then the interpretations window will open in General Mode and initially contain general definitions text.

You can open the interpretations window from the "View Chart" screen provided that you are displaying at least one single wheel or multiwheel chart. However, it is not possible to open the interpretations window from this screen if you are only displaying a grid.

>> To open the interpretations window from the "View Chart" screen

You must be displaying at least one chart in a single or multi-wheel - you cannot open the interpretations window if you are displaying only a grid or other tabulations. The interpretations window will appear when you click on parts of the wheel as follows:

1.   Double-click on any displayed **chart point** (ie. planet, asteroid or angle glyph). This displays an interpretation of that chart point in its house and sign eg. Jupiter in the 11th House in Cancer. If this is a multi-wheel, then the house placement is based on the houses of the anchor chart, which is usually the innermost chart.

2.   Double-click on the **degrees, sign glyph** or **minutes** of any **chart point**. This displays information about the degree occupied by that chart point eg. 17th degree of Pisces.

3.   Double-click on a **sign glyph** on any house cusp. This displays an interpretation of the selected house when ruled by its sign eg. Leo on the 3rd house cusp.

4.   Double click on the **degrees** or **minutes** of any **house cusp**. This displays information about the chart degree of that house cusp eg. 3rd degree of Aries.

5.   Double-click on any unoccupied space inside a **house**. This displays information about the meaning of that house eg. the 7th House.

6.   Double-click inside the aspect ring, or outside the chart. This displays explanatory text about the set of interpretations, such as who wrote it and to what type of charts it applies.

7.   Click once on any **chart point** followed by a single click on any **other chart point** within 3 seconds. This displays an interpretation of the aspect between those two points, if there is an aspect made between them eg. Jupiter Trine The Sun. If the chart points that you click on are in different wheels, then Solar Fire will automatically select the Synastry, Transits to Natal, Progressions to Natal or Directions to Natal set of interpretations, depending on what chart types are involved.

8.   Click once on any **chart point** followed by a single click on either the **sign glyph** on the 1st house cusp, or the **sign glyph** on the 10th house cusp. This displays an interpretation of the aspect between the first point and the Ascendant or Midheaven respectively, if there is an aspect made between them eg. Venus Conjunct Ascendant.

The following diagram shows an example of the "sensitive" areas of a chart, which are numbered according to the list above.

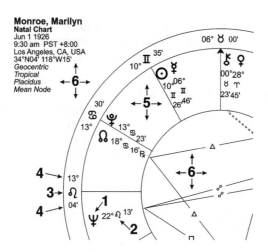

Browsing the Interpretations

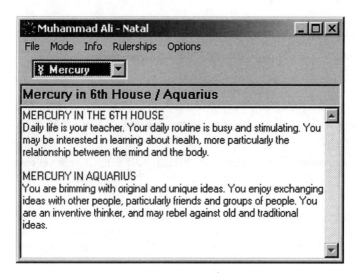

Once the interpretations window is open, it is possible to browse through all the categories of interpretations for a chart as well as all the general definitions, without leaving the window again.

In order to browse through all the available definitions or interpretations relating to the currently selected mode and information type, select any item from any of the drop-down list boxes.

You can also browse through the definitions or interpretations simply by using the cursor keys (UP, DOWN, LEFT and RIGHT). The UP and DOWN keys will move you up and down the items in the currently highlighted drop-down list box. The LEFT and RIGHT keys will move you between the drop-down list boxes eg. if there are two drop down-list boxes using the left key will shift the highlight to the left box, and using the right key will shift the highlight to the right box.

Note that some information types do not have any drop-down list boxes, as there is only one type of information available for them. For example, if you are in Current Chart Mode, then the **Element** information type shows a single set of information about the balance of elements in the current chart. However, if you are in General Mode, then there will be drop-down list boxes allowing you to browse the different elements (fire, earth, air, water) and emphasis types (definition, weak, strong).

Switching Modes

>> To switch between General Mode and Current Chart Mode

Select the desired option from the **Mode** menu.

A tick appears to the left of whichever menu option is selected. Also, when you are in General Mode, the title of the interpretations windows is "General Interpretations", whereas when you are in Current Chart Mode, the title consists of the chart's name and its type eg. "Marilyn Monroe - Natal".

It is not possible to select Current Chart Mode if you have not yet cast or opened any charts. Otherwise you can freely switch between modes as you wish.

In most cases the information type that you are browsing will be retained when you change mode eg. if you are looking at information about the degree of Mercury in a chart (in Current Chart Mode), then when you switch to General Mode you will still see the same text about that degree, but you will be able to browse through the text relating to all the adjoining degrees.

Selecting Information Types

There is a large variety of information types available. These can be accessed from the **Info** menu.

>> **To switch between information types**

Select the desired option from the **Info** menu

A tick appears to the left of whichever menu option is selected.

Most information types show different text depending on whether the mode is set to "General Mode" or to "Current Chart Mode". The information types, and a description of the text which they show in each mode are:

Introduction

General Mode - Title, copyright and explanatory text

Current Chart Mode - Same as General Mode

Degree

General Mode - Information about any degree of the zodiac

Current Chart Mode - Information about the degree of any chart point

Decanate

General Mode - Information about any decanate (10 degree subdivision) of the zodiac and its ruler

Current Chart Mode - Information about the decanate of any chart point, and its ruler

Sign

General Mode - General definition plus weak and strong definition of any sign

Current Chart Mode - Balance of the signs using a scoring system

Element

General Mode - General definition plus weak and strong definition of any element

Current Chart Mode - Balance of the elements using a scoring system

Mode

General Mode - General definition plus weak and strong definition of any mode

Current Chart Mode - Balance of the modes using a scoring system

House

General Mode - General definition plus weak and strong definition of any house

Current Chart Mode - Balance of the houses using a scoring system

Quadrant

General Mode - General definition plus weak and strong definition of any quadrant

Current Chart Mode - Balance of the quadrants using a scoring system

Hemisphere

General Mode - General definition plus weak and strong definition of any hemisphere

Current Chart Mode - Balance of the hemispheres using a scoring system

Aspect

General Mode - General definition of any aspect

Current Chart Mode - Interpretation of the aspect between any two chart points in the current chart

Ray

General Mode - General definition plus weak and strong definition of any ray

Current Chart Mode - Balance of the rays using a scoring system

Lunar Phase

General Mode - Interpretation of any of 8 lunar phases

Current Chart Mode - Interpretation of the lunar phase of the current chart

Sign on House

General Mode - Interpretation of any sign on any house cusp

Current Chart Mode - Interpretation of any house cusp's sign in the current chart

Chart Point

General Mode - Definition of any chart point

Current Chart Mode - Basic technical information and aspect list for any chart point in the current chart

Point in House/Sign

General Mode - Interpretation of any chart point in any sign and any house

Current Chart Mode - Same as above two information categories combined

Point Ruling House

General Mode - No information available (disabled)

Current Chart Mode - Definition of each of the houses ruled by any chart point in the current chart

Dispositor's House/Sign

General Mode - No information available (disabled)

Current Chart Mode - Definition of the house and sign of the dispositor of any point in the current chart

Point's Aspects

General Mode - Any chart point in any aspect to any other chart point

Current Chart Mode - Interpretations of all of the aspects formed to any chart point in the current chart

Point's Rays

General Mode - Definition of each ray relating to any chart point

Current Chart Mode - Same as General Mode

Speaking Interpretations

Speaking options are available only on those computers on which the
Microsoft Speech engine has been installed. This is installed by default on
Windows XP, but not on any earlier versions of Windows).

>> To speak the displayed interpretation text

Select **Speak Interpretations** from the **File** menu.

This will speak the displayed text using the built-in speech synthesizer.
Closing this window stops the speech.

>> To automatically speak the displayed interpretations whenever this dialog opens

Select the **AutoSpeak** item from the Options menu. This may be switched
off simply by re-selecting it.

Changing Rulerships

Some information types, such as decanates, house rulerships, dispositors
and rays, contain information relating to planetary rulerships of signs and
decanates. It is possible to select any available set of rulerships (such as
Modern, Old and Esoteric) to be used in the text for these items as follows.

>> To change rulerships

Select the desired rulership set from the **Rulerships** menu. It is possible to
browse or edit these rulerships, and add or delete rulership sets with a
separate utility, which is described in detail in Changing Rulerships and
Weightings.

Changing the Display Options

You can select a variety of display options as follows:

>> To ensure that the interpretations window remains visible on top of any other window

Select the **Always On Top** item from the **Options** menu. This may be switched off simply by re-selecting it.

>> To make the interpretations window transparent

Select the **Transparent** item from the Options menu. This may be switched off simply by re-selecting it.

(This option is available only for Windows 2000, XP, Vista or later.)

>> To display the interpretations window at full screen size

Click on the maximize button at the top right of the window. You can restore the window to its original size simply by clicking on the restore button at the top right of the window.

>> To alter the font style, size or color

Select the **Font...** item from the **Options** menu. This will display a standard font selection window, from which you can select any available screen font, plus its style, size and color.

>> To alter the size of the interpretations window

Drag the window's borders with the mouse button held down

Sending an Interpretations Report to a Word Processor

Solar Fire's interpretations are designed for personal and professional use rather than for mass-production of printouts for sale.

For beginners they provide a fun-to-use learning tool, and a way to print out chart readings for themselves, friends and family.

For professionals they can be the basis for personalized written interpretations. The text database itself can be revised and expanded to reflect one's own astrological ideas, and the interpretations for any chart can be sent to a word processor and modified for a particular individual.

Today's word processors offer many sorts of font and formatting possibilities. Combining creatively formatted text with the special chart wheels and page designs that you can create in Solar Fire, you can produce distinctive and attractive printouts for gifts and special occasions.

Selecting a Word Processor

You can select which word processor you wish to use when viewing and printing interpretation reports. If you do not select one yourself, then Solar Fire will use the default word processor on your computer system. See Interps for more details on selecting a word processor.

Viewing a Full Interpretations Report

>> To generate a chart interpretations report

Select the **Full Report...** item from the **Interps** menu, or **View Full Report...** option from the **File** menu of the interpretations window. This will display a selection dialog box from which you can choose which categories of interpretations will be included in the report.

You can select any of the available text categories by ensuring that the check box for that category contains an "X". Click on any of these to select or unselect them. If you switch off the "Chart Points" category then it is not possible to include categories relating to rulerships and aspects between points, so these option become disabled (grayed). When you are happy with the selection, click on the **View...** button. Your word processor will be opened up displaying this report. You are then free to browse the report, to print it, or to save it under another name if you wish. Note that, to keep a permanent copy of the report, you must save it under a different name, because Solar Fire always uses the same report name. When you have finished with the report, exit from your word processor.

Note: If you do not exit from your word processor, then the next time that you generate an interpretations report you will see the old report instead of the newly generated one. If this happens, then exit from your word-processor, and generate the report again.

>> To generate a synastry interpretations report

Select the **Synastry Report...** item from the **Interps** menu, or **View Full Report...** option from the **File** menu of the interpretations window when you are already viewing synastry interpretations. This will display a selection dialog box from which you can choose which categories of interpretations will be included in the report, and also the gender of each of the charts.

The interpretation categories may be selected in the same manner as for natal interpretations. However, bear in mind that the some categories do not apply to the synastry report, so that selecting them will make no difference to the final report. In particular, the following items are *not* included in the default synastry report.

- Balances

- House Cusps

- Rulerships & Dispositor

- Rays

Exporting Text to a File

You can send a selection of the available interpretations for the current chart to an external DOS file to be used in a separate text editor, printing utility or word-processor. The resulting text file will have an ANSI format without any carriage return/line feeds within the body of each paragraph. This makes it easy to use if it is imported into a word-processor as it will not be necessary to remove "hard" carriage returns from each paragraph of text.

>> To send interpretations to a text file

Select the **Export Text...** option from the **File** menu of the interpretations window. This will display a selection dialog box from which you can choose which categories of interpretations will be exported.

You can select any of the available text categories by ensuring that the check box for that category contains an "X". Click on any of these to select or unselect them. If you switch off the "Chart Points" category then it is not possible to include categories relating to rulerships and aspects between points, so these option become disabled (grayed). When you are happy with the selection, click on the **Export...** button.

You will then be able to select a directory and filename to which the interpretations text will be sent from a standard Windows "Save File" dialog screen. Initially the filename is set to INTERPS.TXT, but you may change this if you wish, to any valid DOS filename. You might also prefer to select the directory in which your word processor resides in order to make it easier to find the exported file from you word processor.

Once you click on the **Export...** button, the interpretations will be sent to the file that you specified, a series of beeps will be sounded to let you know that it has finished, and you will be returned to the interpretations window.

Note that you cannot export text if you are in General Mode. This export utility can only be used with the interpretations relating to the current chart.

Changing the Interpretations File

When you first install Solar Fire, there are only two interpretations files available, for natal charts and transits to natal charts. However, if you have created additional interpretation files with the interpretations compiler, or purchased any additional interpretations files, then it is possible to select another file. The possible categories of interpretations are

- **Natal**

- **Progressed**

- **Return**

- **Combined**

- **Prenatal**

- **Synastry (Natal to Natal)**

- **Transits to Natal**

- **Progressions to Natal**

- **Directions to Natal**

- **Transits to Natal (Calendar)**

- **Firdaria**

Each of these categories can have a different interpretations file associated with it, which is used whenever a chart of that type is selected. It is possible for all of them to use the same interpretations file, although ideally each category would have its own separate interpretations file, with text that has been written specifically for that chart type.

When Solar Fire is first installed, you will find that all the categories use the same interpretations file (standard.int) apart from Synastry (synastry.int) and Transits to Natal (transits.int) and Progressions to Natal (progress.int).

>> To change the selected interpretations file

Do either of the following.

From the Interpretations window, select the **Open...** item from the **File** Menu.

From the Main Screen, select the required file type from the **Interpretations Files** menu item under the **Interps** menu.

You will then see the File Manager Dialog Box, from which you can choose any other available interpretations file. If you click on the **Select** button, then the chosen interpretations file will become the default for interpretations of the chosen category (if selected from the **Interps** menu), or for the category that is currently being viewed (if chosen from the Interpretations window).

Exiting from the Interpretations Window

You can exit from the interpretation window in two different ways. One way will close and unload the interpretations file, which means that next time you open up the interpretations window a few extra seconds will be taken to load the file again. The other way simply minimizes the interpretations window without unloading the interpretations, so that it can be accessed again almost instantaneously.

>> To exit from the interpretations and unload the interpretations file

Choose the **Exit** option from the **File** menu of the Interpretations window.

>> To minimize the Interpretations window

Click on the minimize button on the top right of the Interpretations window. Once it is minimized, you can retrieve it by double-clicking on its icon, or by using any of the methods previously described to open the Interpretations window.

Chapter 19: Viewing Astro-Locality Maps

Solar Fire contains an astro-locality mapping module called Solar Maps Lite. If you have already purchased the full version of Solar Maps v3 or higher, then you will be able to access its full features instead of the limited features of Solar Maps Lite.

If you own the full Solar Maps program, then you should refer to its manual or on-line help file for instruction on using all of its features. What follows is a brief description of the features of Solar Maps Lite.

Solar Maps Lite allows you to

- Display world maps in rectangular or spherical formats

- Display planetary positions on maps for any natal type chart that has already been calculated in Solar Fire

- Display lines of culmination, anti-culmination, rise or set for the chart's planets and bodies

- Display planetary direction lines in local space

- Display day/night shading for any chart on a rectangular world map

- View solar eclipse paths for any solar eclipse in the period 1951 to 2200

- Measure angular and linear distances between maps locations or planetary lines

- Add, edit or remove cities which are displayed on maps

- Apply alternative pre-defined map and line color selections

>> To start Solar Maps and display the currently select chart

1.   Select the required chart from the list of calculated charts

2.   Select the **Solar Maps** item from the **View** menu.

This will start up Solar Maps, displaying the selected chart over the last selected map.

The Main Solar Maps Window

When Solar Maps starts up for the first time, it needs to prepare the map database. This may take several minutes, and the progress of this operation is shown with a progress bar in the middle of the screen. This is only necessary the first time that Solar Maps is run, and it will normally not occur again.

Like other windows, the Solar Maps main window may be minimized, resized and moved around the screen. Whenever you resize the window, the map will be redrawn automatically to fit the new window size.

The **title bar** - the bar across the top of the window - normally displays information about whatever chart and/or eclipse is currently being displayed, and what kind of astrological lines are being displayed. Some examples are

- Transits 25 Jan1997 - Natal - Lines: MC/IC/Rise/Set

- John Smith - Natal - Lines: Local Space

- John Smith - Natal & Eclipse of 26 Feb 1998 - Lines: MC/IC/Rise/Set

- Eclipse of 26 Feb 1998

The **menu** is the means of accessing all the options within the program. The main headings in the menu are

Chart - Options for selecting and displaying charts and astrological lines on the current map

Map - Options for selecting maps

Eclipse - Options for selecting solar eclipse lines to display on the current map

Options - Special display options

Help - On-line help

The **location information** box displays the current position of the cursor over the map in terms of latitude and longitude. It also displays angular and linear distance between two points when the mouse is anchored and dragged anywhere across the map.

The **line symbols** which appear around the edge of the map (and on some lines within the map itself) indicate the line type of whatever line it is attached to. For example, the As/Venus symbols indicate that the attached line is one along which Venus is rising.

Charts

When you first enter Solar Maps Lite, the chart which is displayed is that which was the current chart in Solar Fire. However, you can select any of Solar Fire's calculated charts without leaving Solar Maps.

>> To select an alternative chart to display

1.   Select the **Select Chart...** item from the **Chart** menu, or click on the **Chart** button

2.   Highlight the required chart and click on the **OK** button

>> To display or remove day/night shading for a chart on a map

Select the **Day/Night Shading** item from the **Chart** menu

This will toggle it on or off. When it is on, the region where the sun is below the horizon is shaded with a cross-hatching pattern. This region is bordered by the lines of rising and setting for the Sun. (Note: This option works only on rectangular world maps. It has no effect on spherical format maps.)

Maps

When you first enter Solar Maps Lite, the map which is displayed is that which was displayed when you last exited Solar Maps.

>> To select an alternative map to display

1. Select the **Select Map...** item from the **Map** menu, or click on the **Map** button, or select a recently used map from the bottom of the **Map** menu

2. Highlight the required map file name and click on the **OK** button

This will cause the newly selected map to be displayed with whatever chart has already been selected.

>> To add, edit or remove city names from a map

Select the **Edit Cities...** item from the **Map** menu

This will display the Edit Cities dialog.

The information that is stored for each entry in the city file is

Name - This name is what appears on the map.

Latitude - The latitude at which the name is to be plotted.

Longitude - The longitude at which the name is to be plotted.

Zone - The normal timezone observed in that city.

Plot If <= - This controls how wide the map must be in order for the name to be plotted. This option is only useful in the full Solar Maps program. It should normally always be set to 360 for Solar Maps Lite.

Alignment - This controls where the symbol is plotted in relation to the city name. If the **Left** option is chosen, then the name is aligned so that the symbol is on the left of the name (ie. +Name). If the **Right** option is chosen, then it is aligned with the symbol on the right (ie. Name+). If the **Centre** option is chosen then the name is centered over the symbol (ie. Na+me).

>> To edit an existing entry in the city file

1. Click on the required entry in the listbox.

2. Edit the information fields.

See the description of fields above.

>> To add a new entry to the list

1. Click on the **"Add City"** button.

2. Enter data into the information fields.

If you have the ACS PC Atlas, then you will see the "ACS PC Atlas" dialog box which allows you to enter the city name and look up its details in the Atlas. These details will be inserted automatically into the information fields on this screen.

>> To delete one or more entries from the list

1. Click on the desired entry or Whilst holding down the **"Ctrl"** key, click on each of the required entries.

2. Click on the **"Delete"** button.

You will be asked to confirm deletion before the selected entries are removed.

>> In order to exit from this screen

Click on the **"OK"** button.

You will be asked whether or not you wish to save the changes that you have made. If you choose to save them, then the entries will be saved and sorted into alphabetical order for next time you use this screen again. If you choose not save them, then any changes that you made using this screen will be lost.

Lines

When you first run Solar Maps Lite, lines of culmination, anti-culmination rise and set are displayed.

>> To select which line types to display

Select the **Displayed Lines...** item from the **Chart** menu, or click on the **Lines** button.

This will display the "Select Lines" dialog, where there are two categories of line types that may be selected. These are

Planet/Angle Lines - These are the lines which describe where on the Earth individual planets are culminating or anti-culminating or are rising or setting. These lines are also sometimes called Astro*Carto*Graphy® lines in other books and programs. The culminating and anti-culminating lines are always lines of longitude, whereas the rising and setting lines are great circles around the globe and appear to curve on a map viewed in Cartesian or Mercator projection.

Local Space Lines - These are the lines indicating the direction in which planets or stars are found when looking from the chart's location. These lines are great circles around the globe, starting from the chart's location. The common convention is to continue the line right around the world, back to the starting location. When viewed in Cartesian or Mercator projection, these lines generally appear to curve.

You can select any combination of the above lines to displays simultaneously.

Eclipses

>> To display a solar eclipse path

Select the **Select Eclipse...** item from the **Eclipse** menu, or click on the **Eclipse** button.

This will display the "Select Eclipse" dialog, from which you can select any partial or total solar eclipse from 1950 to 2200.

When you click on an eclipse in the listbox on the left, the details of that eclipse will be displayed in the box at the right.

Additionally, you may select which of the following items to display by clicking on their check boxes.

Total Eclipse Line - If selected, this will display the central line of total eclipse

Partial Eclipse Lines - If selected, this will display lines of equal magnitude of eclipse in intervals of 25%.

Current Chart - If selected, the currently displayed chart will be retained and plotted at the same time as the eclipse lines.

Note that the Total Eclipse Line option is not available for partial eclipses, and the Current Chart option is only available if you have previously selected a chart.

>> To remove any currently selected eclipse, and leave the map without any eclipse lines displayed

Select the **Clear Eclipse** item from the **Eclipse** menu.

Display Options

Fonts

It is possible to alter the font in which country and city names are written onto the maps, including italicizing or emboldening the typeface or changing its point size.

>> To select font attributes

Select the **Text Font...** item from the **Options** menu

This will display a standard Windows font selection dialog, from which you can select

- Font Name
- Font Style
- Font Size

When you have made your selections, click on the **"OK"** button. The map will be redrawn using the newly selected font for any country or city names that are plotted on the map.

Extra Line Annotation

The number of symbols which are displayed around the outside of the map may be altered. Typically, each astrological line is identified with two symbols - one showing which planet or star it belongs to, and the other showing which line type it is eg. a Venus on the Midheaven line will have a symbol for Venus and a symbol for the MC. It is possible to limit this to displaying a single symbol for the planet, and omitting the line type symbol. This allows the margin around the edge of the map to be reduced, and therefore creates a bigger plotting area for the map. If you have selected settings which give different line types different colors (or line styles or thicknesses), then you may not need the extra symbol to be displayed.

>> To switch the extra line symbols on or off

Select the **Extra Line Annotation** item from the **Options** menu.

This switches the extra line type symbols off if they are on, or switches them on if they are off. A tick appears to the left of this item when it is switched on. The map is automatically redrawn whenever this option is changed.

Note: This option does not affect printed maps. Printed maps always contain the extra line annotation, regardless of how this option is set.

Map Settings

The colors of land and sea areas on the maps and the line types and styles used for planetary lines can be altered according to some pre-defined settings.

>> To choose an alternative set of map and line settings

1.   Select the **Select Settings...** item from the **Options** menu

2.   Highlight the name of a settings file, and click on the **OK** button

This will apply the new color selections and redisplay the current map and chart using these new settings.

Whichever settings you choose will be remembered and re-used in any subsequent sessions with Solar Maps Lite.

Chapter 20: Viewing Stellarium

Stellarium is a free open source planetarium for your computer. It shows a realistic sky in 3D, just like what you see with the naked eye, binoculars or a telescope.

>> To display any calculated chart in Stellarium

Select the required chart from the list of **Calculated Charts** on the main screen.

Select the **Stellarium** option from the **View** menu.

If Stellarium is already installed on your computer, then this will start it up, with location and time set according to the current chart in Solar Fire.

Is Stellarium is not already installed on your computer, then you will be presented with a link to the Stellarium site, from where you may download and install it.

If, for any reason, Stellarium is already installed on your computer, but Solar Fire cannot find it, then you will be prompted to navigate to the folder into which the Stellarium program was installed. Once you have done this, Solar Fire will remember its location in future.

Note: Due to limitations of Stellarium, when a Solar Fire chart is displayed, Stellarium shows the chart time according to your local timezone - not according to the timezone of the chart. However, it is still the correct instant in time, so the celestial phenomena are still all correct for that chart.

Note: Stellarium is a third party product, and Esoteric Technologies has no control over it, or how it may change in future. This link is offered "as-is", and we cannot take any credit for its features, or any responsibility for its flaws. However, we will do our best to maintain compatibility with it in future.

Chapter 21: Generating Chart Reports and Tabulations

This chapter describes how to view and print any of Solar Fire's report or tabulation types relating to a single chart or synastry report types relating to two charts. It is not possible to generate a report relating to more than two charts at a time.

If you wish to generate dynamic transits and progressions reports, rather than a chart report, then refer to page Using Dynamic Reports and Time Maps.

Before generating a report, it is necessary to have either cast or opened the chart or charts that you wish to report on. If you have not yet done so, see Casting a Natal Chart for instructions on casting a new chart, or page Retrieving Charts From a File for instructions on opening an existing chart.

Also it is necessary to have selected the required set of displayed chart points and aspects to be used in generating the report. See Displayed Points for instructions on selecting the set of displayed points and the aspect set.

Report Options

The fixed star paran report lists stars that are in paran to points in the chart. Parans may be of four types - rising, setting, culminating or anti-culminating. It is possible to select which parans to include or exclude from the report. For example, if only rising and settings parans are selected, then the report will list any stars which are rising or settings as the chart points rise or set, but not as the stars or chart points culminate or anti-culminate.

>> To select which parans to use in the fixed star parans report

Click on any of the **Parans to Use** options from the **Reports** menu - Parans that are selected will have a check mark on their left of their entry in the menu. Clicking on an unselected paran will switch it on, and clicking on a selected paran will switch it off. Note that the fixed star paran report lists which parans are currently in use when the report is generated.

Descriptions of the Reports

These are the different types of reports you can choose from:

Chart Analysis

Chart details: name, birth date, birth time, latitude, longitude, etc.

Astronomical information: DeltaT, Ephemeris Time, Julian Day, Sidereal Time at Greenwich, Local Sidereal Time, Obliquity of the ecliptic, Adjusted Calculation Date for midnight and midday ephemerides.

Chart angles: the longitudes of the Ascendant and Midheaven computed to the second of arc.

House cusps: the longitudes of the intermediate house cusps and angles computed to the second of arc.

Chart points: longitudes, daily travel, latitudes, declinations, azimuths and altitudes of all planets and points selected.

Stationary Points: for any points deemed stationary, shows the distance from exact station in time and longitude

Lunar phase: the Sun/Moon angle and its phase out of 8 and 28 phases.

Sign Elements and Modalities analysis: weighted points showing the concentration of planets and points in Fire, Earth, Air and Water; Cardinal, Fixed and Mutable.

House Modalities analysis: weighted points showing the concentration of planets and points in Angular Succedent, Cadent.

Chart Shape: name of chart shape, if any

Note: In the Chart point listing, the daily travel values are normally given in degrees and minutes per day. However, if the rate of travel is less than 1 degree per day, then it is given in minutes and seconds of arc per day instead.

Note: In the Chart points listing, the following flags may be shown immediately after the longitude:

- (no flag) - Direct, not within orb of a station

- R - Retrograde, not within orb of a station

- SD - Within orb of a station - Direct, following the exact station

- DS - Within orb of a station - Direct, prior to the exact station
- SR - Within orb of a station - Retrograde, following the exact station
- RS -Within orb of a station - Retrograde, prior to the exact station

Rulerships Report

This report is available using any available level of rulerships. (It is possible to add your own rulerships to Solar Fire. Refer to page Changing Rulerships and Weightings for instructions on how to do this.) It shows the following:

Planets: accidentally dignified, in mutual reception, in rulership, detriment, exaltation and fall, and the final dispositor.

Chart points: in signs, house, house ruled, dispositor and dispositor's house.

Horary Report

Planetary day, planetary hour, hour of day or night

House Cusps: Almutens (calculated according to the options in the houses.alm almuten definition file)

Chart Points: Ruler, Exalted, Triplicity, Term, Face, Detriment, Fall, Score, Peregrine (calculated according to the options in the essdig.alm dignity definition file)

Chart Hyleg: according to Bonatti's method and Ptolemy's method.

Aspects List

Aspects used: aspect abbreviation or glyph, aspect angle, luminary applying and separating orb (Sun/Moon to other planets), other planet or chart point applying and separating orb, aspect name.

Aspects list: listing of aspects in order from the Moon to the Lunar South Node, showing orb and whether applying or separating.

When this report is produced as a synastry report, aspects shown are between the two charts instead of between planets within the single chart.

Sorted Aspects

Aspects used: aspect abbreviation or glyph, aspect angle, luminary applying and separating orb (Sun/Moon to other planets), other planet or chart point applying and separating orb, aspect name.

Orb used: maximum orb angle

Aspects list: listing of aspects in order of increasing orb and whether applying or separating.

When this report is produced as a synastry report, aspects shown are between the two charts instead of between planets within the single chart.

Aspects Analysis

Aspects used: aspect abbreviation or glyph, aspect angle, luminary applying and separating orb (Sun/Moon to other planets), other planet or chart point applying and separating orb, aspect name.

Major aspect patterns found: Click on the **Patterns...** button to preview all the available aspect patterns and to switch any patterns on or off.

Aspect distribution grid: the number of aspects found among the inner planets, outer planets, and angles.

Aspect frequency analysis: aspect type, actual aspect hits, likely aspect hits, and the percentage of difference from expected frequency of aspect hits.

When this report is produced as a synastry report, aspect patterns do not appear on the report, and the aspect distribution relates to aspects between the two charts.

Note: The "Orb Tightness" of each pattern indicates how close the aspects involved in the pattern are to being exact. A value of 100% would indicate that all the aspects in the pattern are exact, whereas a value of 0% would indicate that all the aspects are at the outer limit of their allowable orbs. In more technical terms, it uses an RMS (root mean square) value of the normalized orbs (where normalized means the ratio of actual orb to maximum allowable orb).

Chart Point Sort

Modulus used: modulus angle

List of chart points: In order of modulus angle, including zodiacal positions

When this report is produced as a synastry report, the points from both charts are listed together, and are flagged to show which chart they belong to.

Sensitive Points

Aspects used: aspect abbreviation or glyph, aspect angle, luminary applying and separating orb (Sun/Moon to other planets), other planet or chart point applying and separating orb, aspect name.

List of sensitive points: zodiacal position, aspect made, chart point aspecting this position

This report is especially useful for quickly finding what is being triggered in a chart by a transiting planet, for example. It is also useful simply as a list of what points in the zodiac are sensitive in chart.

MidPoint Listing

Modulus used: modulus angle

List of midpoints: In planetary order, modulus angle

List of midpoints: In midpoint order, modulus angle

When this chart is produced as a synastry report, the midpoints from the first chart are mixed with the primary positions (ie. the positions of the chart points themselves) of the second chart, and these are flagged to show which chart they belong to. In this manner it is possible to see the positions of the transiting planets relative to a chart's midpoints, for example.

MidPoint Axes

Modulus used: modulus angle

Orb used: orb angle

List of Axes: In planetary order down the screen. Midpoints within orb are listed across the page (and onto next line if line is full).

Example: *Ura* Vp/Sat 0 02d *Asc* 0 05 Mar/Jup 0 09

This shows that Uranus is within 2 minutes of arc of the midpoint of the Vernal Point (0 Aries) and Saturn; within 5 minutes of arc of the Ascendant; and within 9 minutes of arc of the midpoint Mars and Jupiter, within the modulus specified. Also note that the "d" indicates that the midpoint is a conjunction or opposition, regardless of the modulus chosen.

MidPoint Trees

Modulus used: modulus angle

Orb used: orb angle

List of Trees: In planetary order across the screen. Midpoints within orb are listed down the page under each point.

Example, showing the same midpoints as in the previous example:

Ura

Vp/Sat 0 02d

Asc 0 05

Mar/Jup 0 09

Midpoint Modes

Cardinal Points: Zodiacal position of chart points and midpoints which are in cardinal signs, plus modulus angle of points which are in semisquare or sesquisquare to chart points and midpoints.

Fixed Points: As for cardinal points

Mutable Points: As for cardinal points

This report is especially useful for quickly finding any 8th harmonic aspects to midpoints in a chart. For example, in the cardinal section of the report, if two of the entries are:-

  Mar/Nep 14Li59 Mer/Nod 15 25

then a transiting point at 15Cp00is square the Mar/Nep midpoint in the chart with an orb of 1 minute, and is either semisquare or sesquisquare the Mer/Nod midpoint with an orb of 25 minutes.

Arabic Parts

Aspects used: aspect abbreviation or glyph, aspect angle, luminary applying and separating orb (Sun/Moon to other planets), other planet or chart point applying and separating orb, aspect name.

List of Parts: Name and zodiacal position

List of Aspects: Aspects to chart points, orbs

Star Aspects

Aspects used: aspect abbreviation or glyph, aspect angle, luminary applying and separating orb (Sun/Moon to other planets), other planet or chart point applying and separating orb, aspect name.

Chart Points: Zodiacal position and declination

List of aspects: Aspects to fixed stars in current fixed star file, orb and star keywords

Star Parans

Parans Used: List of which parans are included (rise, set, upper culmination, lower culmination)

Paran Orb: maximum paran orb

Chart Points: Zodiacal position and declination

List of parans: Parans to fixed stars in current fixed star file, star keywords

Planetary Nodes

Aspects used: aspect abbreviation or glyph, aspect angle, luminary applying and separating orb (Sun/Moon to other planets), other planet or chart point applying and separating orb, aspect name.

Chart Points: North node position and daily travel, South node position and daily travel

List of aspects: Aspects to other chart points, in order of increasing orb

Asteroids

Aspects used: aspect abbreviation or glyph, aspect angle, luminary applying and separating orb (Sun/Moon to other planets), other planet or chart point applying and separating orb, aspect name.

List of Asteroids in current asteroid file: Longitude, daily travel, latitude, R.A. and Declination, list of aspects from asteroid to other chart points, orbs

Other Bodies

Aspects used: aspect abbreviation or glyph, aspect angle, luminary applying and separating orb (Sun/Moon to other planets), other planet or chart point applying and separating orb, aspect name.

List of Bodies: Name, longitude, daily travel, latitude, R.A. and Declination

List of Aspects: Aspects to chart points, orbs

The bodies which appear in this report are those whose orbital elements are defined in a file called "extras.dat", which resides in Solar Fire's \USERDATA directory. If you have adequate knowledge of orbital elements, it is possible to add or remove bodies from this file, and these changes will be reflected in this report. See Format of the Orbital Elements File for an explanation of the format of this file.

MWA (Munkasey Midpoint Weighting Analysis)

Total Hits, Midpoints in weighted order, Hits in weighted order, Planets in weighted order, sign weights, house weights, harmonic weights.

Unlike the original MWA that includes all of Munkasey's PSPs (personal sensitive points), this version of the report uses only the currently selected chart points.

The weightings are specified in the file MWA.INI in Solar Fire's Settings directory, and adventurous users can edit this file if they wish to alter the weightings.

Difference Listing

Modulus used: modulus angle

List of differences: In planetary order, modulus angle

List of differences: In difference order, modulus angle

The difference between a pair shown in the report as "A/B" is computed as (Position B – Position A), ie. it indicates the zodiacal distance from point A forward through the zodiac to point B.

Extra Ring Points

Aspects used: aspect abbreviation or glyph, aspect angle, luminary applying and separating orb (Sun/Moon to other planets), other planet or chart point applying and separating orb, aspect name.

List of points in current extra ring points file: Longitude, daily travel, latitude, R.A. and Declination, list of aspects from asteroid to other chart points, orbs

Descriptions of the Tabulations

The tabulations are a series of pre-defined collections of page objects organized into useful groupings. These are the same page objects that are used in Solar Fire's pages, and if users wish to create their own collections of page objects and customize them differently from the way they are presented here, then this can be done by designing your own pages using the Page Designer. However, the tabulations presented here allow users to quickly access some of the page objects without having to create new pages for them first.

Each tabulation displays a header for the currently selected chart, showing the name, birth date, birth time, latitude, longitude, etc. These are the different types of tabulations you can choose from:

Stations

For each displayed point, shows the longitude, speed indicator, the zodiacal positions of the last and next station, and the time since the last station and until the next station.

The speed indicator is determined according to the typical speed of each point, and can be Fast, Slow, Stationary or Retrograde.

Rise/Set Times

For each displayed point, shows the longitude, and the paran values for the rise, culmination, set and anti-culmination of that point.

The paran values may be displayed as local times, or LST angles or times, according to the user-setting in the Preferences dialog.

Gauq. Sectors

For each displayed point, shows the longitude, distance in A.U. (usually geocentric, but heliocentric if the chart is heliocentric), the Gauquelin sector (1 to 36) and a flag to show if it is in one of the Gauquelin plus sectors.

Note that (for a planet on the ecliptic) the sectors start at the horizon, and sectors 1 to 9 run from the Ascendant to the Midheaven, 10 to 18 run from the Midheaven to the Descendant, 19 to 27 run from the Descendant to the IC, and 28 to 36 from the IC to the Ascendant.

The Plus sectors are 1, 2, 3, 9, 10, 11, 12, 36.

Modulus Sort

For each displayed point shows the longitude, and the modulus of the longitude according to the current modulus value which may be set by the user on this screen.

There is also a graphical modulus sort strip.

Chart Balances

This shows graphical representations of the balance of modes, elements, rays quadrants and hemispheres. Note the asterisked (*) objects denote that they are showing weighted values ie. adjusting the scores for each category using the user-editable weightings for each point.

House Cusps

For each house cusps, show the longitude and its degree almuten (calculated according to the options in the houses.alm almuten definition file).

Phases/Eclipses

Shows the four last lunar phases and the next phase due (using the standard 4 lunar phases). Also shows the last two and next three eclipses due (both solar and lunar). The times are for either maximum eclipse or for the exact corresponding lunar phase, depending on the eclipse settings in Preferences.

Also shows the last two and next three eclipses due (both solar and lunar).

Essential Dignities

For each chart point: Ruler, Exalted, Triplicity, Term, Face, Detriment, Fall, Score, Peregrine (calculated according to the options in the essdig.alm dignity definition file)

Further Dignities

Shows a collection of page objects with various types of dignities, including planetary sect, planetary hour and day, chart hyleg. mutual receptions, horary consideration and lunar aspects.

AstroDyne Plan&Asp

For each chart point, shows its astrodyne score, giving the overall power score, the % contribution towards the total power score, and a Harmony/Disharmony score.

Also, the strongest, best and worst nine aspects are listed, along with their scores.

AstroDyne Houses

For each house and house type, shows its astrodyne score, giving the overall power score, the % contribution towards the total power score, and a Harmony/Disharmony score.

AstroDyne Signs

For each sign and sign type, shows its astrodyne score, giving the overall power score, the % contribution towards the total power score, and a Harmony/Disharmony score.

Declinations

For each displayed point shows the declination, the longitude, and longitude equivalent of its declination.

There is also a graphical declination strip.

Aspects - Closest

This list all the aspects currently selected, and then lists the aspects within the current chart in order of closeness of orb. Aspects will not appear in this list unless their orb is within i) the maximum orb specified for this object, and ii) the maximum orb allowed for that aspect in the aspect set which is being used. The total number of aspects shown is limited to 24.

Midpoint Trees

This displays midpoint trees for each displayed point in the chart, using the currently specified modulus and orb, both of which may be edited by the user on this screen.

Planetary Hours

This shows the planets of each planetary hour on the chart's date, starting at dawn and ending with dawn of the following day.

Almuten Scores

This object displays planetary scores for various dignity or almuten calculations. The scores are calculated according to the default dignity and almutens scores stored in the file general.alm, which resides in Solar Fire's program folder.

Firdaria (and Firdaria variant)

This lists the starting dates of planetary periods and the ages of the individual at each of these dates, for the current chart. There are two variants of this object, one using planetary periods as they were used by Al Biruni and Schoener, and the other is a variant of this which places the nodes in a different order for night-time charts. (The variants give identical results for daytime charts.)

Vedic Dasas

This displays a list of Dasas (major planetary periods) and Bhuktis (sub planetary periods) using the current default sidereal zodiac for the selected chart.

Nakshatras

This shows the Nakshatras (Vedic lunar divisions) for the current chart according to the default sidereal zodiac. The names and types of the mansions are given, as well as a few keywords describing the attributes of the mansion.

Arabic Mansions

This lists, for each displayed point, the number of the Arabic mansion it occupies (1 to 28), the name of the mansion as given in the Picatrix, the Arabic name, and the English name.

Chinese Mansions

This shows the Chinese Lunar Mansion occupied by each chart point. These mansions are divisions in right ascension, the boundaries of which are defined by the positions of certain fixed stars. The Chinese and English names of the mansion are given, as well as a few keywords describing the attributes of the mansion.

Direction of Divisions

This lists the starting dates of planetary term periods and the ages of the individual at each of these dates, according to the primary direction of the Ascendant of the current chart by oblique ascension.

Miscellaneous

This first object displays the same information as the Planetary Hour/Day object, but also indicates the current planetary rulers of a 36 year cycle. Each 36 year period is ruled by one of the 7 planets from Mars to Neptune, and each year within that 36 year period is sub-ruled by a planet. The periods of rulership start on the tropical Aries ingress each year. This 36 year cycle is described in American Astrology Magazine - Year 1940, in an article by David Anrias (although it is referred to in that article as a 35 year cycle), and is also alluded to in the title of the book "The Initiate in the

Dark Cycle" by Cyril Scott – Publ. Samuel Weiser Inc. This "Dark Cycle" is the 36 year period from 1909 to 1945 which was ruled by Mars.

The second object shows the polarity, element (of the five Chinese Elements) and the animal of the current Chinese lunar year.

Reports or Tabulations for a Single Chart

>> To view a report for a single chart

Do either of the following:

From the main screen, select a chart from the list of "Calculated Charts", and then choose **Current Chart** from the **Reports** menu.

From the "View Chart" screen, select an image of the required single chart, aspect grid or user-defined page from the list box, and select the **Reports** button.

This will display the "Chart Report" screen, which allows reports to be selected, browsed, edited and printed.

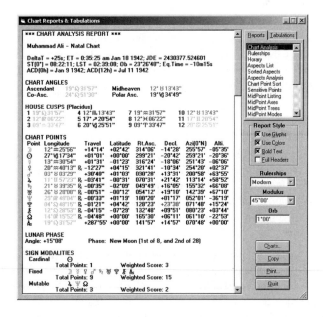

The list box on the top left of the screen contains a list of all the report types that may be displayed.

>> To display any report

Select the required report name from the list box on the top right of the window.

If you select a chart point sort report, or any midpoint type of report, then you can select a modulus angle for the report.

>> To select a Modulus angle

Do either of the following

Click on the **Modulus** drop-down list box and select a pre-defined value - It is possible to select a modulus for any harmonic from the 1st to the 12th

Enter an angle into the **Modulus** box - It is possible to type in any angle from 1 minute of arc to 360 degrees in degrees, minutes and seconds (eg. "67 23" for 67° 23').

If you select a report which requires an orb to be entered, such as a midpoint axes or trees report, or a star paran report then you can enter a limiting orb.

>> To enter an orb

Type the required orb into the Orb box - Any orb may be entered from 0 to 10 degrees, in degrees, minutes and seconds (eg. "0 10" for 10 seconds of arc).

You can browse through the report by clicking on the scroll bars to the right and bottom of the report display box. You can alter the appearance of the report by switching on or off any of the following options:

• **Use Glyphs** - This will substitute astrological glyphs into the report wherever appropriate, replacing abbreviations for planets, asteroids, zodiac signs and aspects.

• **Use Colors** - This allows you to switch on or off the selected colors of each planet, asteroid, zodiac sign and aspects wherever they appear in the report. When this option is switched off, all items appear in black. It is possible to alter which colors are used for each item by selecting **Point Colors...**, **Sign Colors...** and **Aspect Colors...** from the Chart Options menu of the main screen. See Editing a Color File for instructions on how to do this.

- **Bold Text** - This allows you to switch between regular (light) text and bold text.

- **Full Headers** - This allows you to switch on or off the full chart details and full listing of aspects used (in reports which use aspects). This option is useful if you do not need to see the full details, or if you wish to use less paper when printing a report.

>> To select an alternative chart for the same report

Select the **Charts...** button - This will display a list of calculated charts, from which you may select any one.

Note: By switching on the "Auto-apply" option, you may also scroll through charts and see the report automatically updated for each chart you select, without having to close the chart selection dialog.

Note: You can also use this dialog to view or edit the events or comments for any chart by using a right hand mouse click over that chart's entry, which brings up a pop-up menu.

>> To send a copy of the report to the Windows Clipboard

Select the **Copy...** button - Note that glyphs and colors cannot be copied to the clipboard. Abbreviations are used instead of glyphs when the report is copied into the Clipboard. Also, report columns may not align correctly in the Clipboard. If you paste the Clipboard contents into your word-processor, you may have to edit the document to ensure that the columns align correctly, (from where it may be pasted into a word-processor document, for example):

>> To print the report which is currently displayed

Select the **Print...** button. - This will display the "Print" dialog box, allowing you to cancel, alter printer settings, add the report to the batch print queue, or to print it immediately. See Printing from Solar Fire for instructions on printing. The printed report will contain glyphs (if you have the **Use Glyphs** option selected), and colors (if you have a color printer and you have the **Use Colors** option selected). However, the printed report always uses regular (light) text. It is not possible to print the report using bold text.

Synastry Reports

>> To view a synastry report

Do either of the following

From the main screen, choose **Synastry...** from the **Reports** menu - you must then select charts as described in Viewing MultiWheels and Synastry Grids, and then select the **Report** button.

From the "View Chart" screen, select the image of the required biwheel or synastry grid from the list box, and then select the **Reports** button.

This will display the "Reports" screen, which allows reports to be selected, browsed, edited and printed. Refer to the previous section for instructions on how to use this screen.

Chapter 22: Chart Search and Electional Search

These two modules both allow you to search using a variety of simple or advanced criteria, such as for a planet being in specified house or sign, a particular aspect being formed between two planets, a specified aspect pattern existing, the moon being void of course, and many others.

As well as searches using a single condition, you can combine criteria to perform complex searches involving many different factors. For example, you could search for the Moon in either Taurus or Gemini, and the Sun in the 7th house square Uranus.

The **Electional Search** module allows you perform searches through **time**, and presents a list of matching periods of time during which the criteria are satisfied. It also lists times when exact aspects are formed or other exact criteria reached, where relevant. You can search for purely mundane conditions on their own (involving transiting positions), or you can search for transiting positions in relation to a given radix chart.

The **Chart Search** module allows you to search through your stored **charts**, and presents a list of stored charts that satisfy the criteria. In addition to astrological criteria, this module also allows you to use chart data criteria in a search (such as chart name, date, time, house system etc). You can search based purely on the information in the stored charts, or you can search for stored chart positions in relation to a given radix chart.

Chart Search

>> To open the Chart Search dialog

From the main screen, select the **Chart Search** item from the **Chart** menu, or

From the **Chart Database** dialog, click on the **Find...** button and select the **Chart Search** menu item.

This will display the Chart Search dialog, which initially displays the last selection criteria that you used.

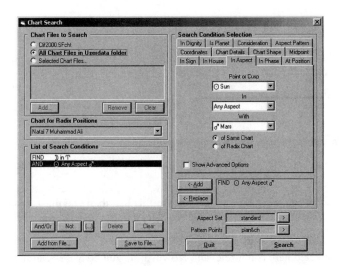

You have three different options to determine which chart file/s are scarched.

• Current chart file – this option shows the name of the currently selected chart file. If selected, only this file will be searched.

• All Chart Files in Userdata folder – If selected, then all charts files in the Userdata folder of Solar Fire will be searched.

• Selected Chart Files – If selected, then only those chart files listed immediately below will be searched. Note that you may select any chart files from any folders.

>> To add a new selected chart file to search

Click on the **Add** button.

If necessary, navigate to the folder in which the required chart file/s reside.

Highlight one (or more) chart files that you wish to add to the search.

Note: You can include multiple chart files at once by using the Mouse + Shift or Ctrl keys.

>> To remove a selected chart file from the search

Highlight the file that you wish to remove from the search.

Click on the **Remove** button.

>> To clear the list of chart files to search

Click on the Clear button.

>> To select a radix chart to use in your search conditions

Select any calculated chart from the **Chart For Radix Positions** drop-down list.

If you wish to use a chart which is not in this list, then you must first cast or open that chart, after which it will be available in this list for selection.

Note: Many searches do not involve radix positions, in which case the chart selected here is not relevant. However, if you do use a search condition that involves a condition including a radix chart position, then this is the chart that will be used.

Electional Search

>> To open the Electional Search dialog

Select the **Electional Search** item from the **Dynamic** menu.

This will display the Electional Search dialog, which initially displays the last selection criteria that you used.

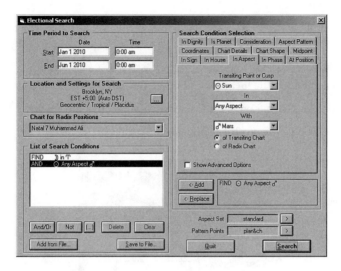

>> **To set the time period for search**

• Enter a start date and time

• Enter an end date and time

Note: The timezone for your entered dates and times is either the current timezone for your default location, or the timezone taken from a specified calculated chart, according to the choice you make below.

Depending on what criteria you select, the search results may vary depending on the location and other settings for which the search is performed. For example, if you are searching for an aspect between a planet and a chart angle such the ascendant, then the timing of aspects formed will vary widely depending on the latitude and longitude used for the calculation. The settings that may be used during the search are as follows:

• Location – the latitude and longitude to use when criteria involve chart angles and/or houses

• Timezone – the default timezone to use for the specified time period to search and for the output results

• House System – the house system to use when criteria involve house cusps or placements

• Zodiac – the zodiac to use when criteria involve celestial longitudes

- Coordinate System – the coordinate system to use when criteria involve calculating chart points

>> To determine the location and other settings for the search

Click on the **"..."** button in the **Location and Settings for Search** frame.

This will open the **Search Location and Settings** dialog.

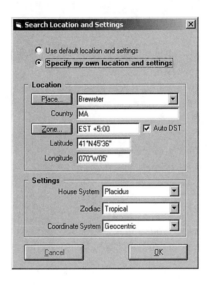

Select one of the following options.

- **Use default location and settings** – Choosing this option ensures that your current default location and settings are used for the search.

- **Specify my own location and settings** - Choosing this option allows you to enter the required place details and other settings in the **Location** and **Settings** frames below.

>> To ensure that the results of the search include automatic timezone change for daylight savings periods

Enable the **Auto DST** checkbox.

If the **Auto DST** option is unchecked, then the results will show times for the specified timezone only, whether or not this is the standard timezone for the given location. This is useful if you would like to see all the results in Universal Time, for example, rather than in the normal timezone for the selected location.

>> To select a radix chart to use in your search conditions

Select any calculated chart from the **Chart For Radix Positions** drop-down list.

If you wish to use a chart which is not in this list, then you must first cast or open that chart, after which it will be available in this list for selection.

Note: Many searches do not involve radix positions, in which case the chart selected here is not relevant. However, if you do use a search condition that involves a condition including a radix position, then this is the chart that will be used.

Specifying Search Conditions

When this dialog box is first displayed, the List of Search Conditions contains whatever search criteria were last used here. You can re-use these criteria, edit them or clear them to start afresh.

To make this search tool as simple to use as possible, there is an option whether to display advanced options or not. The advanced options allow you see and use point and aspect modifiers (explained in more detail later), which give much greater power over the types of conditions that may be specified. It is expected that only advanced astrologers will want to use these, and unless you need this extra power, you may prefer to leave the advanced options switched off.

>> To switch on or off the visibility of advanced options

• Click the Show Advanced Options checkbox.

The Search Condition Selection box contains a series of tabs, each of which allows you to specify a different type of condition.

The types of search conditions available from each tab are described individually in the sections below.

In Sign

This allows you to select

• A Planet, Point or Cusp – any of Solar Fire's standard chart points, or any of the 12 house cusps

• A Modifier – a modifier to apply to the selected point or cusp, such as the ruler of that point, the degree almuten of that point, the antiscia of that point, the contra-antiscia of that point.

• A Sign or Sign Type – any of the 12 signs, any sign element, any sign mode or either sign polarity.

Examples: Mars in Cancer; The Traditional Ruler of the 5th House Cusp in a Fixed Sign; the Antiscia of the Ascendant in Taurus.

In House

This allows you to select

• A Planet, Point or Cusp – any of Solar Fire's standard chart points, or any of the 12 house cusps

• A Modifier – a modifier to apply to the selected point or cusp, such as the ruler of that point, the degree almuten of that point, the antiscia of that point, the contra-antiscia of that point.

• A House or House Type – any of the 12 houses, any house mode or above horizon (7th to 12th) or below horizon (1st to 6th).

Also, for Chart Searches only, whether the house placement relates to the houses of

• The same chart - ie. the houses of the chart you are searching (the selected radix chart is not used)

• The radix chart - ie. the houses of the selected radix chart for this search

Or, for Electional Searches only, whether the house placement relates to houses of

• The transiting chart - ie. the houses varying with time (the selected radix chart is not used)

• The radix chart - ie. the houses of the selected radix chart for this search

Examples: Mars in 4th House; The Traditional Ruler of the 5th House Cusp Above Horizon; the Antiscia of the Ascendant in a Cardinal House.

In Aspect

This allows you to select

• A First Planet, Point or Cusp – any of Solar Fire's standard chart points, or any of the 12 house cusps

• A First Point Modifier – a modifier to apply to the selected point or cusp, such as the ruler of that point, the degree almuten of that point, the antiscia of that point, the contra-antiscia of that point.

• An Aspect or Aspect Type – an individual aspect in the currently selected aspect set, any aspect, any soft aspect, any hard aspect.

• An Aspect Modifier – a modifier to apply to the selected aspect, such as applying only, separating only, or applying or partile.

• A Second Planet, Point or Cusp

• A Second Point Modifier

Also, for Chart Searches only, whether the second point's placement relates to

• The same chart - ie. the aspect occurs between the two points in the charts being searched (the selected radix chart is not used)

• The radix chart - ie. the aspect occurs from the first point in the charts being searched to the second point in the selected radix chart

Or, for Electional Searches only, whether the second point's placement relates to

• The transiting chart - ie. the aspect occurs between the two transiting points (the selected radix chart is not used)

• The radix chart - ie. the aspect occurs from the transiting first point to the second point in the selected radix chart

The aspect types which may be chosen are defined as follows

• Any Aspect – Any one of the aspects which is switched on in the currently selected aspect set, using the orbs defined within that aspect set.

• Any Soft Aspect – Any one of Conjunction, Trine, Sextile, using the orbs defined for those aspects within the currently selected aspect set, regardless of whether or not they are individually switched on in the aspect set.

• Any Hard Aspect – Any one of Opposition, Square, SemiSquare, SesquiSquare, using the orbs defined for those aspects within the currently selected aspect set, regardless of whether or not they are individually switched on in the aspect set.

Examples: Mars conjunct Saturn; The Traditional Ruler of the 5th House Cusp in any applying aspect to the Ascendant; The antiscia of the Ascendant in applying soft aspect to the almuten of the 9th House Cusp.

Note: The aspect orbs that will be used in the search are those natal orbs specified in the currently selected aspect set, as specified in the "Aspect Set" box at the bottom of this dialog. If you wish to change the orbs, then you can either edit this aspect set, or select a different aspect set.

In Phase

This allows you to select

• A First Planet, Point or Cusp – any of Solar Fire's standard chart points, or any of the 12 house cusps

• A First Point Modifier – a modifier to apply to the selected point or cusp, such as the ruler of that point, the degree almuten of that point, the antiscia of that point, the contra-antiscia of that point.

• A Phase – any individual phase division of 2, 4 or 8 in zodiacal longitude.

• A Second Planet, Point or Cusp

• A Second Point Modifier

Also, for Chart Searches only, whether the second point's placement relates to

• The same chart - ie. the phase occurs between the two points in the charts being searched (the selected radix chart is not used)

• The radix chart - ie. the phase occurs between the first point in the charts being searched and the second point in the selected radix chart

Or, for Electional Searches only, whether the second point's placement relates to

- The transiting chart - ie. the phase occurs between the two transiting points (the selected radix chart is not used)

- The radix chart - ie. the phase occurs between the transiting first point and the second point in the selected radix chart

Examples: Moon in Phase 1 of 2 with Sun; The Traditional Ruler of the 5th House Cusp in Phase 3 of 4 with the Ascendant.

Note: The phase is determined by the angle of the first point in relation to the second point ie. by how far the first pint LEADS the second point in the zodiac. Therefore Moon in Phase 1 of 2 with the Sun means that the Moon leads the sun by between 0 and 180 degrees.

Note: With the Moon as the first point, and Sun as the second point, these phases are typically given the following names:

- Phase 1 of 2 – Waxing Moon

- Phase 2 of 2 – Waning Moon

- Phase 1 of 4 – New Moon

- Phase 2 of 4 – First Quarter Moon

- Phase 3 of 4 – Full Moon

- Phase 4 of 4 – Third Quarter Moon

- Phase 1 of 8 – New Moon

- Phase 2 of 8 – Crescent Moon

- Phase 3 of 8 – First Quarter Moon

- Phase 4 of 8 – Disseminating Moon

- Phase 5 of 8 – Full Moon

- Phase 6 of 8 – Gibbous Moon

- Phase 7 of 8 – Third Quarter Moon

- Phase 8 of 8 – Balsamic Moon

At Position

This allows you to select

- A Planet, Point or Cusp – any of Solar Fire's standard chart points, or any of the 12 house cusps

- A Point Modifier – a modifier to apply to the selected point or cusp, such as the ruler of that point, the degree almuten of that point, the antiscia of that point, the contra-antiscia of that point.

- An Aspect or Aspect Type – an individual aspect in the currently selected aspect set, any aspect, any soft aspect, any hard aspect.

- An Aspect Modifier – a modifier to apply to the selected aspect, such as applying only, separating only, or applying or partile.

- A Fixed Zodiacal Longitude

Examples: Mars conjunct 23Ta00'; The Traditional Ruler of the 5th House Cusp in any applying aspect to 17Cp30'; The antiscia of the Ascendant in applying soft aspect to 9Cn23'48".

Note: The aspect orbs that will be used in the search are those specified in the currently selected aspect set, as specified in the "Aspect Set" box at the bottom of this dialog. If you wish to change the orbs, then you can either edit this aspect set, or select a different aspect set.

In Dignity

This allows you to select

- A Planet, Point or Cusp – any of Solar Fire's standard chart points, or any of the 12 house cusps

- A Point Modifier – a modifier to apply to the selected point or cusp, such as the ruler of that point, the degree almuten of that point, the antiscia of that point, the contra-antiscia of that point.

- A Dignity Type – in rulership, in exaltation, in triplicity, in term, in face, in detriment, in fall, is peregrine, is planet of hour, is planet of day, is cazimi, is combust, is under Sun's beams, is oriental, is in accidental dignity by house, is unaspected.

- A Rulership Level – any one of the available rulership level types, such as Modern, Traditional, Esoteric. This is relevant only for those dignity types that vary according to rulership level ie. rulership, exaltation, detriment, fall, and accidental dignity by house. For other dignity types it is ignored.

Examples: Moon in its Modern Rulership; Venus is cazimi; Modern Ruler of the Sun is Oriental.

Note: The orbs used are: cazimi 0°17'; combust 8°30'; under Sun's beams 17°00'.

Is Planet

This allows you to select

•   A Planet, Point or Cusp – any of Solar Fire's standard chart points, or any of the 12 house cusps

•   A Point Modifier – a modifier to apply to the selected point or cusp, such as the ruler of that point, the degree almuten of that point, the antiscia of that point, the contra-antiscia of that point.

•   Any Planet - out to Pluto only

Examples: Modern Ruler of the Moon is Mercury; Almuten is the 10th House Cusp is Saturn.

Consideration

This allows you to select any one of the following considerations:

•   Moon is Void of Course – this occurs after the Moon makes it last aspect in any sign until its ingress into the next sign, using Conjunctions, Oppositions, Trines, Squares and Sextiles, with aspects to the Sun, Mercury, Venus, Mars, Jupiter, Saturn, and optionally also to Uranus, Neptune and Pluto, depending on which user-defined void of course definition has been selected.

•   Moon is VOC (Lilly method) – this is the same as above except that only planets out to Saturn are used (ie. ignoring Lunar aspects to Uranus, Neptune and Pluto), and the signs Taurus, Cancer, Sagittarius and Pisces are deemed never to have void of course occurring in them.

•   Moon is Waxing – this occurs when the Moon leads the Sun by between 0 and 180 degrees.

•   Moon is Fast – this occurs whenever the Moon is traveling at faster than its average rate of travel (ie. faster than 13°10'35" per day).

- Moon is in via Combusta – this occurs when the moon is between 15° Libra and 15° Scorpio.

- Asc is near sign boundary – this occurs when the Ascendant is within 3° of any sign boundary (ie. less than 3° or greater than 27° of any sign).

- Sun is Above Horizon – this occurs when the Sun's is above the Ascendant/Descendant axis.

Aspect Pattern

This allows you to select one of the available aspect patterns to search for.

>> To see a list and preview of each available aspect pattern type

Click on the **View Patterns...** button.

This displays the Aspect Pattern dialog allowing you to browse through the available patterns, and see a preview of the pattern showing its shape and individual aspect makeup.

Note: The chart points that will be used in the search are those specified in the currently specified pattern points set. If you wish to change the selection of points to use, then you can either edit this point set, or select a different point set by clicking on the > button to the right of the Pattern Points box. In particular, it is important to decide whether you want chart angles (such as the Ascendant and Midheaven) to be included in your search. If you are doing an Electional Search, and you include any chart angles, then the search will take much longer (and produce many more hits) because the chart angles move so quickly. If you are doing a Chart Search, this factor is not relevant, but you may still want to decide whether or not you are interested in pattern involving the chart angles, or whether you prefer to limit the search only to planets, for example.

Note: The aspect orbs that will be used in the search are those specified in the currently selected aspect set, as specified in the "Aspect Set" box at the bottom of this dialog. If you wish to change the orbs, then you can either edit this aspect set, or select a different aspect set by clicking on the > button to the right of the Aspect Set box.

Coordinates

This allows you select

• A Planet, Point or Cusp – any of Solar Fire's standard chart points, or any of the 12 house cusps

• A Point Modifier – a modifier to apply to the selected point or cusp, such as the ruler of that point, the degree almuten of that point, the antiscia of that point, the contra-antiscia of that point.

• A Coordinate Type – Longitude, Speed in Longitude, Latitude, Speed in Latitude, Right Ascension, Speed in Right Ascension, Declination, Speed in Declination, Azimuth, Altitude

• A Comparison Type – Less than (<), Less than or equal to (<=), Equal to (=), Greater than or equal to (>=), Greater than (>)

• A Comparison Value – the types of comparison value required depends on the coordinate type. A zodiacal position (including zodiac sign) is required for longitude, an angle from 0° to 360° is required for Right Ascension and Azimuth. An angle from -90° to +90° is required for Latitude, Declination and Altitude, and a daily rate of motion in degrees is required for any speed.

Examples: Sun Longitude is >= 15°Ta00'; Moon Speed in Longitude is >= 13°10'35"; Midheaven Altitude > 75°00'

Note: If you wish to test for a range of values, then you must create two conditions combined with a Boolean operator. For example, to test for the Sun being in the 3rd decanate of Libra, you would need to use two conditions combined with an AND operator ie. Sun Longitude >= 20°Li00' AND Sun Longitude < 0°Sc00'.

Chart Details

Note: The items available in this category depend on whether you are performing a Chart Search or an Electional Search. A Chart Search allows you to select any and all of the items listed below. However, as an Electional Search is a search through time rather than a search of stored charts, most of these items have no relevance to this type of search. Therefore, the *only* chart detail type that is available for selection within an Electional Search is "Time", which may be used to limit the times of day to be searched.

This category allows you to select

- A Chart Detail Type – as listed below

- A Comparison Type – For chart details types which are numerical, date, time, latitude or longitude types, the available comparison types are Less than (<), Less than or equal to (<=), Equal to (=), Greater than or equal to (>=), Greater than (>). For string type chart details, the available comparison types are "contains" (the item being searched contains the comparison value anywhere), "starts with" (the item being searched contains the comparison value starting at the beginning only), "contains word" (the item being searched contained the comparison value as a whole word ie. separated by at least one space from any other characters in the searched value).

- A Comparison Value - the types of comparison value required depends on the chart details type. String type chart details require a character string comparison value. Date type requires a date comparison value. Time type requires a time comparison value. Latitude requires a geographic latitude comparison value and Longitude requires a geographic longitude comparison value.

Chart Detail Types

- **Chart Type** – the name of this chart type eg. Natal, Progressed, Prenatal (string type value).

- **Name** – the chart name (string type value).

- **Date** – the chart date (date type value).

- **Time** – the chart time (time type value)

- **Zone** – the chart's timezone offset in decimal hours (numerical type value)

- **Place** – the chart's place name (string type value)

- **Country** – the chart's country name (string type value)

- **Lat** – the chart's geographic latitude (latitude type value)

- **Long** – the chart's geographic longitude (longitude type value)

- **Coords** – the chart's coordinate system ie. Geocentric of Heliocentric (string type value)

- **Zodiac** – the chart's zodiac type eg. Tropical, Lahiri, Fagan-Allen (string type value)

- **Houses** – the chart's house system name eg. Placidus, Koch, Equal Houses (string type value)

- **Rating** – the chart's source rating eg. AA, A, B, C, DD, X, XX (string type value)

- **File** – the name of the file in which this chart is stored (string type value)

- **Folder** – the name of the folder, including the full pathname, in which this chart's file resides (string type value)

- **Rec** – the record number where this chart is stored in its file (numerical type value)

- **Days to Birthday** – days remaining until next birthday from current date, from 0 to 365 (numerical type value)

- **Comments** – comments text stored with this chart (string type value)

- **Day of Week** - the name of the day of the week for the chart date (ie. "Monday", "Tuesday", etc.)

Examples: Name contains "Bush"; Latitude is > 0°N00'; Days to Birthday is < 30; Rating matches "AA"; Day of Week contains "Sunday"

Note: String comparison types are always case insensitive.

Note: If you wish to test for a range of values, then you must create two conditions combined with a Boolean operator. For example, to test for times between 9am and 5pm, you would need to use two conditions combined with an AND operator ie. Time >= 9am AND Time < 5pm.

Chart Shape

This allows you to select

- One of the available chart shapes

Some chart shape also have a key planet (eg. "lead" or "handle" planet), in which case you can also select

- A planet as the key planet relating to this shape, or "Any Planet" if you don't mind which planet is the key one

Examples: Chart contains "Bowl"; Chart contains "Locomotive" with any planet as "Lead Planet"; Chart contains "Bucket" with Sun as "Handle Planet".

Note: Chart Shape searches always include only a standard planet set (Sun, Mon, Mer, Ven, Mar, Jup, Sat, Ura, Nep, Plu). You cannot change this behavior, as the chart shape definitions rely on using this fixed set, and would not produce meaningful results with any less or more points included.

Midpoint

This allows you to select

• First Midpoint, consisting of 2 Planets, Points or Cusps (A and B) – any of Solar Fire's standard chart points, or any of the 12 house cusps

• Modulus – any degree value available on the drop-down list, or any other value typed in by the user

• Orb – any degree value available on the drop-down list, or any other value typed in by the user

• Second Midpoint, consisting of 2 Planets, Points or Cusps (A and B) – any of Solar Fire's standard chart points, or any of the 12 house cusps

Also, for Chart Searches only, whether the second midpoint's placement relates to

• The same chart - ie. the contact occurs between the two midpoints in the charts being searched (the selected radix chart is not used)

• The radix chart - ie. the contact occurs from the first midpoint in the charts being searched to the second midpoint in the selected radix chart

Or, for Electional Searches only, whether the second midpoint's placement relates to

• The transiting chart - ie. the contact occurs between the two transiting midpoints (the selected radix chart is not used)

• The radix chart - ie. the contact occurs from the transiting first midpoint to the second midpoint in the selected radix chart

Examples: Mon/Ven contacts Sun/Mer in 90° modulus within 1° orb;

Note: To specify a normal chart point instead of a midpoint, simply ensure that both the A and B points are the same point.

Creating the List of Search Conditions

After creating a search condition, as described in the previous section, you must add it to the list of search conditions before the search can be started.

If you have only a single condition to search for, and the list of search conditions is empty, then the condition will be automatically added to the list when you click on the search button.

Otherwise, if you create a search condition, and click on the search button before adding it to the list, then you will get a warning message reminding you that you have not added it yet, and allowing you to cancel the search in order to do so, if you wish.

You have the ability to either add your new condition to the end of the list, or to replace any existing condition on the list with your new condition.

Adding, Replacing, Deleting or Clearing Conditions

>> **To add a new condition to the end of the list**

Compose your new condition using the **Search Condition Selection** options.

Click on the **Add** button.

>> **To replace an existing condition with a new condition**

Highlight the existing condition you wish to replace.

Compose your new condition using the **Search Condition Selection** options.

Click on the **Replace** button.

>> **To clear the list of conditions**

Click on the **Clear** button.

>> **To delete an existing condition**

Highlight the existing condition you wish to delete

Click on the **Delete** button.

Combining Search Conditions with Boolean Logic

If you have more than one search condition, then you must ensure that they are combined using the correct logical (Boolean) operators.

• The AND operator requires that BOTH conditions which it links are satisfied in order to pass the test.

• The OR operator requires that EITHER ONE or BOTH conditions which it links may be satisfied in order to pass the test.

• It is also possible to apply a NOT operator, which simply reverses the individual condition to which it is applied.

>> To apply the NOT operator to a condition

Highlight the condition you wish to negate.

Click on the **Not** button.

>> To toggle between the AND or OR operator between two conditions or bracketed group of conditions

Highlight the second condition of the two you wish to act on (or the first condition of the second group of conditions, if it forms part of a bracket group).

Click on the **And/Or** button.

>> To toggle bracketing on subgroups of conditions

Highlight all the conditions you wish to bracket or unbracket together (must be a sequential group of conditions in the list).

Click on the **(...)** button.

If that group is not already bracketed, then it will be bracketed. If it is already bracketed, then it will be unbracketed.

Saving and Restoring Lists of Search Conditions

When you exit from the search screen, the list of conditions is automatically saved and then redisplayed the next time you return to the same search screen. However, it is also possible to save and restore lists of conditions to and from files, so that you can re-use them at any later time without having to re-enter each individual search condition again.

>> To save the current list of search conditions

Click on the **Save to File** button

Either specify a new file name of your choice, or else select an existing file name to overwrite

Click on the **Save** button

>> To restore a previously saved set of search conditions

Click on the **Add from File** button

Select the required file name

Click on the **Open** button

Note: When you restore a set of criteria, they are added to the end of your existing list. This is useful if you have stored "snippets" of conditions that you wish to combine. However, if you prefer to overwrite your existing list, then you must clear the list before you restore the set of criteria.

Selecting the Aspect Set and Pattern Points

If you intend to use criteria that involve aspects (In Aspect, At Position, Aspect Pattern), then you can specify which set of aspects you wish to use. This will determine which individual aspects are available for selection, and what orbs each aspect has.

>> To select which aspects and orbs to use

Click on the > button to the right of the **Aspect Set.**

This will display the "File Management" dialog box from which an aspect set may be selected, edited or created.

If you intend to use criteria that include an aspect pattern, then you can specify which chart points to allow as part of the aspect pattern.

>> To select which pattern points to use

Click on the > button to the right of the **Pattern Points**.

This will display the "File Management" dialog box from which a point set may be selected, edited or created.

Running the Search

>> To start the search

Click on the **Search** button.

You will see a results dialog appear, into which the results are added as the search progresses.

Working with the Results of a Chart Search

When the Chart Search starts running, the Chart Search Results dialog appears.

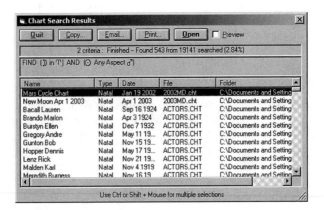

As the search progresses, the top caption shows the progress, indicating how many matching charts have been found, how many have been searched, and what percentage of those searches have resulted in matches.

Each matching chart that is found is added to the main list below, as it is found.

>> To stop the search while it is still running.

Click on the **Stop** button.

After the search has been stopped, or finishes on its own, the caption on the **Stop** button changes to **Quit**.

>> To preview charts in the results list

Click on the **Preview** checkbox to toggle it on or off.

When it is checked, whenever you click on a chart in the results list, the chart preview window will be displayed or updated with the currently highlighted chart. The Chart preview window may be moved and resized according to your preferences. See ??? for more information about the Chart Preview dialog.

>> To resize the width of a column

Use the mouse to drag the column border between any two column headers, or

Double-click on a column border to make the column automatically resize to fit the largest item of data that is displayed in that column.

>> To edit the column selection and order

Use a right hand mouse click when the cursor is over the column headers.

This will display the Choose Columns dialog.

You can select or unselect any of the available columns by either clicking in the checkbox to the left of the column name, or by using the **Show** or **Hide** buttons.

You can change the order of a column by highlighting it and then using the **Move Up** or **Move Down** buttons to re-order it relative to the other columns.

Note: If the selected columns' widths are cumulatively wider than the displayed width of the list, a horizontal scroll bar will appear at the bottom of the list, allowing you to scroll to see the extra columns. Alternatively you can increase the displayed width of the list by resizing the width of the entire dialog.

>> To copy selected charts from the results list into another chart file

1.   Select the required charts (use Ctrl or Shift + Mouse to make multiple selections).

2.   Click on the **Copy...** button. This will display the File Manager with a list of target chart files.

3.   Either select one of the files on the list, or select the **Create** button to create a new empty chart file to copy the charts into.

A "Copy Charts" dialog box will be displayed, giving the options of copying all of the selected charts without confirmation, of being asked for confirmation of the copying of each individual chart, or of canceling the copying process. If the **Yes** button is selected then, for each selected chart in sequence, a dialog box will be displayed asking whether or not that individual chart should be copied. If the **No** button is selected then all of the selected charts will be copied immediately. If the **Cancel** button is selected then no charts are copied.

Note that when charts are copied to another chart file, any chart comments and events that are associated with the charts are copied as well, provided that the destination chart file is of a format that can store these.

>> To email charts in the results file

Select the **Email...** button and from the drop-down menu select either the **All Charts...** option or the **Selected Charts...** option.

You will then see the **Email Charts** dialog with various options for sending the charts by email. See ??? for more information about this dialog.

>> To print a chart details summary of charts from the results list

The summary may be printed at three different levels of detail:

Brief Listing - Each chart occupies a single line of output, and contains only the essential details that would be required to recast the chart: Name, date, time, timezone, latitude and longitude.

Full Listing - Each chart occupies two lines of output, and contains the same information as the brief listing plus the coordinate system (geocentric/heliocentric), zodiac type, house system, place name and country/state.

Full with Comments - The details of each chart occupy two lines of output, containing the same information as the full listing, and any chart comments that are associated with the chart occupy additional text lines below the chart details.

1.   Select the **Print Details...** button and from the drop-down menu select either the **All Charts...** or **Selected Charts...** option.

2.   Select the **Print Details...** button and from the drop-down menu select one of the listing options **Brief Listing...**, **Full Listing...** or **Full with Comments...**.

3.   The "Print" dialog box will appear, from which you can alter printer settings, add this job to the print queue, or print it immediately. See Printing from Solar Fire for further information on printing.

>> To open a selected chart in the Chart Database screen

Double-click on the selected chart, OR

Select the required chart.

Click on the **Open** button and choose the option to open the chart file.

>> To open selected charts and add them to the main list of calculated charts

Select the required chart or charts (use Ctrl or Shift + Mouse to make multiple selections).

Click on the **Open** button and choose the option to add the charts to the list of calculated charts.

Working with the Results of an Electional Search

When the Electional Search starts running, the Electional Search Results dialog appears.

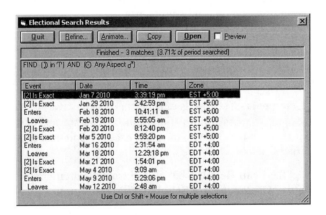

As the search progresses, the top caption shows the progress, indicating how many matching periods have been found, and what percentage of the time searched has resulted in a match. Each matching period that is found is added to the main list below, as it is found.

There are three types of events listed:

- **Enters** - this gives the date and time after which the search condition (or combined search conditions if more than one) become satisfied.

- **Leaves** - this gives the date and time after which the search condition (or combined search conditions if more than one) are no longer satisfied.

- **Is Exact** - this gives the date and time on which the search condition (or one specific search condition if more than one) is exact. This entry is preceded by a number in square brackets eg. [1], [2] etc. The number inside the brackets refer to which particular one condition in the list of conditions is exact, according to the order in which they are specified. For example, if you have searched for (Jup Cnj Sat and Mar Opp Sat) then "[1] Is Exact" refers to (Jup Cnj Sat) and "[2] Is Exact" refers to (Mar Opp Sat).

Note: "Is Exact" events only appear for those types of conditions which can be considered to have exact hits, rather than just having a period of time during which they are in orb or in effect. The only types of conditions which do have exact events are

- **In Aspect** - this has an exact event when the aspect orb is zero, in addition to Enters/Leaves events when entering or leaving orb according to the orbs specified in the aspect set.

- **At Position** - this also has an exact event when the aspect orb is zero, in addition to Enters/Leaves events when entering or leaving orb according to the orbs specified in the aspect set.

- **Coordinates** - if the search condition uses a "Comparison Type" of "=" (equals) then this only produces exact events. If the search condition uses a "Comparison Type" involving greater than or less than operators, then it only produces Enters/Leaves events.

- **All others types of conditions** - can produce only Enters/Leaves events.

>> To stop the search while it is still running.

Click on the **Stop** button.

After the search has been stopped, or finishes on its own, the caption on the **Stop** button changes to **Quit**.

>> To preview charts in the results list

Click on the **Preview** checkbox to toggle it on or off.

When it is checked, whenever you click on a chart in the results list, the chart preview window will be displayed or updated with the currently highlighted chart. The Chart preview window may be moved and resized according to your preferences. See Current Chart Preview for more information about the Chart Preview dialog.

>> To resize the width of a column

Use the mouse to drag the column border between any two column headers, or

Double-click on a column border to make the column automatically resize to fit the largest item of data that is displayed in that column.

>> To refine the search within one of the periods found

Highlight either the entering or leaving line of a found matching period.

Click on the **Refine** button.

This will re-open the Electional Search dialog, with the start and end dates and times set to the these entering and leaving times. This allows you to easily perform a further search within this time period.

>> To view one of the entering, leaving or exact events in the animation module

Highlight a line on the list of matches (either entering, leaving or exact)

Click on the **Animate** button.

This will open the animation screen displaying a chart set the date and time of the selected event. You can then step the chart forward or backward through time as you desire.

>> To copy the results to the clipboard as text

Click on the **Copy** button.

This will copy the search results to the clipboard as text. You can then paste the contents of the clipboard into another application (such as a word processor), where you can edit or print it, for example.

>> To open selected entering or leaving events and add them as calculated charts on the main screen

Select the required lines on the list of matches (use Ctrl or Shift + Mouse to make multiple selections).

Click on the **Open** button.

Chapter 23: Using Dynamic Reports and Time Maps

This chapter describes how to generate, view and print a report of transits or progressions to any chart (hereafter referred to as the "radix" chart). It also describes how to view the output in the form of a "Time Map".

Before generating a dynamic report, it is necessary to have either cast or opened the chart for which you wish to generate the report. If you have not yet done so, see Casting a Natal Chart for instructions on creating a new chart, or page Retrieving Charts From a File for instructions on opening an existing chart.

Report Header

The full header of the dynamic report usually takes up about half a page, and includes details of all the selections you made to generate the report. It is possible to prevent this information from being printed in order to save this space. If this option is switched off, then only the base chart name and the name of the saved selection are printed.

>> To switch the full transit header option on or off

Choose **Full Transit Header** from the **Dynamic** menu - This will switch it on if it was off, or off if it was on.

Note: If you want to show your report to others who may need to know the settings you used to generate your report, then ensure the report header option is switched on.

Report Accuracy

It is possible for Solar Fire to calculate its dynamic reports using two different methods

With **Maximum Accuracy** switched **on** - In this case all dynamic report calculations are performed using an iterative method that ensures that the time given for each events is accurate to within one second of time. However, the "cost" of this accuracy is that it is considerably slower than less accurate methods.

With **Maximum Accuracy** switched **off** - In this case some dynamic report calculations (ie. aspect hits) are performed using a quadratic curve-fitting method, which approximates the correct result, and is generally not quite as accurate as the iterative method, but has the advantage of being much quicker. The loss of accuracy is usually very small - typically giving results within several seconds of the maximally accurate result, although in some isolated cases it could be out by up to ten seconds or more.

Typical users of Solar Fire will probably prefer to have the Maximum Accuracy option switched off, because it makes dynamic report and calendar generation much quicker, and still retains a level of accuracy which is more than adequate for most astrological purposes. However, those users who do need results which are always accurate to the nearest second of time should switch Maximum Accuracy on.

Note: All sign ingresses and planetary stations in dynamic reports and calendars are always calculated to maximum accuracy, regardless of whether the Maximum Accuracy setting is on or off.

>> To alter the report accuracy setting

Choose **Maximum Accuracy** from the **Dynamic** menu - This will switch it on if it was off, or off if it was on.

Note: This option also affects the calendar module, because it uses dynamic reports which run in the background to generate its calendar events.

Generating a Dynamic Report

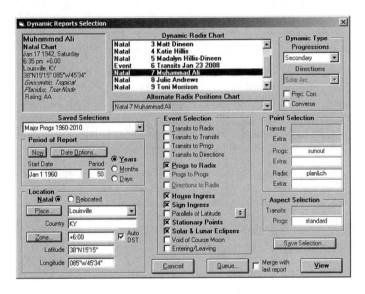

>> **To generate a dynamic report**

Choose **Transits & Progressions...** from the **Dynamic** menu - This will display the "Dynamic Report Selection" dialog box that allows the selection of a radix chart and options to be used in generating the report.

Select a chart from the **Dynamic Radix Chart** list box.

Optionally select a different chart from the **Alternate Radix Positions Chart** drop-down listbox. Usually this should be the same chart, but if you choose a different chart, then the generated dynamic report will show dynamic events of the Dynamic Radix Chart in relation to the chart points of the alternate chart. For example, if you choose "Sarah Jones" as your dynamic radix chart, and "David Smith" as your alternate radix chart, then when you generate a progressions report, it will show Sarah's progressed planets making aspects to David's natal planets.

Optionally, choose an item from the drop-down list of **Saved Selections** - Doing so will cause all the options on this screen to be updated according to what was last saved in this Saved Selection. Having done this, you may still alter any of the options on the screen without causing any changes to the Saved Selection. For example, if your Saved Selection has a report period of 1 year, you might wish to alter this to 2 years for this particular report, or you may wish to add Eclipses to the report. These new options will remain in effect until you either choose another item from the drop down list of Saved Selections, or alter any of the other options yourself. (If you select the same Saved Selection again, then the options will be reset to what they were when you last selected it.)

Either use the **Date Options** button to choose an automated date setting (see below for a full description), or else enter the **Start Date** for the report manually. There are some shortcuts to setting the date quickly and easily as follows: Select the **Now** button to get today's date; double-click on the **Days** option button to set the date back by one day; double-click on the **Months** option button to set the date back to the first day of the month (or to the previous month if the day is already the 1st of the month); double-click on the **Years** option button to set the date back to the first day of the year (or to the previous year if the day is already the 1st of January).

Set the length of the reports by selecting any one of the **Days**, **Months** or **Years** option buttons, and enter the number of days, months or years in the **Period** box. This must be a positive integer. The period for which the report will run will be this number of years, days or months, depending on which of these periods has been selected with the option buttons.

Select Location type to be either **Natal** or **Relocated**. If a dynamic report is being generated for an individual, then it should normally be relocated to wherever they are living during the period of the report. However, if the chart's subject is someone who is living in the same location as they were born during the time of the report, then the natal option is appropriate. If only progressions are being generated for an individual, then the location should normally be the same as the natal chart location. However, if the radix chart is that of a person who moved during the first few months of their life, it may be appropriate to relocate it. If the **Natal** option is selected then all the boxes relating to location, including time zone, longitude and latitude will contain the location details from the selected base chart. Note that although it is technically correct to alter the time zone if the current time zone is different from the natal one, in practice this is only necessary if you are examining lunar or chart angle transits, as the difference in the resultant times is otherwise not significant. If the **Relocated** option is selected then all the boxes relating to location, including time zone, longitude and latitude will contain the current default values. (See Saving and Restoring Settings for details on default values.) Any of these values may be altered in the same manner as when creating a new chart. See Casting a Natal Chart for instructions on how to alter location values.

The **Auto DST** option allows you to choose whether or not the results of the report will be shown in the given timezone only, or whether the timezone should be adjusted automatically to take account of daylight savings periods for the given location.

In the **Event Selection** area, click on the options which you wish to include. These options are:

Transits to Radix - transits of planets/asteroids/angles to points in the selected radix chart

Transits to Transits - transits of planets/asteroids/angles to one another

Transits to Progressions - transits of planets/asteroids/angles to their progressed positions

Transits to Directions - transits of planets/asteroids/angles to their arc directed positions

Progressions to Radix - progressions of planets/asteroids/angles to points in the selected radix chart

Progressions to Progressions - progressions of planets/asteroids/angles to one another

Directions to Radix - arc directed positions of planets/asteroids/angles to points in the selected radix chart

Note that at least one of the above options MUST be selected in order to produce a report. Also note that, unless the radix chart is a natal or event type chart, then it will only be possible to select the Transits to Radix or Transits to Transits options. In this case, the other options will be disabled (grayed).

House Ingress - If selected, then the report will contain an entry for each chart point that crosses a house cusp in the radix chart, either direct or retrograde.

Sign Ingress - If selected, then the report will contain an entry for each chart point that crosses a zodiac sign cusp in the radix chart, either direct or retrograde.

Parallels of Declination or Latitude - If selected, then the report will contain entries for parallels and contra-parallels of declination or latitude, as well as for aspects of longitude. The selection of either declination or latitude may be made by clicking on the up-down arrow button to the right of this option. This button toggles the setting between declination and latitude.

Stationary Points - If selected, then the report will contain entries showing the dates when planets or asteroids are geocentrically stationary. (This has no effect if the radix chart is heliocentric.)

Solar & Lunar Eclipses - If selected, then the report will contain entries showing the date and time and zodiacal position of maximum eclipse of exact associated lunar phases, depending on the eclipse settings in Preferences.

Void of Course Moon – If Selected, then the report will contain entries showing the date and time of the last aspect made by the Moon as it enters its void of course state, as well as the sign ingresses, which indicate where the Moon ends it void of course state. (Void of Course is calculated according to the user-selected options).

Entering/Leaving - If selected, then the report will contain an entry for each chart point as it enters transiting orb and leaves transiting orb, as well as when the transit, progression or solar arc direction is exact. Also, any aspects which are already in orb at the beginning of the report period will be listed. If this option is not selected, then the report contains entries only for exact hits. The angle of the transiting orb used for the report is taken from the current aspect set file. This orb may be altered by editing the aspect set file. See Aspect Set for instructions on how to edit the aspect set file.

Note: If you need to ensure that slow moving transits are always shown in a short time-period report, whether or not they actually make any exact hits during that time period, then make sure the Entering/Leaving option is selected.

Note: Only one of the parallels options can be selected at one time. It is not possible to produce a report containing both parallels of declination and of latitude.

If you have selected any events involving Progressions or Directions, then in the **Dynamic Type** box, select which type of progressions or directions you wish to use by selecting one of the available types from the drop-down list boxes. The progression types are:

Secondary - This is the most commonly used type of progression, based on a day for a year ie. one day per solar cycle.

Tertiary - This method of progression is based on the mean rate of a day for a lunar month.

Minor - This method of progression is based on a mean lunar cycle for a year.

User Rate - This method allows you to define whatever rate of progression you choose. The rate used here must be set in the **User Progression Rate** option of the **Preferences** dialog.

The direction types are:

Solar Arc - This is the most commonly used method. Chart point longitudes are directed by the secondary progressed arc in longitude, and chart point declinations are directed by the secondary progressed arc in declination.

Ascendant Arc - Chart points are directed by the ascendant arc (which is itself derived from the secondary progressed solar arc.)

Vertex Arc - Chart points are directed by the vertex arc (which is itself derived from the secondary progressed solar arc.)

User Arc - Chart points are directed by a user-defined annual arc rate. The rate used here must be set in the **User Direction Rate...** option of the **Preferences** menu.

Primary Mundane - This method directs chart points along their respective diurnal arcs according to the rotation of the earth about its axis. This option is different from all the others in that aspects formed using this method are mundane aspects rather than aspects of zodiacal longitude. The rate of direction can be selected from the **Primary Direction Rate** option of the **Preferences** menu. See Rate for Primary Directions.

Profections (Annual) – This directs the chart by 30 degrees per year. Conventionally, you would use this direction method to find when the directed Ascendant makes conjunctions to points in the radix chart.

Optionally, select the **Prec. Corr.** or **Converse** options and an arc multiplier. If the **Prec. Corr.** option is checked, then the calculations will be done according to the position of the planets in the Sidereal zodiac, rather than the Tropical zodiac. However, the resulting report will still be calculated in Tropical Zodiac. Note that if the radix chart which you are using already uses a Sidereal zodiac, then this option will have no effect, and the resulting report will be in the Sidereal zodiac. If the **Converse** option is checked, then the calculation of the transits and progressions will be done by searching backwards from the converse entered time in relation to the time of the dynamic radix chart. An additional arc multiplier button (**Mult**) is visible whenever Solar Arc, Ascendant Arc or Vertex Arc directions have been selected for inclusion in the report. Clicking on this button produce a drop-down menu with the possible arc multipliers - x1 (Normal), x2 (Double Arc), x0.5 (Half Arc), x-1 (Negative Arc), x-2 (Negative Double Arc), x-0.5 (Negative Half Arc).

You may wish to alter the **Point Selection**. The items that you can select are:

Transits - Transiting points. You may, for example want to include just transits from the outer planets only. On the other hand, for a very short-term report, you may want to include transits by the Moon.

Extras - Extra transiting points. This can include any combination of midpoints between planets or other chart points, as well as fixed stars, asteroids and extra bodies.

Progs - Progressing and Directed points. You can specify a different set of points from the transiting points.

Extras - Extra Progressing and Directed points. This can include the same types of points as for the extra transiting points.

Radix - Points in the radix chart that you want to include in the report. You could exclude the MC and Ascendant if the birth time was uncertain; add asteroids, use inner planets only, etc.

Extras - Extra radix points. This can include any combination of midpoints between planets or other chart points, and fixed stars, arabic parts, asteroids, extra bodies, fixed zodiacal positions and house cusps.

The names of the currently selected sets are displayed, and it is possible to select different sets, browse or edit them etc. by clicking on the name of the desired set. Doing so will cause the File Manager screen to be displayed See Using the File Manager for instructions on using the File Manager to alter any settings.

You may also wish to alter the **Aspect Selection.** The items that you can select are:

Transits - Aspects formed from transiting points to radix points.

Progs - Aspects formed from progressed or directed points to radix points. This can be a different set of aspects from the transiting aspects.

Optionally select the **Merge** checkbox – If you do so, then the new report that you generate will be merged with the previously generated dynamic report, and all events for both reports will be displayed together. This option is useful for generating reports that require combinations of settings that are not possible in a single report. For example, you could produce a report using Solar Arc directions, and then merge this with another report using Ascendant Arc directions. The final result is a report containing both types of directions.

Finally select the **View** button - The "Dynamic Events Report" screen is displayed, and the report is generated as you watch.

Instead of viewing the report immediately, you have the option of adding the report to the print queue, to be printed later.

>> To add the report to the print queue

Select the **Queue**... button - This will display a dialog box asking you to confirm whether or not you wish to add this dynamic print job to the Solar Fire print batch queue. If you select the OK button, then it will be added to the queue, and it will not be calculated or printed at this time. It is possible, at any later time, to start printing all the jobs that are on the batch print queue by selecting the **Start Print Queue...** option from the **View** menu of the main screen. Note that any dynamic report that is calculated on the batch queue will be sorted into date order. If you wish to see the report in any of the other available sort orders, you must generate the report using the **View** button.

Automated Date Options

It is possible to allow the start date for the report to be set automatically, based on the current date or the date of the radix chart begin used. If one of these automated options is chosen, and the current settings are saved as a **Saved Selection**, then the next time this **Saved Selection** is used, the report start date will be updated automatically as required.

Clicking on the **Date Options...** button displays the Report Start Date dialog.

The available options are

• **Fixed date as entered** – using this option has the same effect as manually entering a start date. The date you enter remains fixed for all subsequent reports unless you manually update it again.

• **Relative to the current date** – this allows you to set a report period that moves forward in time as the current date changes. This is useful for creating a limited period report that always remains up-to-date.

• **Relative to the radix chart date** – this allows you to set a report period which is fixed relative to the birth date. This is useful for creating a report that always starts at or near the radix chart's birth date, ie. a lifetime report.

The adjustment options for relative dates are as follows.

• **Go to** – allows you to adjust from the reference (current or radix) date back to the beginning of the day, month, quarter, half year or year.

• **Adjust date by** – allows you to adjust from the reference date by any integer multiple of days, months or years. This may be a positive or negative multiple, for an adjustment forward or backward in time respectively.

Examples:

If the settings are Relative to Current Date, Go To Start of Month, Adjust by –1 months, then any current date in December 2005 results in an automate report start date of 1st November 2005 ie. the first day of the month preceding the current month.

If the settings are Relative to Radix Chart Date, Go To Start of Month, Adjust by +1 months, then a radix chart date of 28th December 1957 results in an automated report start date of 1st January 1958 ie. the first day of the month following the birth date.

Saving and Deleting Selections

Solar Fire is supplied with a list of predefined dynamic report selections. It is possible to select any of these, edit them, delete them, or to create your own selections. Each named selection in the list is simply a record of all the selections that can be made on this screen, including start date, period, location details, event types etc. In this manner, it is possible to customize your own set of dynamic report options and to save them for easy access in future sessions.

>> To save or re-save the currently selected dynamic options

Select the **Save Selection...** button. You will be asked to enter a description under which to save this selection. If you then select the **OK** button, it will then be saved to the list.

>> To delete a saved selection

Highlight the desired selection in the **Saved Selections** list and use the **Del** key.

Viewing the Report

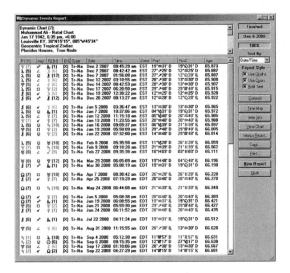

During report generation, you can stop further report calculation by selecting the **Cancel** button. When the report is finished, it is possible to exit from this screen by selecting the **Quit** button.

The status of report generation is shown in the three boxes at the top right hand side of the screen. The top box shows the type of calculations being performed, the second box shows the date for which calculations are currently being performed, and the lower box shows an approximate percentage completed so far, both by percentage number, and with a graphical "flood-fill" bar, for the current calculation type.

There is a limit of 10,000 dynamic events in any one report. If this limit is reached, or if your computer runs out of memory before this limit is reached, then you see a dialog box indicating the problem, and the report will be truncated at that point.

When the report calculation is complete, the report is sorted into whichever sort order was last chosen. It is possible to sort the report into a variety of different orders as follows.

>> To change the sort order

Select the required sort order option from the drop-down list. Possible orders are

- **Date** - Entries in the report will be sorted according to date and time, in ascending order of time.

- **E/X/L Event** - Entries in the report will be sorted into groups of in orb at the beginning of report (B), entering orb (E), exact (X) and leaving orb (L) events for the same transit or progression, and then the groups are sorted into date order of the first item in the group. If the Entering/Leaving option was not selected for this report, then this order is the same as Date order.

- **Point 1** - Entries in the report will be sorted into groups of entries for each point in the first column of the report. These are the dynamic chart points. The entries are sorted by date within each dynamic point group.

- **Point 2** - Entries in the report will be sorted into groups of entries for each point in the third column of the report. These are normally the radix points, but may also be dynamic points if the event is a transit to transit, transit to progression, transit to solar arc or progression to progression. The entries are sorted by date within each point group.

- **Weighting** - Entries in the report will be sorted into an order calculated according to weightings ascribed to each transiting point, aspect and radix point. The weightings relate to the speed of movement of each chart point, so that transits involving (slow moving) Pluto are at the top of the report, and within the transits of each planet, transits involving the (fast moving) ascendant are at the top. In many instances this order will approximate to the level of significance of the transit. However, due to the subjective nature of determining the importance of particular transits, this report should only be used as a potential aid - not as a definitive statement of the relative importance of each transit!

- **Event Type** - Entries in the report will be sorted into groups of the same event types, for example all the transits to radix (Tr-Na) will appear first, the transits to transits (Tr-Tr) next etc. The entries are sorted by date within each group.

- **Aspect** - Entries in the report will be sorted into groups of aspect. For example, all conjunctions appear at the top, oppositions next etc. The order in which of the aspects appear is determined by Solar Fire's internal aspect ordering, which is the same order in which aspects appear in the aspect editor, for example.

You can alter the appearance of the report by switching on or off the **Use Glyphs**, **Use Colors,** and **Bold Text** option. These work in the same way as for the Chart Reports, as described in Generating Chart Reports.

If you wish to keep the report to view again later, then you can click on the screen's minimize button (at the top right of the screen). This will turn the screen into an icon at the bottom of your Windows desktop area, and you may view it again at any time by double-clicking on its icon. Note, however, that if you generate another dynamic report, then it will overwrite your existing report. If you wish to save it then you must print it or copy it to the clipboard before producing another dynamic report.

Description of Report Layout

The report appears on the screen in two parts - at the top is a small window giving a report header. This contains details of the radix chart, the points and aspects selected and the types of events selected, and the period of the report. Below this is the large window, containing the body of the report. You can browse through the report by clicking on the scroll bars to the right of the report display boxes.

A typical report line has the following items:

Point1	**Asp**	**Point2**	**Hit**	**Type**	**Date**	**Time**	**Zone**	**Position1**	**Pos**
Ura (10)	Sqr	Ven (7)	(X)	(Tr-Na)	Jun 12 1993	11:07: 23pm	BST +1:00	19Cp23 R	19L

In this sample report line, transiting Uranus (retrograde) at 19°23' of Capricorn in the 10th house is making an exact square to natal Venus (direct) at 19°23' of Libra in the 7th house on 12th June 1993.

The possible items in each line are defined in the following table.

Point1	The dynamic point and the house it is occupying on the radix chart
Aspect	The aspect formed between Point1 and Point2
Point2	The radix point (or second dynamic point) and its house in the radix chart
EXL	(X) for exact hit, (E) for entering orb, (L) for leaving orb, (B) for already in orb at beginning at report, (S) for sign ingress, (H) for house ingress.
Type	A combination of abbreviations from the list below, indicating the type of dynamic event and radix chart for Point1 and Point2.
Date/Time	To date of the event
Time	The time of the event on the given day
Zone	The timezone abbreviation for the given time of the event
Age	Age of native in decimal years at time of event
Position1	Zodiacal position of Point1 - R indicates retrograde, D direct. If the aspect is a parallel or contra-parallel, then this shows the declination or latitude. If this relates to a primary mundane direction, then this shows the position of Point1 in its diurnal arc in pseudo degrees (0°=Eastern horizon,90°=Upper culmination).
Position2	Zodiacal position of Point2 - R indicates retrograde, D direct. If the aspect is a parallel or contra-parallel, then this shows the declination or latitude.
Chart 1	Indicates the chart number and name of the dynamic radix chart. This column only appears if an alternate radix positions chart has been selected, or if the report is merged with other reports which use a different dynamic radix chart.
Chart 2	Indicates the chart number and name of the alternate radix positions chart. This column only appears if an alternate radix positions chart has been selected.

Possible Type abbreviations are as follows.

- Tr - Transits
- Sp – Secondary Progressed
- Tp – Tertiary Progressed
- Mp – Minor Progressed
- Up – User Rate Progressed
- Sa – Solar Arc Directed
- Aa – Ascendant Arc Directed
- Va – Vertex Arc Directed
- Ua – User Arc Directed
- Pm – Primary Mundane Directed
- Pv – Primary van Dam
- Pf - Profected
- Na – Natal Radix
- Pn – Progressed Radix
- Di – Directed Radix
- Re – Return Radix
- Co – Composite Radix
- Ha – Harmonic Radix
- AH – Age Harmonic
- A1 – Age+1 Harmonic
- Prefix "c" – Converse
- Prefix "p" – Precession Corrected (Prec. Corr.)
- Postfix "x2", "x0.5", "x-1", "x-2", "x-0.5" – indicate the arc multiplier that was used, if any. (Applies to Solar Arc, Ascendant Arc and Vertex Arc directions only.)

Some examples of these types are as follows.

- Tr-Na - Transits to Natal

- Sp-Na - Secondary Progressed to Natal

- cpVa-Na - Converse Precession Corrected Vertex Arc Directions to Natal

- Sax0.5-Na – Ascendant Arc Directions (Half Arc) to Natal

- Tr-Pn – Transits to a Progressed Radix chart

- Tr-Pr – Transits to progressions (same radix chart)

Point1 and **Point2** may be any of the following types.

- **Any chart point** (planet, asteroid, Transneptunian, angle) - Shown by either it's glyph or by it's abbreviation (eg ♅ or "Ura")

- **A midpoint between any two points** - Shown by either their glyph or by their abbreviations (eg. ♅/☽ or "Ura/Mon")

- **A fixed star** - Shown by either s* where * is a number of by its first six letters (eg. "s12" or "Mirach")

- **An Arabic Part** - Shown by either p* where * is a number of by its first six letters (eg. "p7" or "Brothe")

- **An asteroid** - Shown by either a* where * is a number or by its first six letters (eg. "a3" or "Apollo")

- **A fixed position** - Shown by either f* where * is a number or by its position (eg. "f1" or "00Ar00")

- **A house cusp** – shown by a number from 1 to 12.

Note: If you have a listing with a large number of fixed stars, Arabic Parts, asteroids or fixed positions, then you may wish to switch between the alternate display styles to help you identify which item is which on the list.

>> To switch between the alternate display styles for Point1 and Point 2

Click on the **Use Glyphs** option in the Report Style frame

Editing the Report

You can delete lines from a report, change the widths of the columns, reorder the columns, and add or remove columns.

You can also change the width of the entire report by resizing the entire report window.

>> To delete lines from the report

It is possible to delete lines from the report, on a line-by-line basis. In order to delete a line, you must first

Select the line by clicking on it. The line is shown to be selected by a dashed rectangle enclosing it. Then simply use the **Del** key. The line will be deleted, and the other report lines adjusted as necessary to fill the gap. Note that deleted lines cannot be undeleted. You will need to regenerate the entire report in order to get any deleted lines back.

>> To change the width of a column

Drag the column border on the report header bar with the mouse

>> To reorder, add or remove columns

Use a right hand mouse click on the report header bar.

This will display the **Choose Columns** dialog.

You can select any combination of columns to display by checking or unchecking them in the checkboxes to the left of the items in the list, and change the order of the columns by highlighting a column and then using the **Move Up** or **Move Down** buttons repeatedly until the desired new position is reached.

Note: If not all columns are visible in the report after adding or resizing them, you can increase the visible area by resizing the entire report window.

Item Info

It is possible to view further information on items in the dynamic report, such as interpretations or a list of aspects to eclipses. This option also makes it possible to see the full name of any fixed star, Arabic Part or asteroid that appears in abbreviated form in a line of the dynamic report

>> To view further information on an item

Select a report line by clicking on it and then select the **Item Info** button, or double-click on a line in the report

The Item Info dialog box will be displayed.

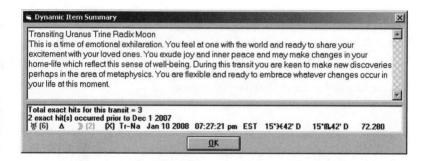

The top box in this screen will show in words, what dynamic event this line contains, followed by an interpretation of that event, if interpretation text exists for that type of event.

The bottom box will list any similar events that are found in the report, eg. if the selected line is transiting Saturn square natal Moon, then any other exact, entering or leaving hits of this transit will also be listed. Also, if the selected event is a transit to a radix chart, then the total number of exact hits that will occur during this transit is listed, plus the number of hits that occurred before the report period, and/or the number that will occur after the report period.

If the event is an eclipse or a stationary point of a planet (ie. going direct or retrograde), then a list of aspects of points in the radix chart to the eclipse or stationery position is shown. The aspects used in this list are those in Solar Fire's currently selected aspect set.

When you have finished looking at the information in this dialog box, clicking on the **OK** button will cause it to disappear.

View Chart

It is possible to calculate and display a full chart for date and time of any event in the report. The type of chart depends on what type of dynamic event is selected, for example for transits to a natal chart, you see a biwheel showing a transit chart on the outside and the natal chart on the inside; for a stationary point you see a single wheel showing transits; for transits to progressions you see a biwheel with transits on the outside and progressions on the inside, etc.

>> To display a chart for any event in the dynamic report

Select a report line by clicking on it

Select the **View Chart** button

This will cause any required chart or charts to be calculated and added to the list of Calculated Charts, and the "View Chart" screen to be displayed. When you have finished looking at the chart and **Quit** from this screen, you are returned to the dynamic report screen.

Viewing a Dynamic Interpretations Report

You can send all the available interpretations for a dynamic report to be viewed in a separate word-processor. You may also wish to select which word processor to use (see Selecting a Word Processor), and whether or not the report will be formatted using Rich Text Format (see Interps).

>> To view an interpretations report

Select the **Interps Report...** button. Your word processor will be opened up displaying this report. You are then free to browse the report, to print it, or to save it under another name if you wish. Note that, to keep a permanent copy of the report, you must save it under a different name, because Solar Fire always uses the same report name. When you have finished with the report, exit from your word processor.

Copying to the Clipboard

>> To copy the report to the Windows clipboard

Select the **Copy** button.

From the clipboard, the report may be pasted into a word-processor or page layout program, for example. Note that glyphs and colors cannot be copied to the clipboard. Abbreviations are used instead of glyphs when the report is copied into the Clipboard. Also, report columns may not align correctly in the Clipboard. If you paste the Clipboard contents into your word-processor, you may have to edit the document to ensure that the columns align correctly.

Printing the Report

>> To print the report in the displayed sort order

Select the **Print...** button.

The printed report will contain glyphs (if you have the **Use Glyphs** option selected), and colors (if you have a color printer and you have the **Use Colors** option selected). However, the printed report always uses regular (light) text. It is not possible to print the report using bold text.

Note that it is not possible to add a report to the print batch queue from this screen. To do so you must use the **Queue...** button on the "Dynamic Selections" dialog box.

Time Map

>> To view a graphical display of the dynamic events in your report

Select the **Time Map** button.

After a brief calculating period, the TimeMap screen will appear.

The time scale for the time map corresponds to the period of the dynamic report upon which it is based. The list of dynamic events is the same as those in the dynamic report, expect that all the Entering, Exact and Leaving events of a particular transit or progression are grouped together into single entries. Also, to optimize space, the events are listed using astrological glyphs, using subscripts to indicate what kind of dynamic event they relate to. These subscripts are

t - transiting

p - progressing

d - directed

n - natal

r - radix

It is possible to alter the display to show either transiting hit numbers or dates/times on which certain events occurred, on the map. The Hit Nos option shows which hit in a series of direct/retrograde transits to a point is occurring. For example, if the transit has three hits (1st hit direct, 2nd hit retrograde, and 3rd hit direct), then these events will be labeled 1:3, 2:3, and 3:3 respectively. If the transit has only one hit, then it will be labeled 1:1. This enables you to see at a glance whether there are associated hits which occur before or after the duration of the time map. Note, however, that progressions and directions and special dynamic events do not have hit numbers shown, as these will generally always be single events. The Date option shows the day and month of each major event on the map. For example an event which occurs on the 23rd March will be labeled either 23/3 or 3/23 depending on the date order in your Windows setup. However, if the duration of the time map is less than 7 days, then this option shows the time in 24 hour format, instead of the date. For example an event which occurs at 3:46pm is labeled 15:46. It is possible to scroll through this list by using the scroll bars on the right of the screen. It is also possible to reorder and delete lines in the map.

>> To delete one or more lines from the map

Select the required lines by clicking on them

Select the **Delete**... button

You will be asked to confirm whether or not you wish to delete them. Note that clicking on any line selects it on the first click, and unselects it on a subsequent click.

>> To move a line on the map

Drag and drop the required line as follows

Position the mouse over the line you wish to move and hold down the left hand button

Drag the mouse to the required position in the map

Release the mouse button

>> To print a copy of the time map

Optionally use the **Printer...** button to alter printer settings such as paper orientation

Select the **Print** button

This will print the entire list, in the displayed order, using as many pages as are required. Each page will have a time scale printed at the top.

>> To view further information on an item

Double click on a line

The Item Info dialog box will be displayed, showing interpretations and event information. This may be used in the same manner as in the dynamic report screen.

>> To return to the dynamic report screen

Select the **Quit** button.

Chapter 24: Using the Graphic Ephemeris

This chapter describes how to generate, view and print a graphic ephemeris of longitudes of transits, progressions or directions, and of declinations or latitudes of transits and progressions, for any chart.

It is also possible to generate a graphic ephemeris of transits without reference to any chart, which can be printed out as a pro-forma ephemeris for use with any chart. A graphic ephemeris may also be added to the print batch queue, to be printed later.

Before generating a graphic ephemeris, you should cast, open or generate the subsidiary chart that you wish to base the ephemeris on, so that it is showing in the "Calculated Charts" list box on the Main Screen.

>> To generate a graphic ephemeris

Choose the **Graphic Ephemeris** menu item from the **Dynamic** menu. This will display the "Graphic Ephemeris Selection" screen that allows the selection of a base chart and various other options.

Choosing Ephemeris Options

>> To select a base chart

Click on the required base chart in the list of **Dynamic Radix Charts**.

You may also optionally select a different chart from the **Alternate Radix Positions Chart** drop-down listbox. Usually this should be the same chart, but if you choose a different chart, then the generated ephemeris will show dynamic events of the Dynamic Radix Chart in relation to the radix chart points of the alternate chart. For example, if you choose "Sarah Jones" as your dynamic radix chart, and "David Smith" as your alternate radix chart, then when you generate an ephemeris, it will show Sarah's progressed planets making aspects to David's natal planets.

>> To select previously saved options

Choose an item from the **Saved Selections** drop-down list on the left hand side of the screen. This will immediately update all the selections on the screen with whatever was stored under that saved selection description.

>> To set the date from which the ephemeris will start

Select the **Now** button - If the **Now** button is selected, then the Date will be updated to correspond to the computer's internal clock. This button is useful if you wish to produce an ephemeris covering a period from today onwards.

Enter a Date - Enter a date in any acceptable format. Most commonly used formats are acceptable. If the format is not acceptable then an error dialog box will be displayed. Acceptable formats are described in detail in Entering a Date.

Alternatively, to facilitate the setting of the date, there is a special feature to help you quickly set the date back by a day, to the beginning of a month, or to the beginning of a year. To set the date back by one day, double-click on the **Days** option button. To set the date back to the first day of the month (or to the previous month if the day is already the 1st of the month), double-click on the **Months** option button. To set the date back to the first day of the year (or to the previous year if the day is already the 1st of January), double-click on the **Years** option button.

Once you have the desired start date then you can set the duration of the ephemeris to be any number of days, months or years.

>> To select the duration of the ephemeris

1.   Select any one of the Days, Months or Years option buttons

2.   Enter the number of days, months or years in the **Period** box. This must be a positive integer. The period that the ephemeris will cover will be this number of years, days or months, depending on which of these periods has been selected with the option buttons.

>> To select the location for which you wish the ephemeris to apply

Select either the **Natal** or **Relocated** option button - If a dynamic report is being generated for an individual, then it should normally be relocated to wherever they are living during the period of the report. However, if the chart's subject is someone who is living in the same location as they were born during the time of the report, then the natal option is appropriate.

If only progressions are being generated for an individual, then the location should normally be the same as the natal chart location. However, if the base chart is that of a person who moved during the first few months of their life, it may be appropriate to relocate it.

If the **Natal** option is selected then all the boxes relating to location, including time zone, longitude and latitude will contain the location details from the selected base chart. Note that although it is technically correct to alter the time zone if the current time zone is different from the natal one, in practice this is only necessary if you are examining lunar or chart angle transits, as the difference in the resultant times is otherwise not significant.

If the **Relocated** option is selected then all the boxes relating to location, including time zone, longitude and latitude will contain the current default values. (See Saving and Restoring Settings for details on default values.) Any of these values may be altered in the same manner as when creating a new chart. See Casting a Natal Chart for instructions on how to alter location values.

>> To select the ephemeris dynamic type

Select one of the following options from the **Ephemeris Selection** list:

Transits - to display transiting planetary positions

Progressions - to display any type of progressed planetary positions

Directions - to display any type of directed planetary positions

If you select progressions, then the **Progressions** drop-down listbox in the **Dynamic Type** box will become enabled, and you can select any of the available progression types from that list. The progressions may be secondary, tertiary, minor, user-defined rate, age or age+1 harmonic.

If you select directions, then the **Directions** drop-down listbox in the **Dynamic Type** box will become enabled, and you can select any of the available direction types from that list. The directions may be solar arc, ascendant arc or vertex arc.

Also note that, unless the base chart is a natal or event type chart, then it will only be possible to select the **Transits** option. In this case, the other options will be disabled (grayed).

If you wish to view **Prec. Corr.** or **Converse** planetary position, then you can optionally also click on their check boxes in the **Dynamic Type** box, and you can also choose an arc multiplier using the **Mult** button if your are using Solar Arc, Ascendant Arc or Vertex Arc directions.

>> To select the graph coordinate type

Select **Longitude, Declination** or **Latitude** from the drop-down list box below the dynamic type selection. (Only longitude is available if you have chosen to use directions.)

If you select longitude, then you have the option of selecting an ephemeris modulus angle. If you select declination or latitude, then you can select an angle extent.

>> To select the ephemeris modulus angle

Select a pre-defined modulus angle from the **Modulus Angle** drop-down list

Alternatively, you can type any desired angle from 10 minutes of arc to 360 degrees directly into the **Modulus Angle** box. You can type in degrees and minutes and seconds, separating each with a space (eg. 22 30 for 22°30'), and you can also use decimal format (eg. 22.5 for 22°30').

The graph will display the zero line at the top, and extends downwards by the amount of the specified modulus angle.

>> To select the angle extent

Select a pre-defined angle from the **Angle Extent** drop-down list

Alternatively, you can type any desired angle from 10 minutes of arc to 90 degrees directly into the **Angle Extent** box. You can type in degrees and minutes and seconds, separating each with a space (eg. 22 30 for 22°30'), and you can also use decimal format (eg. 22.5 for 22°30').

The angle extent determines how many degrees are displayed on either side of the zero line. For example, selecting 30 degrees for a declination graph will create a graph from 30 degrees south to 30 degrees north.

Note: The graph always shows an equal angle extent above and below the zero line. You cannot produce a graph that shows only one hemisphere.

>> To select other display options

Click on the **Radix Positions** check box in order to have the radix chart's planetary positions displayed on the ephemeris.

Click on the **Radix Aspects** check box in order to have an aspect glyph displayed wherever a dynamic planetary position crosses a radix position.

Click on the **Sign Labels** check box in order to have zodiac sign labels for each planetary line (both radix and dynamic), and sign change bullets on each planetary line wherever the planet crosses into a new sign.

Click on the **Lunations** check box to have New and Full moon position markers on the graph. These appear as small circles containing an N for a new moon (without eclipse), F for a full moon (without eclipse), ✔ for a solar eclipse on the new moon, and ☄ for a lunar eclipse on the full moon. NB – This option setting is included as part of the Saved Selection, so if you wish its setting to be remembered as part of the current selection, you must use the **Save Selection** button after changing it.

Click on the **Deg Gridlines** check box in order to have dashed lines drawn across the ephemeris at each degree division. Having this option switched on helps locate positions within the ephemeris more easily, but may be distracting when viewing the ephemeris on a small screen.

Click on the **Date Gridlines** check box in order to have dashed lines drawn down the ephemeris at each date division.

Click on the **Back Shading** check box to have the entire ephemeris data area shaded with a light grey. This option affects the aesthetic appearance of the ephemeris only.

>> To select which chart points to use in the ephemeris

Click on the required point type (**Transits**, **Progs** or **Radix**) inside the Points Selection box. This will display the File Manager which lists all the available point files. To select a file, highlight it and click the **Select** button. To see what is in a file and optionally make changes, click the **Edit** button. For more details on selecting and editing point files, see Editing a Chart Points File.

Note: Only those point types which are applicable to the current selections will be enabled.

>> To save these selections for future use

Click on the **Save Selection...** button. You will be asked to enter a description under which to save this selection. Type in a brief description, and then click on the **OK** button. The description will appear in the **Saved Selections** list on the left of the screen, ready to reselect in future.

>> To delete a saved selection

Highlight the desired selection in the **Saved Selections** list, and press the **Del** key.

Viewing and Printing the Graphic Ephemeris

Once all the options have been set in the **Graphic Ephemeris Selection** screen, it is possible to view the ephemeris, to print it now or later, and to copy it to the clipboard for pasting into other programs.

>> To add the ephemeris to the print batch queue

Click on the **Queue...** button. This will display a dialog box asking you to confirm whether or not you wish to add this job to the Solar Fire print batch queue. If you select the OK button, then it will be added to the queue, and it will not be calculated or printed at this time. It is possible, at any later time, to start printing all the jobs which are on the batch print queue by selecting the **Start Print Queue...** option from the **View** menu of the main screen.

>> To view the graphic ephemeris

Click on the **OK** button. The "Graphic Ephemeris" screen is displayed, and the ephemeris is generated as you watch. Once the ephemeris is finished, you have the option of resizing the screen. If the screen is smaller than the available screen size, then clicking on the screen's maximize button will generate a larger display, which may be easier to read.

>> To step the graphic ephemeris forward or backward in time

Click on the >> or << buttons in the top corners of the screen. These will recalculate and display the graphic ephemeris for the time periods adjoining the time period of the current graph.

>> To print the graphic ephemeris

Click on the **Print...** button. The usual print dialog box will appear enabling you to select **Setup...** or **Print**. However, the **Queue** button will be disabled. In order to queue the ephemeris, you must return to the **Graphic Ephemeris Selection** screen.

>> To copy the ephemeris as a graphic

Position the mouse anywhere over the graphic ephemeris and click once on the right-hand mouse button. This will display the copy dialog with the options to copy the graph to various locations in various formats. See Copying, Publishing and Sending Graphics for a full description of these options.

Chapter 25: Searching for Eclipses

This chapter describes how to use Solar Fire's eclipse database to list eclipses and eclipse data, cast eclipse charts, and search for eclipses that make aspects to any specified position or any points in a specific chart.

>> **To enter the eclipse module**

Select the **Eclipses...** item from the **Dynamic** menu

You will then see the Find Eclipses dialog from which you can make various selections.

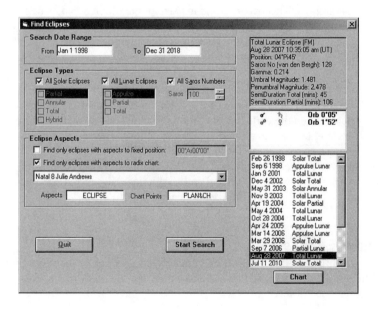

- **Dates** - You must always specify a date range in the **From** and **To** fields. These accept dates in the same way as all other date entry fields in Solar Fire. See Entering a Date for details on entering dates.

- **Eclipse Types** – You can select any combination of eclipse types and/or Saros Numbers by using the check boxes for each option, and optionally entering a specific (van den Bergh) Saros Number. See a description of eclipse types below.

• **Eclipse Aspects** – If you wish to find only those eclipses that make an aspect to a fixed position, then check the first box, and enter the required zodiacal position. If you wish to find all eclipses that make an aspect to a planet or point in a chart, then check the second box and select a chart from the drop-down list of calculated charts. You can select which set of aspects are used by clicking on the Aspects box, and which set of chart points are used by clicking on the Chart Points box.

Solar Eclipse Types

• **Partial** – There is no region of complete obscuration of the Sun. This occurs when the axis of the Moon's shadow passes outside of the disk of the Earth. Maximum partial eclipse therefore occurs in polar regions.

• **Annular** – This occurs when the size of the Moon's disk is less than the size of the Sun's disk, so that when the Moon is directly in front of the Sun, a ring of sunlight (annulus) is still visible around the Moon.

• **Total** – This occurs when the Moon's disk is larger than the Sun's disk, and completely obscures the Sun for a period of time.

• **Hybrid** - Hybrid eclipses are also known as annular/total eclipses. They occur when the vertex of the Moon's umbral shadow pierces Earth's surface along the central path of an annular eclipse. The eclipse's character then changes to total along the section of the path where the umbral vertex extends beneath Earth's surface. The central paths of hybrid eclipses usually (but not always) begin and end as annular eclipses, but become total along some middle portion of the path.

Lunar Eclipse Types

• **Appulse** – This occurs when the Moon passes across the penumbra of the Earth' shadow, and this darkens part of the Moon's surface, but obscures none of it completely.

• **Partial** – This occurs when the Moon passes partly across the umbra of the Earth's shadow. Part of the Moon's surface becomes completely obscured.

• **Total** – This occurs when the Moon passes completely into the shadow of the Earth, and the whole disk of the Moon becomes completely obscured.

When you have made all your selections, click on the Start Search button. Solar Fire will list all of the eclipses that match your selection in the list box on the bottom right of the dialog.

When you highlight any eclipse on this list, the full details of that eclipse will appear in the box at the top, right of the dialog, and any aspects that are made between the eclipse point and the (optionally) selected chart will be displayed below that. The items displayed are as follows.

• **Eclipse Type** – Solar / Lunar and whether Partial / Annular / Total / Hybrid / Appulse.

• **Date and Time** – The date and time (Universal Time, timezone +0:00) of maximum eclipse, given to the nearest whole minute or else the date and time to the nearest second of exact lunar phase, depending on the eclipse setting under Preferences.

• **Position** – The zodiacal position of the Sun (in Solar Eclipses) or Moon (in Lunar Eclipses).

• **Saros Number** – The number of the Saros cycle to which this eclipse belongs. The Saros is a period of approximately 18 years and 11 days, after which eclipses are repeated with only slightly altered characteristics. The standard astronomical numbering system is that first described by Prof G. van den Bergh in *"Periodicity and Variation of Solar (And Lunar) Eclipses"* publ. Haarlem, Netherlands, 1955. An alternative numbering system was described by Robert Carl Jansky in *"Interpreting the Eclipses"* publ. Astro Computing Services 1979, and extended by Bernadette Brady in *"The Eagle and the Lark"* publ. Samuel Weiser Inc, 1992.

• **Gamma** – In a lunar eclipse, this is the distance of the Moon from the axis of the Earth's shadow, at the time of greatest eclipse. In a solar eclipse, this is distance of the shadow cone axis from the centre of Earth at the instant of greatest eclipse. Units are of equatorial radii.

• **Magnitude** – The fraction of the Sun's diameter obscured by the Moon.

• **Umbral Magnitude** – The fraction of the Moon's diameter obscured by the umbra.

• **Penumbral Magnitude** – The fraction of the Moon's diameter obscured by the penumbra.

• **Duration Total** – The duration of total or annular eclipse phase at the point of greatest eclipse.

- **Semi-Duration Total** – The half-time of totality (complete obscuration of moon) of eclipse. Adding this time to the time of maximum eclipse would give the time of ending of totality.

- **Semi-Duration Partial** – The half time of partial (partial obscuration of moon) phase of eclipse. Adding this time to the end of totality would give the time of ending of the partial phase of the eclipse.

>> To calculate a chart for one or more listed eclipses

1.   Highlight the required eclipse (or multiple eclipses) in the list box.

2.   Click on the **Chart** button.

This will calculate a chart for the time of maximum global eclipse (or multiple eclipse charts if you have highlighted multiple eclipses).

If you were finding eclipses only with aspects to a specified radix chart, then the location and timezone of the eclipse chart will be adopted from the specified radix chart. Otherwise, the current default location and timezone are adopted.

If you wish to see the same eclipse chart for another location, then use the Chart / Locality menu items to relocate the eclipse chart to the required location.

Chapter 26: Real Time Clock and Animation

This chapter describes how to use Solar Fire's real time astrological clock, and how to animate charts and page displays by running or stepping them forward and backward through time. This module also allows the one-step construction of biwheels, triwheels and quadriwheels showing transits, progressions and directions around natal chart.

Some things that can be done in this module are as follows.

• Display a real time astrological clock for the current location

• Display a real time astrological clock for any other location and timezone

• Display a natal chart ready to step forward or backward in time

• Display a progressed or directed chart ready to step forward or backward in time

• View pop-up interpretations of a chart (see Viewing Interpretations)

• Display and operate a dial pointer (see Using Dials and Pointers)

• Display a biwheel with a natal chart (or radix chart) on the inner ring, and current transits on the outer ring, ready to step forward or backward in time

• Display a triwheel with a natal chart (or radix chart), current secondary progressions and transits, ready to step forward or backward in time

• Display a quadriwheel with a natal chart (or radix chart), current secondary progressions, solar arc directions and transits, ready to step forward or backward in time

• Display other combinations of fixed and dynamic charts in uni, bi, tri and quadriwheels

• Display any astrological page ready to step forward and backward in time

• Run, step or jump the charts or pages through time

These options are described more fully below.

Note that the wheel styles and other color options used in this module are always the same as those that are in effect on the View Chart screen, and can be altered by using a right hand mouse click somewhere over the display to bring up the Chart Options menu.

How to Set Up Animations

>> To display a real time astrological clock for the current location

Select the **Real Time Clock** item from the **Dynamic** menu

This will display a chart for the current default location, updated at regular intervals.

>> To display a real time astrological clock for any other location and timezone

1.   Cast a new natal chart for the required location for any date and time

2.   Select that chart as the current chart

3.   Select the **Animate Chart...** item from the **Dynamic** menu

4.   Click on the **Clock** option button at the top right of the screen

This will display a chart for the required location, showing the correct current local time for the timezone of the chart, updated at regular intervals. For example, if your default location is Sydney, Australia (AEST –10:00), and it is currently 3pm in Sydney, and you cast a chart for London, UK (GMT +0:00), then display that chart in the real time clock, then the clock time will be displayed as 5am GMT, which is the correct current time for London.

>> To display a natal chart ready to step forward or backward in time

1.   Select the required natal chart as the current chart

2.   Select the **Animate Chart...** item from the **Dynamic** menu

This will initially display the chart exactly as it has been cast. If you use the time controls to alter or step the time, then the chart's date and time are used as the starting point, and then adjusted according to the options you choose.

>> To display a progressed or directed chart ready to step forward or backward in time

1.   Select the required progressed or directed chart as the current chart

2.   Select the **Animate Chart...** item from the **Dynamic** menu

This will initially display the chart exactly as it has been cast. If you use the time controls to alter or step the time, then the chart's date and time are used as the starting point, and then adjusted according to the options you choose.

>> To display a biwheel with a natal chart (or radix chart) on the inner ring, and current transits on the outer ring, ready to step forward or backward in time

1.   Select the required natal chart as the current chart

2.   Select the **Animate BiWheel...** item from the **Dynamic** menu

This will display the natal chart as a fixed chart on the inner ring, and the current transits on the outer ring. If you use the time controls to alter or step the time, then the current date and time are used as the starting point, and the transits chart is then adjusted according to the options you choose.

>> To display a triwheel with a natal chart (or radix chart), current secondary progressions and transits, ready to step forward or backward in time

1.   Select the required natal chart as the current chart

2.   Select the **Animate TriWheel...** item from the **Dynamic** menu

This will display the natal chart as a fixed chart on the inner ring, and the current secondary progressions on the middle ring, and transits on the outer ring. If you use the time controls to alter or step the time, then the current date and time are used as the starting point, and the progressions and transits charts are then adjusted according to the options you choose.

>> To display a quadriwheel with a natal chart (or radix chart), current secondary progressions, solar arc directions and transits, ready to step forward or backward in time

1.   Select the required natal chart as the current chart

2.   Select the **Animate QuadriWheel...** item from the **Dynamic** menu

This will display the natal chart as a fixed chart on the inner ring, and the current secondary progressions on the middle inner ring, solar arc directions on the middle outer ring and transits on the outermost ring. If you use the time controls to alter or step the time, then the current date and time are used as the starting point, and the progressions, directions and transits charts are then adjusted according to the options you choose.

>> To display other combinations of fixed and dynamic charts in uni, bi, tri and quadriwheels

If you are already displaying a dynamic wheel with the required number of charts, then click on the **Charts...** button to display a dialog which allows you to select alternative charts.

Alternatively, you can select the **Animate Page...** item from the **Dynamic** menu. You will be prompted to select the required page type from the list of available pages, and then the required chart types. (See below)

>> To display any astrological page ready to step forward and backward in time

If you are already displaying a dynamic wheel or page with the required number of charts, then click on the **Page...** button to display a dialog that allows you to select alternative pages. Note that you will only be able to select another page which requires the same number of charts as the wheel or page you are currently viewing.

Alternatively, you can select the **Animate Page...** item from the **Dynamic** menu. You will be prompted to select the required page type from the list of available pages, and then the required chart types. (See below)

Selecting Alternative Chart Types

The dynamic chart selection dialog is similar to the multiwheel selection dialog, except for the additional option of selecting a dynamic method to apply to some or all of the charts in the wheel or on the page.

You can select the following chart types or methods:-

- **Transits** – This will display a chart of transiting positions, varying with the animation date and time. When this option is selected, there is no need to select a base chart.

- **Fixed Base Chart** – This will display the selected base chart as fixed, so that it does not vary with the animation date and time. This option should be selected, for example, with a natal chart that you wish to place in the centre of a multiwheel, with transits or progressions around it.

- **Secondary Progressions** – This will display a chart of the progressed positions calculated from the selected base chart.

- **Mean Tertiary Progressions** – As above

- **True Tertiary Progressions** – As above

- **Minor Progressions** – As above

- **User Progressions** – As above. The user progression rate is one of the settings that may be specified in the Preferences dialog of Solar Fire.

- **Solar Arc Directions** – This will display a chart of the directed positions calculated from the selected base chart.

- **Ascendant Arc Directions** – As above

- **Vertex Arc Directions** – As above

- **User Rate Directions** – As above. The user direction rate is one of the settings that may be specified in the Preferences dialog of Solar Fire.

- **Annual Profections** – As above. The profection rate is equivalent to a direction arc of 30 degrees per year.

- **Age and Age+1 Harmonic** - These will display a chart of the age and age+1 harmonic positions calculated from the selected base chart.

When you select a progression or direction method, you may also choose whether to apply converse or precession correction options, by checking the appropriate boxes as required. If Solar Arc, Ascendant Arc or Vertex Arc methods are chosen, then you can also use the **Mult** button to select an arc multiplier if you wish. These options have the same effect as the same named options when casting subsidiary charts under the **Chart** menu. See Casting Subsidiary Charts for further information on these options.

The **Selected Chart** list at the bottom of the dialog contains a list of which chart types have already been selected. If you have selected a uniwheel or page which requires only one chart, then this list will only have a single item in it. If there are multiple items in the list, then you must click on the one you wish to select or edit before changing your selection of base chart and/or dynamic chart method.

>> To select a transits chart to animate

In the Selected Charts list, click on the item that you wish to change to transits.

In the Dynamic Methods list, click on the Transits item.

It is not necessary to select a base chart in this case, because transits depend only on the animation date and time, and are calculated independently of any base chart.

>> To select a fixed base chart

In the Selected Charts list, click on the item that you wish to change to a fixed base chart.

In the Base Charts list, click on the required base chart.

In the Dynamic Methods list, click on the Fixed Base Chart item.

Any chart that you select this way will remain fixed, even though you may be running an animation. This option is only to be used when you have other dynamic charts in the same wheel page, such as transits or progressions to the base chart, and you want the base chart to remain fixed as a radix chart whilst the other dynamic charts are animated as the date and time change.

Note: If you use the fixed base chart option when you are only viewing a single chart on a wheel or page, then the animation features will have no effect.

>> To select a dynamic chart to animate

In the Selected Charts list, click on the item that you wish to change to an animated chart.

In the Base Charts list, click on the required base chart.

In the Dynamic Methods list, click on the required dynamic method (such as Secondary Progressions, Solar Arc Directions etc,), and optionally also select the Prec. Corr. and Converse options.

Any chart calculated by this method will be derived as a subsidiary chart of the selected base chart, and updated according to the animation date and time.

Exporting Animated Charts

It is possible to export any animated charts into Solar Fire's list of calculated charts from where they may be saved to a chart file or used anywhere else in Solar Fire.

It is also possible to automatically export the animated charts and simultaneously display them in the Chart View screen, from where various extra functions are available, such as rectify assist, reports, and copy/send.

These functions are useful when you have used the animation module to find particular charts of interest, and then wish to be able to save them or use them in other parts of Solar Fire.

>> To export the current animated chart/s to the list of calculated charts

Click on the **Export** button, and select **To Calculated Chart List** from the pop-up menu.

>> To export the current animated chart/s and display them as a fixed Chart View page

Click on the **Export** button, and select **To Fixed Page...** from the pop-up menu.

How to Control the Animation

When the real time clock is running, you cannot perform any of the animation functions. Before using the animation features, you must ensure that the Animation option is chosen at the top right of the screen.

If this is a multiwheel animation, and includes a fixed natal chart that has stored life events, then it is possible to select any life event from a list to set the animation time and date automatically.

>> To set the time and date to that of a stored life event

Click on the **Events...** button, and select one of the events from the **Event Selection** dialog box.

Note: You can also add new life events from this dialog if you wish.

>> To set the time and date to a particular value

Enter new values directly into the date and time boxes. (See Entering a Date and Entering a Time for details on acceptable formats for dates and times).

>> To set the time step interval

1.   In the **Step By** drop-down box, select one of the pre-defined time intervals.

2.   Optionally enter a numeric multiple into the box immediately to the left.

For example, to specify a 5 minute interval, select the "Minutes" item from the list, and then enter the value 5.

>> To run the chart through time

The left and right arrows will start the animation running backward or forward in time respectively, with the display being recalculated at the specified intervals. Click on the red square Stop button to halt the animation.

>> To step the chart forward or backward

The left and right arrows with the adjacent vertical bars will step the animation backward or forward in time respectively, one step for each mouse click.

Alternatively, after ensuring that the displayed wheel or page has the focus (by clicking on it), you can use the left or right arrow keys to step back or forward with one step per keypress.

>> To change the rate of animation

Use the mouse to slide the Animation Speed control left or right.

When at its leftmost position, this will attempt to update the display as often as the power of your computer will allow. When moved further right, the display is only updated after a fixed interval of time has elapsed. If your computer is not a very recent, powerful model, you may wish to leave this control at or near its fastest setting. If your computer is especially powerful, you may prefer to choose a slower setting so that the animation does not run overly fast.

>> To reset the date and time to now

1.   Click on the **Clock** option button – this will reset the date and time to match your computer's system clock, and the timezone of the first displayed chart. Note that this means that the displayed time and date will be correct for the location of the chart according to its timezone, and may therefore be different from your current local time, but the planetary zodiacal positions will still be the correct ones for the current instant.

2.   If you wish to animate again from this date and time, then click on the Animation option button.

Chapter 27: Using Calendars

This chapter describes how to generate, view and print a calendar containing transits, progressions and/or directions for any radix chart. Calendar data may also be exported to other calendaring programs, such as MS Outlook and others.

Before generating a calendar, it is necessary to have either cast or opened the chart/s for which you wish to generate the calendar. If you have not yet done so, see Casting a Natal Chart for instructions on creating a new chart, or page Retrieving Charts From a File for instructions on opening an existing chart.

>> To open the Calendar module

Choose **Calendar...** from the **Dynamic** menu - This will open the "Calendar" screen, and display calendar entries for the current chart and date.

>> To change the calendar duration

Either, choose the **Day, Week** or **Month** items from the View menu

Or, click in the **Day, Week** or **Month** button on the top, left toolbar.

- **Day** - shows one calendar day only

- **Week** - shows a 7 day period with the current date in the middle ie. 3 days to either side of the current calendar date

- **Month** - shows the full calendar month for whatever month the current date falls into

>> To change the current calendar date

Do any of the following

- Click on the drop-down arrow to the right of the date entry, and use the standard calendar control to select a new date

- Click on the "-" (minus sign) button - this moves the current calendar date **back** by one day, week or month, depending on the current calendar duration

- Click on the "+" (plus sign) button - this moves the current calendar date **forward** by one day, week or month, depending on the current calendar duration

>> To change the current radix chart for the calendar

Select the required chart from the drop-down listbox just above the calendar viewing frame.

Calendar Information

Each calendar day displays the following information.

- The day number - at top left.

- The time zone - at top centre - this is the time zone for which any calendar entries showing times relate to.

- Lunar zodiacal info - at top right. This shows the Moon glyph, followed by its current sign glyph, or two glyphs if the moon makes an ingress into a new sign during this calendar day. Where there is an ingress, the exact time of ingress is shown below this. If the Moon goes void of course during the day, then the time that this occurs is also shown.

- Lunar phase information - at bottom centre. This shows a small graphic representation of the current lunar phase, plus a further description of the phase. If any of the four major phases occur on this day, then the time of the exact phase is given. On any other day, the name of the current phase, and the lunar phase angle at midday are shown instead.

- Dynamic calendar events - in the central section. This lists all the transits, progressions and/or directions and other dynamic events which are currently selected in the Calendar Preferences.

Dynamic Calendar Events

Each entry is given in one of the following formats

- For the first item on a line - Event Type, Point1, Aspect, Point2, Time (optional)

If there is enough space, then there may be additional entries on the same line which relate to the same Event Type and Point1.

- For additional entries on the same line - , Aspect, Point2, Time (optional)

Event Types which appear here are the same event types as those which appear in the dynamic reports, and are described fully in the description of report layouts.

>> To view an interpretation of an individual calendar event

Hover the mouse over that calendar event

This causes a tooltip to pop up showing the interpretation of that event. The interpretation is automatically taken from whichever interpretation file is currently selected for use with the calendar.

>> To view a report containing all events and their interpretations

Select the **View Interpretations Report...** item from the **View** menu.

Your word-processor will be opened up displaying this report.

Note: To keep a permanent copy of the report, you must save it under a different name, because Solar Fire always uses the same report name.

Setting Calendar Preferences

>> To open the Calendar Preferences dialog

Select **Edit Settings...** from the **Preferences** menu item of the Calendar screen.

This will display the Calendar Options dialog.

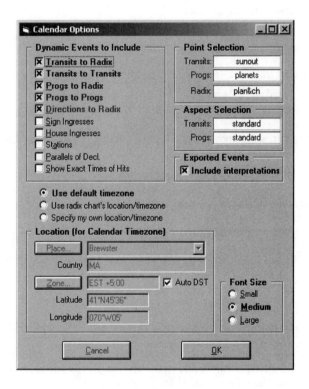

Many of the options available here are the same as those in the Dynamic Reports module.

Note: The options that you select and set here are always remembered for future sessions. To revert to any previous settings, you must reselect those settings yourself, using this dialog.

Dynamic Events To Include

Check the options which you wish to include. These options are:

- Transits to Radix - transits of planets/asteroids/angles to points in the selected radix chart.

- Transits to Transits - transits of planets/asteroids/angles to one another.

- Progressions to Radix - progressions of planets/asteroids/angles to points in the selected radix chart.

- Progressions to Progressions - progressions of planets/asteroids/angles to one another.

- Directions to Radix - arc directed positions of planets/asteroids/angles to points in the selected radix chart.

- Sign Ingresses - movements of points across sign boundaries.

- House Ingresses - movements of points across house cusps of the radix chart.

- Stations - times when points become stationary.

- Parallels of Declination - aspects of declination (in addition to aspects of longitude, which are always included).

- Show Exact Times of Hits - whether or not to show the time (to the nearest minute) of each event, rather than just the day on which it occurs.

Timezone/Location Options

- Use default timezone – to use your current default location and timezone settings for the calendar events.

- Use radix chart's location and timezone - to use the current chart's location and settings for the calendar events.

- Specify my own location/timezone - allows you to enter the required place details and other settings in the Location frame below.

Location (for Calendar Timezone)

You can select location details in a similar manner to choosing a location for a new natal chart.

The location is relevant only 1) for the selection of which timezone to use, and the switching dates between daylight savings and normal time for that location, and 2) for the calculation of transiting angles. However, it is not recommended to include chart angles as transiting points.

Normally the **Auto DST** option would be switched on. If the **Auto DST** option is unchecked, then the results will show times for the specified timezone only, whether or not this is the standard timezone for the given location. This is useful if you would like to see all the results in Universal Time, for example, rather than in the normal timezone for the selected location.

Point Selection

• **Transits** - Transiting points. You may, for example want to include just transits from the inner planets only. On the other hand, for a more detailed calendar, you may want to include transits by the Moon.

• **Progs** - Progressing and directed points. You can specify a different set of points from the transiting points.

• **Radix** - Points in the radix chart that you want to include in the report. You could exclude the MC and Ascendant if the birth time was uncertain; add asteroids, use inner planets only, etc.

Note: Given the large number of transiting angle events that occur every day, it would only be possible to display only a very a small proportion of such events in the calendar dialog, so it is strongly recommended that you do not include chart angles as transiting points

Aspect Selection

• **Transits** - Aspects formed from transiting points to radix points.

• **Progs** - Aspects formed from progressed or directed points to radix points. This can be a different set of aspects from the transiting aspects.

Exported Events

• **Include Interpretations** - If this option is selected, then calendar data that is exported to other applications will include Solar Fire's interpretation of each event, in addition to the event details themselves. Switching this off reduces the volume of exported information, by limiting it to include only the name, date and time of each event.

Font Size

- **Small** - allows up to about 10 lines of event data per calendar day

- **Medium** - allows up to about 8 lines of event data per calendar day

- **Large** - allows up to about 6 lines of event data per calendar day

Note: The font size selection affects only the lines containing the dynamic events. The day number, lunar sign and phase information always remain at a fixed font size.

Note: To display more events per calendar day, you can also switch off the **Show Exact Times of Hits** option, as this usually allows more individual events to be listed per line of event data.

Exporting Calendar Events

>> To copy or send a copy of the calendar image

Choose **Copy/Send Image...** from the **Export** menu of the Calendar dialog

This invokes the **Copy Image To** dialog that allows you to select whether to send the currently displayed image to the clipboard, to a file, or to an email attachment, with various selectable options. See Copying, Publishing and Sending Graphics.

>> To send calendar events to MS Outlook

Choose **Send Calendar Events / To MS Outlook...** from the **Export** menu of the Calendar dialog.

This will display the MS Outlook Export Options dialog, giving you the ability to add or remove calendar entries in MS Outlook.

This feature allows you to label all Solar Fire's generated entries so that you can then easily remove them all later, without interfering with any other existing Outlook calendar entries. It is recommended that you use "Solar Fire" as the whole label name, or at least as the start of a longer label name, to reduce the risk of accidentally deleting entries which were not generated by Solar Fire.

Note: You can, if you wish, export more than one person's calendar events to Outlook. In that case, it is recommended that you append the chart name to the label before exporting, so that you can tell the entries apart in MS Outlook eg. "Solar Fire - Sarah" and "Solar Fire - John". Doing this also allows you to remove just one person's entries (by using ""Solar Fire - John" in the delete dialog), or all entries at once (by using "Solar Fire" in the delete dialog.)

>> To delete existing calendar events from MS Outlook

Optionally edit the category label in the **Existing Outlook Calendar Entries** frame.

Click on the **Remove** button.

You will get a notification message telling you how many entries were deleted.

Note: This removes all entries that start with the given text, so entering "Solar Fire" will delete all entries for "Solar Fire - John" and "Solar Fire - Susan", for example.

>> To add the existing calendar events to MS Outlook

Optionally edit the category label above the **Export** button.

Click on the **Export** button.

Note: If you wish interpretation text to be included with each event, make sure you have switched on the Include Interpretations options in the Calendar Preferences dialog.

>> To export calendar events to another calendaring application

Either choose **Send Calendar Events / To iCalendar file...** from the **Export** menu of the Calendar dialog.

Or choose **Send Calendar Events / To vCalendar file...** from the **Export** menu of the Calendar dialog.

You will be prompted to enter a filename and location to save the file to.

Once you have exported the data, you will need to import it into whatever application you wish to use it with, instructions for which you must obviously obtain from that application's own documentation.

iCalendar and vCalendar Formats

iCalendar is a standard for calendar data exchange, sometimes also referred to as "iCal". vCalendar was the precursor of the iCalendar exchange format. It is implemented and supported by many different calendaring, including Apple's iCal application, Facebook, Google Calendar, Lotus Notes, Microsoft Entourage, Microsoft Exchange, Mozilla Calendar Windows Calendar, Microsoft Works Calendar, Microsoft Outlook, and many others.

Chapter 28: Printing from Solar Fire

This section describes how to send a chart page, report or time map to the printer which is attached to your computer system, how to add a print job to the batch print queue, to be printed at a later time instead of immediately, and how to alter printer settings such as the number of copies of each page to be printed, the page orientation and the print resolution.

If you wish to set page margins, then you must do this before printing. See Setting Page Margins for information on how to do this.

Before printing a chart, grid or report relating to a chart or grid, it is necessary to have either cast, opened or generated the charts which you wish to print, or to have generated the report which you wish to print.

You can print from any screen with a **Print...** button, or with a **Print** menu option.

Printing from a View Screen

You can print any wheel, grid, user-defined page, dynamic report, Time Map, ephemeris page or Planetarium view by clicking on the **Print** button on the screen. In most cases a print dialog box will appear, which you can use as described in following sections.

>> To print any chart or grid or page layout for which an image has already been created

From the "Chart View" screen, select the required image from the list of images

Select the **Print...** button

>> To print any report, from the "Chart Report" screen

Select the desired report from the list of reports

Select the **Print...** button

Printing without Viewing

If you just want printouts, you can print single and multiple wheels and grids without first viewing them on the screen. These printouts will use whatever displayed points, aspects set, wheel style, display options, colors, fonts and other options that are currently selected in the Chart Options and Preferences menus.

>> To print one or more charts or aspect grids from the main screen

Select the chart(s) from the list of "Calculated Charts".

Select the **Print Chart...** or **Print Grid...** options from the **Chart** menu.

>> To print a multiwheel chart or synastry grid from the main screen

Follow the instructions in Viewing MultiWheels and Synastry Grids to select the required charts.

Select the **Print...** button.

Using the Print Dialog Box

Most **Print** options in Solar Fire will display the "Print" dialog box, which allows the user to add the print job to the batch print queue, to alter printer settings, or to print immediately.

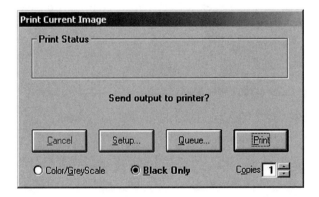

If you wish to exit from this dialog box without taking any action, then the **Cancel** button may be used.

>> To select a Color/Greyscale/Black options

Choose one of the two options provided.

Color/Greyscale - if you have a color printer (on which the color printing ability is enabled), then the output will be printed using the colors selected in your current color scheme for printers. If your printer is not a color printer (or is a color printer, but on which the color printing ability is disabled), then it will appear in greyscale equivalents to the colors selected in your current color scheme for printers.

Black Only - this converts all color output to black. This produces the clearest output on most monochrome printers.

>> To send output to the printer immediately

Optionally select a **Color/Greyscale/Black** option.

Optionally enter a number of **Copies** to print.

Select the **Print** button - This will start the print job, and messages will appear on the screen to indicate the status of printing. Generally the printer will not actually start printing until the "Print" dialog box disappears. It is not possible to cancel printing once it has started, although it is possible to delete an item from the Windows print queue if it has not already been sent to the printer in its entirety. See your Windows manual for information on the Windows print queue.

If the printer is switched off, not connected to the computer, or has other problems, then Windows will issue a message asking whether you wish to cancel or retry. You may then attempt to remedy the problem and select the **Retry** button, or select the **Cancel** button if you wish to continue working without fixing the problem now. If the **Cancel** button is selected then the output will not be sent to the printer, but it will remain on the Windows print queue (not to be confused with the Solar Fire batch print queue). Please refer to your Windows manual for instructions on using the Windows Printer object to deal with the Windows print queue.

>> To add this output to the print batch queue

Optionally enter a number of **Copies** to queue for printing.

Select the **Queue...** button - This will display a dialog box asking you to confirm whether or not you wish to add this print job to the Solar Fire print batch queue. If you select the OK button, then it will be added to the queue, and it will not be printed at this time. It is possible, at any later time, to start printing all the jobs which are on the batch print queue by selecting the **Start Print Queue...** option from the **View** menu of the main screen.

Note: If you have specified more than one copy, then the print queue will have the specified number of copies added to it instead of just one.

>> To alter printer setup options

Select the **Setup...** button

See Altering Printer Settings for information on altering printer settings.

Note: The number of copies you set in the printer settings is ignored by Solar Fire. To print multiple copies, you must set the number of copies required in this dialog instead.

Note: The number of copies you select in this dialog is always automatically reset to one when it is next opened. This is done deliberately to prevent you accidentally printing multiple copies when you have simply forgotten to reset it from last time you printed.

Setting Page Margins

It is possible to set page margins which apply to all types of Solar Fire's printed output, including charts, reports and time maps.

>> To set page margins

Select the **Page Margins...** option from the **Charts** menu - This will display a "Page Margins" dialog box in which it is possible to view the current page margins or to set new ones.

There are four margins (left, right, top and bottom), each of which may be different, if desired. These margins are expressed in terms of a ratio of page dimensions (based on the printable page area, not the full page size), so a setting of 0.1 indicates a margin of 1/10th of the printable page size, for example.

Each margin must be between 0 and 0.4 inclusive. A page margin of 0 indicates that printed output will extend right to the edge of the printable area of the page.

For example, if you wish to set a 10% left hand binding margin, but to otherwise use the full printable area, then enter

0.1 0.0 0.0 0.0

When you select the **OK** button you will be asked to confirm your settings before they are saved. Note that the page margin settings are saved for subsequent sessions only if you choose to **Save Settings** or if **Save Settings on Exit** is on.

Altering Printer Settings

>> To alter printer settings

Do either of the following

From Solar Fire's Print Dialog box, select the **Setup...** button

Select the **Printer Setup...** option from the **Options** menu of Windows Print Manager in the Control Panel

This will display a "Print" dialog box that allows the selection of an alternative printer, and the number of copies of each page to print and whether to collate the pages in order.

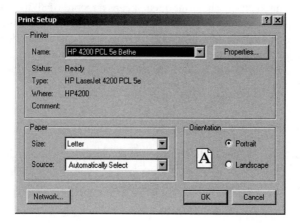

If you wish to exit from this dialog box without altering any settings, then the **Cancel** button may be used. If you wish any changes that you make to take effect, then the **OK** button should be used.

There is also a **Properties...** button which allows page orientation and size and other options to be selected. Use this option if you wish to alter the page orientation from portrait (normal orientation) to landscape (page sideways) or vice-versa. However, note that if you use landscape format to print charts, then any reports subsequently printed will also be in this orientation unless you switch this option back first.

Please refer to your Windows manual for further information on how to specify printer settings.

Any alterations made with this option result in changes to the printer setup being stored in Windows, and these changes will therefore affect any other Windows applications that use the printer.

Using the Batch Print Queue

The batch print queue is a means of storing instructions for the printing of a series or charts and/or reports and then allowing them to be printed all together at a convenient time. The purpose of the option is to allow the user to generate a large number of charts and reports in a short space of time, without having to wait for each one to print before generating the next one. Then at a convenient time, the user may take a break whilst the whole batch of charts and reports in printed out without requiring any further user interaction. The print queue keeps a record of all the chart display options that were in effect at the time when each item was added to the queue, and uses the appropriate options for each chart individually as it is printed, when the queue is released. After the batch queue has finished printing, the chart display options are automatically restored to the settings that were in effect immediately before the queue was released.

Adding Items to the Print Queue

For instruction on how to add items to the batch print queue, see Printing from Solar Fire. It is possible to put any type of chart or grid image and most types of reports onto the batch print queue.

Starting the Print Queue

This section describes how to start the batch print queue, which will print all the items that have been added to the print queue during this session, or since the batch print queue was last printed or cleared.

>> **To start the print queue**

From the main screen, select the **Start Print Queue...** option from the **Chart** menu - This will display a dialog box asking for confirmation of whether to start printing items on the batch print queue. Select the **Cancel** button to quit without starting the queue, or the **OK** button to start printing.

Clearing the Print Queue

This section describes how to clear all the items from the print batch queue that have been added since it was last printed or cleared. If the print batch queue is cleared, then all the items on the print queue will be lost.

>> **To clear the print queue**

From the main screen, select the **Close Print Queue...** option from the **Chart** menu - This will display a dialog box asking for confirmation of whether to clear all the items from the batch print queue. Select the **Cancel** button to quit without clearing the queue, or the **OK** button to clear it.

Chapter 29: Using the File Manager

This chapter describes how to use the file manager. The file manager is a common access point to various file management functions for all the file types which exist within the program. It is possible to create new files, delete existing files, copy files, rename files or select files to be the current file, from within the file manager. For certain file types it is also possible to edit the file.

The file manager is accessed from a variety of different menu options and screens within the program.

Choosing any of the following types of options from the main screen menu, or from other locations in Solar Fire, will invoke the file manager.

Chart File...
Displayed Points...
Displayed Transiting Points...
Extra Ring Points...
Aspect Set...
Aspected Points...
Fixed Star File...
Arabic Parts File...
Asteroid File...
Extra Bodies File...
Wheel Styles...
Dial Styles...
Point Colors...
Aspect Colors...
Sign Colors...
Interpretations File...

In the dynamic report selection and graphic ephemeris selection screens, clicking on any of the following boxes will also invoke the file manger.

Transiting Points
Extra Transiting Points
Progressing Points
Extra Progressing Points
Radix Points
Extra Radix Points
Transiting Aspects
Progressing Aspects

The file manager will also be invoked if the **File...** button is selected from any screen.

When the file manager screen appears its title line will display the name of the file type that has been chosen, and the list box will contain an entry for each file name of this file type. The file name that is highlighted is always initially the "current" file (ie. the last selected file). If there are no files of this type then the list box will be empty, and it will only be possible to create files.

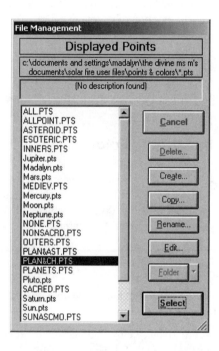

The File Manager dialog can be resized horizontally or vertically as required by dragging its borders with the mouse. It is possible to leave the file manager at any time by selecting the **Cancel** button.

Selecting a File

Selecting a file causes the contents of that file to be read into the program to be used wherever appropriate. For example selecting a "Displayed Points" file called "plan&ast.pts" updates the list of points that will be displayed on any subsequently drawn chart.

Also that file becomes the "current" file, and the display box on the main screen is updated to show the name of this file as the currently selected file.

>> To select a file

Select a file from the list of file names and click on the **Select** button, or double-click on a file on the list of file names. If you are selecting a chart file, then you also have the option of choosing a directory of folder to look in first.

After file selection, the file manager screen is hidden.

Note: If you need more space to see long file or directory names, then resize the dialog box by dragging its border with the mouse.

Selecting a Directory or Folder

When selecting Chart Files, it is possible to access directories other than Solar Fire's standard USERDATA directory. This can be useful if you wish to read from or save charts to a diskette, networked computer, or any other location on your own computer, for example.

>> To select a directory or folder

If the directory selection box is not already visible, then click on the **Folder...** button to make it visible.

You can select an alternative drive by finding it on the drop-down list box of drives, and any directory on that drive by navigating through the directories or folders on that drive.

>> To re-select a recently used folder

Click on the down arrow button to the right of the **Folder...** button.

This will display a pop-up menu allowing you to select from any of the ten most recently used folder names.

Creating a File

>> To create a new file

Select the **Create...** button.

This will display the "Create File" dialog box, which allows the entry of the file name to create. Note that the file name must be a valid file name, without a file extension (the file manager automatically adds the appropriate file extension for this file type). A valid file name can consist of up to 80 characters. If the name is not valid then an error dialog box will be displayed.

When the file has been created its name is added to the list of file names on the file manager screen, and it may be edited if it is of an edible file type.

The initial contents of a newly created file depend on the file type:

For a "Charts" or "Places" file, the file will be empty after it is created, and it will be possible to add entries by saving charts or entering places into the place database screen, respectively.

For "Displayed Points", "Displayed Transiting Points", "Aspected Points", "Radix Points", "Transiting Points" and "Progressing Points" files, the file will contain a selection of points containing all the planets, Chiron, the North Node, the Ascendant and the Midheaven.

For "Point Colors", "Aspect Colors" and "Sign Colors" files, the file will contain colors all set to black.

For "Aspect Set" files, the file will contain a list of standard 12th harmonic aspects.

It is not possible to create an "Interpretations" file. If you wish to do so, you must use the Interpretation Editor, which is a separate utility program.

If you wish to create a new file that is to be only slightly different from an existing file, it may be easier to copy the existing entry to the new file name instead of creating the new file name. This will result in less editing being required.

Deleting a File

>> **To delete a file**

Select the file from the list of file names.

Select the **Delete...** button.

This will display a dialog box asking for confirmation of deletion. When the file has been deleted its name is removed from the list of names on the file manager screen.

Copying or Renaming a File

Copying a file results in a new file being created with a copy of the contents of the selected file, whereas renaming a file results in the name of an existing file being changed.

It is possible to use these options to copy or rename files to or from floppy disks or other directories or folders on the computer's hard disk.

>> To create a copy of an existing file under a new file name

Select a file from the list of file names

Select the **Copy...** button

This will display a standard file save dialog box allowing you to enter a new name and/or location

>> To rename a file

Select a file from the list of file names

Select the **Rename...** button

Then follow the same procedure as for copying a file.

Note: If any files other than chart files are copied or renamed to other directories or floppy disks then the file manager will not be able to display them in its list of selectable files. The file manager only displays the names of files that are in the Solar Fire's default USERDATA directory.

Editing a File

You can edit the contents of any file for which the **Edit** button in the File Management dialog box is enabled. It is not possible to edit "Charts" or "Places" files from the file manager. Charts files can only be manipulated in the Chart Database screen, and Places files in the Place Database screen.

The manner in which each of the various file types can be edited is described in the following sections.

Chapter 30: Changing Chart Options

It is possible to alter any of the following items that relate to the manner in which charts and reports are calculated and displayed.

* Chart points displayed

* Points displayed in transits charts

* Current chart's displayed points

* Points included in an extra wheel ring

* Aspects used and their orbs

* Chart points which have aspects drawn to them

* Fixed Star file, Arabic Parts file, Asteroids file and Extra Bodies file

* Style of displayed chart wheels

* Style of displayed chart dials

* Selection of whether to display houses proportionally

* Application of house cusps adjustment when houses are over-full

* Selection of whether aspect lines appear in displayed charts

* Selection of whether aspect glyphs appear in displayed charts

* Selection of aspect highlighting and filtering options

* Special chart superimposition options when displaying multi-wheels

* Colors schemes used for chart points, aspects, zodiac signs and as backgrounds

* Fonts used for screen displays and printouts

The selection of each of these is described in detail in the following sections. It is possible to save any of these selections so that they will be used automatically when the program is next started up. See Saving and Restoring Settings for instructions on how to do this.

Displayed Points

Displayed points are the planets, asteroids and other points which appear on a displayed chart or synastry grid or in any report.

A set of displayed points is a named file containing a list of which points are switched on and which are switched off.

The name of the currently selected set of displayed points is shown in the information box on the main screen of the program.

When the program is first installed, there are a variety of named displayed point sets which may be selected. It is possible to alter which points are displayed by selecting an alternative set of displayed points, or by editing an existing one or creating a new one.

>> To alter the displayed point set, from the main screen

1.   Choose the **Displayed Points...** option from the **Chart Options** menu

2.   Then follow the instruction relating to displayed points in Using the File Manager.

Current Charts Displayed Points

It is possible to select a set of displayed points which will be used only with the currently selected chart. This is useful, for example, when you wish to display a chart of the current transits in a biwheel with a natal chart. In this case, you might prefer the transits chart to display only the outer planets, because the inner planets and chart angles move so quickly as to be of much lesser importance.

>> To alter the current chart's displayed point set, from the main screen

1.   Select the chart that you wish to use from the list of **Calculated Charts**

2.   Choose the **Current Chart's Displayed Points...** option from the **Chart Options** menu

3.   Then follow the instruction relating to displayed points in Using the File Manager.

Whenever this chart is subsequently displayed, it will always contain the newly selected displayed points instead of the current set of displayed points which are used in all other cases.

If you wish to reset the displayed points for this chart to be the current set of displayed points again, then you must re-use this option to select whichever set of displayed points is the current set.

Displayed Transiting Points

A set of displayed transiting points is a named file containing a list of which points are switched on and which are switched off.

Displayed transiting points are the planets, asteroids and other points which can appear on a displayed multi-wheel chart when both of the following are true.

• the chart is deemed to be a "transits" chart by Solar Fire.

• when that chart is not the house cusp anchor chart for that wheel (which is usually means when it is not the innermost chart).

The criteria by which Solar Fire deems a chart to be a "transits" chart are either one of the following.

• Any natal type chart that has an event type of "Event".

• Any natal type chart that has an event type of "Unspecified", and that contains either "transit" or "event" anywhere in its name.

Unless either of these conditions is met, Solar Fire assumes that the chart is not a "transits" chart, and therefore uses only the default Displayed Points set.

However, when either of these conditions is met, then the points which are actually displayed are all those points which are switched on in BOTH the default Displayed Points AND in the Displayed Transiting Points. Therefore, **you should use this selection to switch OFF only those points that you DO NOT wish to see in a transits chart** (eg. chart angles, and perhaps other fast moving points such as the moon), and you should leave ALL other points switched ON, even if you do not normally display them in a chart. Doing this will allow you to later choose a set of ordinary Displayed Points containing some additional points, and have those additional points automatically also appear in transits charts, without having to also reselect a set of Displayed Transiting Points.

When the program is first installed, there are a variety of named displayed point sets which may be selected. It is possible to alter which points are displayed by selecting an alternative set of displayed points, or by editing an existing one or creating a new one.

>> To alter the displayed transiting point set, from the main screen

1.   Choose the **Displayed Transiting Points...** option from the **Chart Options** menu

2.   Then follow the instruction relating to displayed points in Using the File Manager.

Extra Ring Points

Extra Ring Points is a selection of points or bodies of various types that can be displayed in a special chart wheel which includes an extra ring in addition to the normal ring which displays the standard chart points.

The types of extra points that can be selected are standard chart points, midpoints, fixed zodiacal positions, fixed stars and astronomical objects, Arabic parts, asteroids, bodies calculated from orbital elements, prior lunar phases, eclipse points and planetary nodes.

When the program is first installed, there are a variety of named extra ring point sets which may be selected. It is possible to alter these selections by editing an existing set or creating a new one.

>> To alter the extra ring points set, from the main screen

1.   Choose the **Extra Ring Points...** option from the **Chart Options** menu

2.   Then follow the instruction relating to extra ring points in Editing an Extra Ring Points File.

Aspect Set

Aspect sets are named files containing a list of which aspects are switched on and off and what orbs each aspect has. The aspect set controls which aspects are displayed on charts or synastry grids and in any reports. It is also used when any dynamic transits or progressions report is created.

The name of the currently selected aspect set is shown in the information box on the main screen of the program.

When the program is first installed, there are a variety of named aspect sets which may be selected. It is possible to alter which aspects are displayed and their orbs by selecting an alternative aspect set, or by editing an existing one or creating a new one.

>> **To alter the aspect set, from the main screen**

1.   Choose the **Aspect Set...** option from the **Chart Options** menu

2.   Then follow the instruction relating to aspect sets in Using the File Manager.

Aspected Points

Aspected points are the planets, asteroids and other points to which aspects are drawn on a displayed chart.

A set of aspected points is a named file containing a list of which points are switched on and which are switched off.

It is possible for an aspected point set to be different from a displayed point set. In this case the displayed chart will not have aspects drawn between every chart point. This is useful in order to switch off aspects to the Ascendant and Midheaven, for example, when they are still required to be displayed in the chart.

The name of the currently selected set of aspected points is shown in the information box on the main screen of the program.

When the program is first installed, there are a variety of named aspected point sets which may be selected. It is possible to alter which points are aspected by selecting an alternative set of aspected points, or by editing an existing one or creating a new one.

>> **To alter the aspected point set, from the main screen**

1.   Choose the **Aspected Points...** option from the **Chart Options** menu

2.   Then follow the instructions relating to aspected points in Using the File Manager.

Files

This menu option allows you to select any of four different types of files to use as the default, or to edit or browse their contents. These file types are as follows.

- **Fixed Stars** – files containing selections of fixed stars or other astronomical objects

- **Arabic Parts** – files containing lists of Arabic part definitions

- **Asteroids** – files containing lists of asteroids

- **Extra Bodies** – files containing orbital elements for various bodies

See Using the File Manager for more details on how to select, edit and use these file types.

Wheel Styles and Dial Styles

It is possible to select from a range of available chart and dial styles to be used whenever Solar Fire displays or prints charts. Solar Fire comes supplied with several different pre-defined chart styles, and it is also possible to create your own designs with the separate Wheel Designer program. The most common types of wheel styles that you might like to use are the Anglo/American style, European Style and French style.

You can select any available pre-defined style for use with single chart displays, bi-chart displays, tri-chart displays, quadri-chart displays, small wheel displays (which includes dual wheels on a page and wheel and grid on the same page), and preview wheel displays, such as on Solar Fire's main screen.

>> To select a particular style of display for all subsequent wheel or dial display and printing

1.   Click on the **Wheel Styles** or **Dial Styles** button, or choose the required chart combination option from the **Wheel Styles** or **Dial Styles** option of the **Chart Options** menu

2.   Then follow the instruction relating to wheel and dial styles in Using the File Manager.

Once a particular style is selected, all subsequent displays of that chart combination type will use that selected style. For example, if you select a "French" style for biwheel chart combinations, then all subsequent biwheel displays will use the "French" style.

Proportional Houses

Most house systems, apart from equal house systems, have houses that vary in size. In some cases, especially at high latitudes, there can be a considerable "distortion" so that a couple of houses are very narrow, whilst others are very wide. It is possible to display Solar Fire charts either with equal-sized (non-proportional) houses, or with proportional houses. However, when displaying a chart using a wheel style which contains a zodiac ring (such as a French or European style), then this option is automatically overridden, as in this case the house cusps must always maintain their positions in relation to the zodiac ring. When a chart is displayed with non-proportional houses, the planets will not be drawn in their correct geometrical positions. Instead they will be moved, wherever possible, to fall within the correct house cusps. Also, in this case, the tick marks on the inside rim of any single wheel display will also be moved to correspond to the displayed position of the planet. Therefore, when displaying non-proportional charts, it is advisable to either switch on the House Expansion option, or to carefully check whether planets are in their correct houses by looking at their angles, as this will not necessarily be obvious from their plotted positions. Generally, this problem does not occur if the chart is drawn with proportional houses, as the tick marks will clearly show exactly where each planet is in relation to the house cusps, even if the planet symbol is not in its correct house.

>> To alter the current Proportional Houses setting, from the main screen

Choose the **Proportional Houses** option from the **Display Options** submenu of **Chart Options** menu. This will switch on the option if it is currently off, or switch it off if it is currently on. When this option is switched on, a tick appears to the left of this item on the menu.

Once this setting is altered, any chart or grid subsequently displayed on the screen will be affected. To alter the house display on a chart which has already been displayed previously, the **ReDraw** button must be selected from the "Chart View" screen before the change will come into effect.

House Expansion

A chart may sometimes have many planets or other chart points in a single house. In this case, when you view the chart you may find that some of these points spill over into adjacent houses. If this happens, you can switch this option on to prevent this from happening. When switched on, this option will cause any over-full houses to be expanded to accommodate all the required points, so that it is clear in which house they reside.

>> **To change the current house expansion setting, from the main screen**

Choose the **House Expansion** option from the **Display Options** submenu of the **Chart Options** menu

This will switch on the option if it is currently off, or switch it off if it is currently on. When the house expansion option is switched on, a tick appears to the left of this item on the menu.

Once this setting is altered, any chart subsequently displayed on the screen or printed will be affected. To alter this option on a chart which has already been displayed on the screen previously, the **ReDraw** button must be selected from the "Chart View" screen before the change will come into effect.

Aspect Lines

Any single-wheel chart which you view on the screen or print may optionally display aspect lines inside the central ring of the chart.

>> **To alter the Aspect Lines setting, from the main screen**

Choose the **Aspect Lines** option from the **Display Options** submenu of the **Chart Options** menu

This will switch on the option if it is currently off, or switch it off if it is currently on.

Once this setting is altered, any single-wheel chart subsequently displayed on the screen or printed will be affected. To alter this option on a chart which has already been displayed on the screen previously, the **ReDraw** button must be selected from the "Chart View" screen before the change will come into effect.

Aspect Glyphs

Any single-wheel chart which you view on the screen or print may optionally display aspect lines inside the central ring of the chart. When they are displayed (ie. when the Aspect Lines option is on), it is also possible to choose whether or not to show the aspect glyphs in the middle of each aspect line.

>> To alter the Aspect Glyphs setting, from the main screen

Choose the **Aspect Glyphs** option from the **Display Options** submenu of the **Chart Options** menu. This will switch on the option if it is currently off, or switch it off if it is currently on.

Once this setting is altered, any single-wheel chart subsequently displayed on the screen or printed will be affected. To alter this option on a chart which has already been displayed on the screen previously, the **ReDraw** button must be selected from the "Chart View" screen before the change will come into effect.

Aspect Highlighting and Filtering

This option allows you to highlight aspects according to their tightness of orb, use different line styles for applying and separating aspects, and to display conjunction lines. The filtering features allow you to flexibly switch on or off aspect lines according to a range of useful criteria, such as limiting the orb, displaying only aspects belonging to a particular harmonic, or only those aspects emanating from a selected chart point. This can be performed quickly and interactively whilst displaying a chart (without having to change the currently selected aspect set), and is therefore a powerful tool in assisting the analysis of aspects.

>> To open the Aspect Highlighting and Filtering Dialog

Choose **Aspect Highlighting and Filtering...** from the **Chart Options** menu.

If you wish to apply highlighting or filtering to a chart interactively, then you should first display the required chart in the View Chart or Animation window, and use a right hand mouse click over the chart to bring up the Chart Options menu.

The **Apply** button is enabled when you are already viewing a chart on the Main Screen, in the View Chart, Animation or any Chart Preview window. It may be used to apply any changes you make without closing this dialog.

The **Transparent** option (only available in Windows 2000, XP or later) allows the dialog to be made semi-transparent. This is useful in helping you to see otherwise hidden parts of pages when you are using the **Apply** button to preview any changes without closing this dialog.

Aspect Highlighting

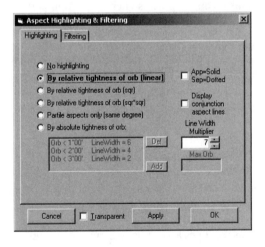

- **No highlighting** – the aspect lines are not highlighted. All aspect line thicknesses are set to their standard default line width.

- **By relative tightness of orb** – the aspect line thickness are scaled according to how tight they are (by taking the ratio of the actual orb to the maximum possible orb ie. by relative orb ratio). The tightest orbs have the thickest lines, and the widest orbs have the thinnest lines. The maximum line width multiplier can be set to control the factor by which the line width is increased for the tightest orbs. The **Linear** option thickens the lines in direct proportion to the relative orb ratio eg. an aspect whose orb is half of its maximum allowed orb has its thickness multiplied by half the maximum line width multiplier. The **Sqr** option thickens the line in proportion to the square of the relative orb, so an aspect whose orb is half of its maximum allowed orb has its thickness multiplied by one quarter of the maximum line width multiplier. The **Sqr*Sqr** option thickens the line in proportion to the fourth power of the relative orb, so an aspect whose orb is half of its maximum allowed orb has its thickness multiplied by one eight of the maximum line width multiplier.

• **Partile aspect only (same degree)** – only those aspects that are partile (ie. those which are in the same whole degree of their sign at each end of the aspect) are highlighted by the line width multiplier. All other aspects are set to their standard default line width.

• **By absolute tightness of orb** - the aspect line thicknesses are scaled according to their actual orbs in degrees. When this option is selected, the list box below contains a list of orb limits and the corresponding line width multipliers to apply. This list may be edited by the user. Use the **Add** button to add a new line, the **Del** button to remove a line, and use the **Max Orb** box to set the orb in degrees and minutes.

• **App=Solid; Sep=Dotted** – When this box is checked, all applying aspects are shown as solid lines, and all separating aspects are shown as dotted lines. This can be used in addition to the line thickness options.

• **Display Conjunction Aspect Lines** – When this box if checked, an aspect line is drawn between points which are conjunct. *Note:* If the points are very closely conjunct, then these conjunction lines will not be easily visible.

Aspect Filtering

- **No filtering** – the aspect lines are not filtered. The aspects displayed are those that are enabled and within orb according to the currently selected aspect set.

- **By applying/separating** – only those aspect types shown in the drop-down list box at the right are displayed. This may be All Aspects (no filtering), Applying only, Separating only. This option may be used together with some of the other options below. For example, if you are filtering by aspect harmonic, then you can use this to limit the aspect to applying or separating aspect of that harmonic.

- **By % of maximum orb** – only those aspects whose orbs are less than the prescribed percentage of their maximum possible orb are displayed. The prescribed percentage may be adjusted by the user either by typing a new number into the adjoining box, or by using its spin buttons.

- **By absolute maximum orb** - only those aspects whose orbs are less than the prescribed orb are displayed. The prescribed orb may be adjusted by the user by typing a new maximum orb angle into the adjoining box.

- **By aspect harmonic** – only those aspects that belong to the selected harmonic family are displayed. When this option is selected, the orbs from the current aspect set are used, but the enabled or disabled aspect settings are ignored.

• **By individual aspect** - only the selected aspect type is displayed. When this option is selected, the orbs from the current aspect set are used, but the enabled or disabled aspect settings are ignored.

• **By aspect pattern** – only those aspects that form the selected aspect pattern type are displayed. If a chart does not contain the selected aspect pattern, then no aspects are displayed in that chart. If a chart contains multiple instances of the selected aspect pattern, then all instances are shown. When this option is selected, the orbs from the current aspect set are used, but the enabled or disabled aspect settings are ignored.

• **By chart point** – only those aspects that emanate from the selected chart point are displayed. When this option is selected, only those aspects that are enabled in the current default aspect set are displayed.

• **Switch filtering off after close** – ensure this box is checked unless you want the filtering options you set to be maintained permanently. As most filtering is done on a temporary basis, this options helps you avoid forgetting to set the filtering off when you finish, which might result in unexpected or missing aspect lines when you subsequently view charts.

• **Auto apply changes** – setting this option on saves you from having to click on the **Apply** button after every change you make. This is especially helpful if you wish to scroll through many filtering options (such as through the whole list of aspect patterns, to see if any are present in the chart being examined).

Multiwheel Superimposition

This is a special option that determines the manner in which charts are aligned with one another (ie. superimposed). The usual manner of superimposition is "zodiacal", meaning that when charts are displayed in a biwheel, for example, 0 Aries in one chart is aligned with 0 Aries in the other chart. This method is the one used in almost all astrological books and publications.

However, it is also possible to align charts by other methods, for example according to their house cusps, or according to the position of points within the charts.

The options available are

• **Zodiacal (Normal)** – This is the default option when the program is first installed, and should always be selected unless you specifically wish to use non-standard superimposition methods.

- **By Sign of Selected Point** – This will align 0 degrees of the sign of the selected superimposition point in the superimposed chart with 0 degrees of the sign of the selected base point in the base chart. In this case the superimposition adjustment will always be an exact factor of 30 degrees.

- **By Exact Position of Selected Point** – This will align the exact zodiacal position of the selected superimposition point with the exact position of the selected base point in the base chart. In this case the superimposition adjustment can be any angle.

The last two options require a specific chart point to be selected. For example, if the "Exact Position of Selected Point" option is selected, then the selected superimposition point and base point might both be set to Ascendant. In this case, when a biwheel is displayed, the outer chart will have its ascendant aligned exactly to the ascendant of the inner chart, so that the houses of each chart coincide with one another.

This option never affects a single chart on its own – it only affects multiwheels, reports or page objects that show chart inter-relationships. Specifically, the items affected are:

- Biwheels – The outer chart is adjusted. The inner chart remains fixed.

- Triwheels - The two outer charts are adjusted. The inner chart remains fixed.

- Quadriwheels - The three outer charts are adjusted. The inner chart remains fixed.

- Quinquiwheels - The four outer charts are adjusted. The inner chart remains fixed.

- Synastry aspects – Chart B is adjusted. Chart A remains fixed.

Further options are as follows.

Use Radix Point in Subsidiary Charts – This option only affects subsidiary charts (such as progressed charts) that are superimposed onto other base charts. In this case it is possible to superimpose the charts by aligning the subsidiary (progressed) point with the base chart, or alternatively by aligning the radix position of the selected point of the progressed chart. For example, if we view John's progressed chart in a biwheel around Susan's natal chart, and we have selected to superimpose by exact position of ascendants, then, when this option is switched off, John's *progressed* ascendant will be aligned to Susan's natal ascendant. However, when this option is switched on, John's *natal (radix)* ascendant will be aligned to Susan's natal ascendant, instead.

Display Superimposed Positions – This option determines whether the planets and zodiac of the superimposed chart retained their original zodiacal positions in the wheel or reports, as opposed to the entire chart being shifted in the zodiac to appear as if it was aligned with the zodiac of the base chart. For example, if we view John's natal chart in a biwheel around Susan's natal chart, and we have selected to superimpose by exact position of ascendants, then, when this option is switched off, John's ascendant will be notated with its original (un-superimposed) zodiacal position, and the zodiac of the outer chart will be shown as offset from that of the inner chart. However, when this option is switched on, John's ascendant will be notated with its superimposed position (ie. identical to Susan's ascendant position), and the zodiac of the outer chart will appear to align exactly with the zodiac on the inner chart. The purpose of this option is to allow inter-chart aspects to be seen much more readily than would otherwise be the case.

Note: Using these options can cause much confusion if you are not familiar with the concept of superimposition. After use, please remember to switch this option back to **Zodiacal (Normal)** in order to avoid the likelihood of mistaking a superimposed zodiac with an erroneously calculated chart!

Color Schemes

A "color scheme" is a set of color selections for aspects, chart points, sign glyphs, sign fills as well as a background color or graphic which is displayed on the chart viewing screen.

You can select existing color schemes or create and save your own schemes. The name of the currently selected color scheme for both screen and printer is shown in the information box on the main screen of the program.

>> To select, edit or create a color scheme

Choose **Color Scheme...** from the **Chart Options** menu

This will display the color scheme selection dialog.

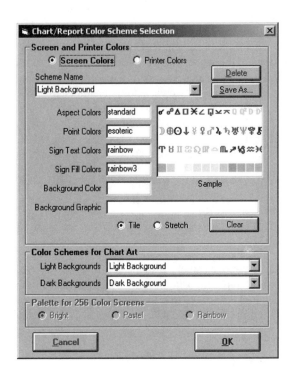

The elements in the **Screen and Printer Colors** frame are as follows.

• **Screen Colors / Printer Colors** – You can assign different color selections to be used for the screen and the printer. This is useful, for example, if you wish to print in monochrome even though you have a color printer, or if you want the colors on the printer to be darker than the colors on the screen to make them more legible on a white page. This is especially useful if you have selected a dark background color for the screen, but still wish to print onto white paper. In this case you can choose light colors to contrast well with the screen background, and dark colors to contrast well with the printed white page. Note that any colors you select apply only to either the Screen or the Printer, depending on which option is selected. Thus, when you change screen colors, the colors that appear on the printer will remain unchanged unless you also change the printer colors.

• **Scheme Name** – When this program is first installed, there are a number of predefined color schemes that can be selected from this drop-down list box. Selecting a named scheme from this list will result in the subsequent items on this dialog being updated to reflect all the color selections stored in that selection. If you have made changes to any color selections, then you can save the new color scheme by clicking on the **Save As...** button and specifying a name for the scheme. If you specify an existing scheme name, then that scheme will simply be replaced with your new scheme. You can also delete any named scheme by first selecting it from the list, and then clicking on the **Delete** button. Note that the list of scheme names is different for screen and printers.

• **Aspect Colors** - Aspect colors are the colors in which aspect symbols and aspect lines will appear in any displayed chart or grid. A set of aspect colors is a named file containing a list of which color is assigned to each aspect. When the program is first installed, there are a variety of named aspect colors sets which may be selected. It is possible to alter the colors in which aspects are displayed by selecting an alternative set of aspect colors, or by editing an existing one or creating a new one. To alter the aspect colors set, click on the box containing the name of the current aspect colors, and then follow the instruction relating to aspect colors in Using the File Manager.

• **Point Colors** - Point colors are the colors in which planets, asteroids and other points will appear in any displayed chart or grid. A set of point colors is a named file containing a list of which color is assigned to each point. When the program is first installed, there are a variety of named point colors sets which may be selected. It is possible to alter the colors in which points are displayed by selecting an alternative set of point colors, or by editing an existing one or creating a new one. To alter the point colors selection, click on the box containing the name of the current point colors, and then follow the instruction relating to point colors in Using the File Manager.

• **Sign Text Colors** - Sign text colors are the colors in which zodiac sign glyphs will appear in any displayed chart. A set of sign colors is a named file containing a list of which color is assigned to each sign. When the program is first installed, there are a variety of named sign colors sets which may be selected. It is possible to alter the colors in which signs are displayed by selecting an alternative set of sign colors, or by editing an existing one or creating a new one. To alter the sign colors set, click on the box containing the name of the current sign text colors, and then follow the instruction relating to sign colors in Using the File Manager. Usually you will want to choose colors which contrast well with the background color or graphic eg. if the background is white, then dark sign colors will be most legible.

• **Sign Fill Colors** - Sign fill colors are the colors in which zodiac signs in chart zodiac rings will appear in any displayed chart. A set of sign colors is a named file containing a list of which color is assigned to each sign. When the program is first installed, there are a variety of named sign colors sets which may be selected. It is possible to alter the colors in which signs are displayed by selecting an alternative set of sign colors, or by editing an existing one or creating a new one. To alter the sign colors set, click on the box containing the name of the current sign text colors, and then follow the instruction relating to sign colors in Using the File Manager. Usually you will want to choose colors which blend well with the background color or graphic eg. if the background is white, then light sign text colors will be most appealing.

- **Background Color** – The background color of the Chart View screen may be set with this option. You can select any color, but usually it is best to choose either a fairly light color or a fairly dark color. If you choose a moderately light or dark color, then you may have difficulty viewing aspects, points and wheels on the page. This option determines whether charts and page objects are drawn with dark (black) outlines or light (white) outlines. When you choose a light color, charts are drawn with dark lines, and when you choose a dark color, charts are drawn with light lines, in order to maximize the visibility of the displayed items. Note that if you choose a dark background graphic, then it will be necessary also to choose a dark background color to ensure that the chart is drawn with light lines.

- **Background Graphic** – You can select any graphic of type *.jpg, *.wmf, *.gif, from any location, to display as the background to the Chart View screen. Ideally you should choose a graphic which does not have large contrasts in color, to avoid the possibility of making the charts or page objects difficult to see. If you choose a dark graphic then you will also need to select a dark (eg. black) background color to ensure that the page objects are drawn with light colored lines. Similarly, if you choose a light graphic then you will also need to select a light (eg. white) background color to ensure that the page objects are drawn with dark colored lines. You have the option to stretch the graphic to fit the size of the display, or to tile it, in which case the graphic is repeated as many times as needed to fit the full display area. You can clear any graphic selection by clicking on the **Clear** button.

The **Color Schemes for Chart Art** frame allows you to choose special color settings for any pages which have been designed with full-page background graphics - as is the case for the "Chart Art" pages in Solar Fire. It is necessary to have a special color setting for these because Solar Fire would normally display line and text colors according to the current color scheme selected above, but these settings may clash with the colors of the background graphic of the page. For example if your current color scheme is for a light background color then lines are displayed in black, but if the Chart Art page has a dark colored background graphic, then black lines would not be very visible on top of that. Therefore most page objects have a "Force Color" property which may be set in order to ensure that one of the following schemes is applied to that object instead of the default color scheme selected above.

•   **Light Backgrounds** - You can choose any color scheme that has been designed to work with light backgrounds.

•   **Dark Backgrounds** - You can choose any color scheme that has been designed to work with dark backgrounds.

Note: If you use a background graphic, then you may notice that some chart wheels are displayed transparently, so that the graphic shows through them, and some are opaque, so that the background graphic is not visible inside them. This behavior depends on whether the rings within the wheel have been designed to be transparent or to have a fill color. You can alter any wheel design to make it transparent or opaque by setting the its ring fill color option in the wheel designer. See Editing a Wheel Design File for further information.

Color Depth

Solar Fire can be used on any computer that is capable of displaying at least 256 colors or greater color depths known as "HiColor" and "TrueColor", and in this case you will be able to generate more attractive displays. In most cases, whenever you select a color from one of Solar Fire's color selection options (eg. sign colors, aspect colors, planet colors etc.), the color which is actually displayed on the screen will be whichever of the available colors matches your selected color most closely. If your display supports only 256 colors, then you may find that some of the displayed colors are different from your original selections. If you are using HiColor or TrueColor, then you will find that the displayed colors match your original selections very well.

If you have a 256 color display, then Solar Fire allows you to choose from three different palettes (color ranges) in order to help you most closely match the colors that you have chosen. The color palettes which are available for displays with 256 colors are as follows.

Bright Colors - A selection of colors which are at the brighter end of the scale

Pastel Color - A selection of colors which are softer in tone

Rainbow Colors - A selection of colors which covers a wide range of tones

If you are viewing a chart, you will need to click on the ReDraw button to see the effect of the new palette.

Note: Changing the color palette does not change your original color selection, it only affects how your color selection is currently displayed. For example, if you choose the color orange for a planet, then displaying it with the **Pastel Colors** palette shows it as a browny color, because that is the closest match to orange in that palette. However, if you then switch to the **Bright Colors** palette and redraw the chart, it is displayed as orange, because an orange color is included in that palette.

Changing the number of colors your monitor can display

Most modern computer displays allow you to select how many colors they will display, so if you are currently displaying only 256 colors, then you can probably alter your display settings to allow more colors to be displayed.

Warning: It is not recommended that you try the following unless you are proficient in the use of Windows, and able to deal with potential problems caused by changing the display driver. For further assistance, you should contact your computer dealer, or a qualified Windows instructor.

>> To select a greater color depth for your display

Exit from Solar Fire

From the **Control Panel**, select the **Display** icon

Click on the **Settings** Tab

Select a color setting from the **Color Palette** drop-down box

Note: If you do not exit from Solar Fire before changing color depth, then some colors may be displayed incorrectly. If so, you should exit from Solar Fire and then start it up again. This will clear the problem.

Fonts

It is possible to choose which text font style you wish to use on chart captions displayed on the screen, as well as another text font style for any charts and reports which are printed on your printer. You can also select a base font size for printed reports and tabulations.

When the Solar Fire program is first installed on you computer, it sets your screen font as "ET Sans Serif 2" and your printer font as "ET Symbol 2". However, you are free to select alternative fonts if you so wish. If you select any other fonts, then Solar Fire will use your selected font for displaying any normal text, but will continue to use the astrological fonts when displaying any astrological symbols.

These two fonts contain all the astrological symbols that are needed by the program, without which you will not be able to display charts and reports with astrological symbols. Therefore you must not delete them from your computer. If, for any reason, these fonts are removed, then Solar Fire will display spurious symbols instead of the correct astrological symbols.

>> To examine or alter the existing font selections

Choose the **Fonts...** option from the **Chart Options** menu. This will display the "Font Selection" screen, which allows the selection of any available font for your printer or screen.

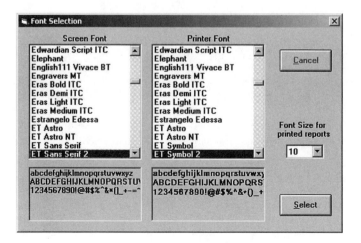

When this screen is first displayed, the current font selections will be highlighted in each of the list boxes.

>> To change a font selection

Select a font name from either list box.

An example of text in the selected font is shown in the display boxes below each list. Some printer fonts cannot be displayed on the screen, in which case the display box will contain a message to this effect.

>> To alter the base font size used for printing reports, time maps and graphic ephemerides

Select a font size from the drop-down list.

Note: This base font size does *not* affect printed charts or user defined pages, as these use font sizes which vary according to user-defined font size selections in the wheel and page designs, and also on the size of the displayed page.

>> To activate the new font selections

Click on the **Select** button.

Chapter 31: Changing Preferences

It is possible to perform any of the following actions from the **Preferences** menu

- Editing current settings

- Save all the current settings

- Restore the previously saved settings

- Switch on or off an option to save settings automatically upon exit

- Edit the toolbar buttons

- Switch on or off various panels on the main screen

The selection of each of these is described in detail in the following sections. It is possible to save any of the switchable preferences so that they take effect automatically when the program is next started up by using the **Save Settings** option.

Saving and Restoring Settings

Whenever the program is started up, all current settings are read in from the SOLFIRE5.INI file, which resides in the Windows directory of your computer. The program's settings may be saved or restored at any time. Whenever the settings are saved, the SOLFIRE5.INI file is updated, so that these will be retained for use next time the program is started up.

These settings include such things as chart calculation options, compliments text, date entry and display options, atlas type selection, email options etc.

Some additional items are also stored in the SOLFIRE5.INI file, but these are stored automatically whenever they are changed, and do not depend on the user selecting a save option. These include things like the default place, report screen's modulus and orb, the dynamic report entry screen's selection, the dynamic report sort order etc.

>> To save all the current settings in the program

Choose the **Save Settings...** option from the **Preferences** menu. This will display a dialog box asking you to confirm whether or not you wish to overwrite the previously stored selections. Selecting the **Cancel** button will prevent any action from being taken. Selecting the **OK** button will save the current settings.

>> To restore all the previously saved settings in the program

Choose the **Restore Settings...** option from the **Preferences** menu. This will display a dialog box asking you to confirm whether or not you wish to overwrite the current selections. Selecting the **Cancel** button will prevent any action from being taken. Selecting the **OK** button will restore the previously saved settings and make them the current settings.

Note that it is not possible to save or restore settings individually - all settings are saved or restored together.

Save Settings on Exit

It is possible to ensure that any alteration made to settings and defaults (described above) are saved automatically whenever the user exits from the program.

>> To switch the Save Settings on Exit option on or off

Choose the **Save Settings on Exit** option from the **Preferences** menu. This will switch on the option if it is currently off, or switch it off if it is currently on. When the save on exit option is switched on, a tick appears to the left of this item on the menu. If there is no tick then it is currently switched off.

Editing Settings

Choose the **Edit Settings...** option from the **Preferences** menu. This will display the Preferences dialog with various tabbed panels grouping the available options into various topics.

Calculations

Lunar Node Type

The lunar node is one of the chart points which may be displayed in any chart or grid. It is possible to select the lunar node as either the true node or the mean node.

- **True Node** - is the real position of the moon's node at any time.

- **Mean Node** - is the position of the moon's node according to a mathematical formula which ignores many of the minor perturbations in its orbit.

Any chart display or report indicates which type of lunar node has been used during its calculation. The lunar node type is not saved with a chart - it is only applied when a chart is being calculated.

Black Moon Type

The Black Moon is one of the chart points which may be displayed in any chart or grid – also sometimes known as the Black Moon Lilith. This point is the empty focal point of the Moon's orbit around the earth, which is also the apogee of the Moon's orbit.

It is possible to select the Black Moon as either the true (osculating) apogee or the mean apogee.

- **True Apogee** - is the position of the moon's apogee, taking into account short term fluctuations (osculations) in the plane of the moon's orbit.

- **Mean Apogee** - is the position of the moon's apogee according to a mathematical formula which ignores many of the minor perturbations in its orbit.

The selected Black Moon type is not saved with a chart - it is only applied when a chart is being calculated.

Note: Other objects called Lilith are also sometimes used in astrology.

- The asteroid Lilith - asteroid number 1181

- The Dark Moon Lilith – a possible second satellite of the earth (not confirmed by modern astronomy), as first postulated by Waltemath, and written about by Delphine Jay

These are NOT the same as the Black Moon Lilith.

Part of Fortune Type

The way in which the Part of Fortune, as displayed in charts, is calculated may be selected by the user. The options are as follows.

Different Day/Night - According to researchers of ancient astrological texts, the correct method of calculating the Part of Fortune is to use Asc+Moon-Sun for daytime charts, and Asc+Sun-Moon for nighttime charts.

Fixed Formula – (Daytime Only) Many astrological programs in the past (including earlier versions of Solar Fire) have used a calculation for the Part of Fortune which is based on a single formula for both day and night charts ie. Asc+Moon-Sun. Although this is now thought to be incorrect, many astrologers have become accustomed to using it in this way, so this option is included for their convenience.

Any charts subsequently opened or calculated will use the newly selected calculation type.

Note that this option affects the position of the Part of Fortune as shown in charts and all reports with the exception of the Arabic Parts report of Solar Fire. If you wish to alter the calculation of the Part of Fortune in the Arabic Parts report, then you must use the Arabic Parts Editor.

Optional Correction Factors

Apply Geocentric Correction to Latitude
Apply Parallax Correction to Moon

Apply Geocentric Correction to Latitude

It is possible to calculate charts based either on geographic (also known as geodetic) latitude or geocentric latitude.

Atlases such as the ACS International Atlas, the ACS American Atlas and Solar Fire's own place databases, contain geographic latitudes. Geographic latitudes are based on the measurement of the angle of the local horizon (also known as the geodetic horizon) onto the celestial sphere. It is assumed that all latitudes entered into Solar Fire are geographic latitudes, and all displayed latitudes, such as in chart details text, are geographic latitudes.

However, because the earth is not perfectly spherical it is also possible to define a latitude based on where the horizon would be if the earth was a perfect sphere, which also corresponds to the angle of a line from that location to the centre of the earth. This is known as a geocentric latitude. The geocentric latitude is never more than 12 minutes of a degree different from the geographic latitude.

There are arguments for and against using each of these types of latitude. Astrologers are divided about which is the most appropriate to use.

Solar Fire always displays latitudes as a geographic latitudes. However, when this option is on, any chart calculations performed will have a correction applied to the latitude to convert it from geographic to geocentric. Any chart that has had this correction applied will have a "G" appended to its latitude. For example, a geographic latitude of 34°S55' is displayed as 34°S55'G when this option is on.

In order to determine exactly what the geocentric correction is, you must view a "Chart Analysis" report for the chart. If the geocentric correction has been applied, then this will be specified in the report, and the corrected geocentric latitude will shown as well as the originally entered geographic latitude.

Any charts opened or calculated, or dynamic reports generated are calculated according to the current setting of this option.

Apply Parallax Correction to Moon

Traditionally, the planet's positions are calculated as if they were observed from the centre of earth (hence "geocentric"). However, as the moon is much closer to the earth than the other planets, certain geometrical effects come into play that are negligible for the other planets. In particular, due to the moon's proximity to the earth, it appears to be in a slightly different zodiacal position depending on where on earth it is observed from. This effect is known as lunar parallax (or also as a "topocentric" coordinate system).

Typically, this can make a difference to the moon's longitude of the order of 1 degree. Thus, if the moon is near the end of a sign, applying this correction can actually put the moon into the next sign in same cases.

Any charts opened or calculated, or dynamic reports generated are calculated according to the current setting of this option. When this option is switched on for a particular chart, the chart details text has an additional line indicating that the parallax correction has been made.

Note that, although the altitude of the observer also makes a small difference to the parallax calculation, it is negligible in comparison with the observer's location, so is ignored by Solar Fire. For example, an altitude of 3000 meters makes a maximum difference of only 2 to 3 seconds of arc in the moon's position, and it is usually less than this.

Void Of Course

The Moon is generally said to be "void of course" after it has made its last aspect to another planet in its current sign, and the void of course period ends when the Moon makes it ingress into the next sign. However, the precise interpretation of this condition varies according to different authorities. In Solar Fire, the Moon is considered to be void of course when it is not applying to any aspect (within the given set of aspects to any planet within the given set of planets) whose position of perfection currently falls within the same sign. The possible user-defined options are as follows.

- **Modern** - uses Conjunctions, Oppositions, Trines, Squares and Sextiles, with aspects to the Sun, Mercury, Venus, Mars, Jupiter, Saturn, Uranus, Neptune and Pluto.

- **Traditional** - uses Conjunctions, Oppositions, Trines, Squares and Sextiles, with aspects to the Sun, Mercury, Venus, Mars, Jupiter, Saturn.

- **Lilly** – uses Conjunctions, Oppositions, Trines, Squares and Sextiles, with aspects to the Sun, Mercury, Venus, Mars, Jupiter, Saturn. The signs Taurus, Cancer, Sagittarius and Pisces are deemed never to have void of course occurring in them.

Vulcan Calculation

As Vulcan is a hypothetical planet, there is no officially accepted ephemeris for the calculation of its position. However, two of the more widely used methods of calculating its position have been included in Solar Fire, and it is possible to choose which of these methods you would like to be used whenever Vulcan's position is calculated. The possible methods are

L.H.Weston - Professor Weston produced a set of orbital parameters for Vulcan based on a number of supposed sightings during last century and early this century. This proposed orbit has Vulcan orbiting the Sun once every 19.5 days, and having a maximum orb of about 8° from the Sun, as observed from the earth. The complete theory is published in the booklet "The Planet Vulcan", published by the American Federation of Astrologers, Inc. Some doubt has been cast on the correspondence of this proposed orbit with the observations on which it is based, but no alternative has yet been proposed.

D.Baker - Dr Baker has documented a theory for Vulcan based on a quantum mechanical type of behavior. Vulcan is positioned 3° from Mercury in the direction of the Sun. If Mercury is within 3° of the Sun, then Vulcan is conjunct the Sun. It is always on the same side of the Sun as Mercury. The full rationale behind this concept is explained in his *Dictionary of Astrology*.

When this option is changed, any charts that are subsequently opened or calculated will use the newly selected calculation method, but charts that have already been calculated retain the option that was in effect when they were calculated.

Ray Weightings

The Rays are the seven primary energetic influences proposed and described in various works relating to esoteric astrology and philosophy.

Each sign is considered to be influenced by a subset of rays, and possibly in varying proportions. Two of the most commonly used schemes for assigning weightings to the rays influencing each sign are provided as options.

• **Equal** – This scheme is based directly on tabulations in the book "Esoteric Astrology" by Alice A. Bailey, and assumes that each ray influencing a sign does so in equal proportion.

• **D.Baker** – This scheme is based on the works of Dr. Douglas Baker, and assumes that the rays influence each sign disproportionately.

Sign	Equal	D.Baker
Aries	1 = 50%; 7 = 50%	1 = 40%; 7 = 40%; 6 = 20%
Taurus	4 = 100%	4 = 70%; 1 = 20%; 5 = 10%
Gemini	2 = 100%	2 = 80%; 4 = 10%; 3 = 10%
Cancer	3 = 50%; 7 = 50%	3 = 40%; 7 = 40%; 6 = 20%
Leo	1 = 50%, 5 = 50%	1 = 40%; 5 = 30%; 2 = 30%
Virgo	2 = 50%; 6 = 50%	6 = 60%; 2 = 30%; 5 = 10%
Libra	3 = 100%	3 = 80%; 1 = 10%; 5 = 10%

Scorpio	4 = 100%	4 = 80%; 6 = 20%
Sagittarius	4 = 33.3%; 5 = 33.3%; 6 = 33.3%	4 = 40%; 5 = 30%; 6 = 30%
Capricorn	1 = 33.3%; 3 = 33.3%; 7 = 33.3%	3 = 40%; 1 = 40%; 5 = 20%
Aquarius	5 = 100%	5 = 40%; 7 = 40%, 4 = 20%
Pisces	2 = 50%; 6 = 50%	2 = 50%; 6 = 40%; 1 = 10%

Whichever option is selected here will affect any Ray tabulation page objects and interpretation reports that include a balance of Rays section, when they are subsequently produced.

MC in Polar Regions

Historically, astrology has been developed mainly in temperate latitudes, and therefore the mathematical problems that occur in polar regions have not received much attention in astrological texts. As a result, many modern astrology programs have failed to deal with these issues in a consistent manner.

The crux of the problem is that the normal (temperate latitude) way of defining chart angles and houses breaks down in polar regions. In these latitudes, it becomes possible for the Ascendant to retrograde, and for certain portions of the zodiac never to rise at all.

Generally, except in some very specific polar locations, it is always possible to identify the Ascendant as that part of the zodiac that is rising across the horizon (even though it may in fact be retrograding), and this happens to occur always in the Eastern horizon.

However, there are two different ways of determining the Midheaven (MC), which sometimes give diametrically opposed answers for its position in the zodiac.

•   **Always towards equator** – In this case the MC is defined as the intersection of the prime meridian with the ecliptic, towards the equator (or more precisely the ecliptic). This means that the MC is always due south in northern polar regions (and conversely is due north in southern polar regions), even though, on those days when the Sun does not rise, the MC also remains below the horizon. Another consequence of this definition is that the MC is the same for any location along a line of longitude, right from one pole to the other.

•   **Always above horizon** – In this case the MC is defined as the intersection of the prime meridian with the ecliptic, above the horizon. This means that the MC is always above the horizon (even when the Sun does not rise during the day), but as a consequence, the position of the MC in the zodiac jumps by 180 degrees (ie. has a discontinuity) as you move along a line of longitude from the equator to the winter pole.

When this option is changed, any charts that are subsequently opened or calculated will use the newly selected calculation method, but charts that have already been calculated retain the option that was in effect when they were calculated.

Progs/Dirns

Chart Angle Progression Type

When charts are progressed, it is normal to progress all the planets according to the prescribed progression rate, but to apply a separate calculation to determine the position of the Midheaven (MC), and then to derive the other chart angles (Ascendant, Vertex, Equatorial Ascendant) from that newly calculated MC. Solar Fire includes 5 different methods by which the MC's progressed position may be calculated. These methods are as follows.

True Solar Arc in Longitude - The MC's longitude is progressed by the same longitude arc as the Sun. This method is possible the most commonly used method today.

True Solar Arc in Right Ascension - The MC's right ascension is progressed by the same right ascension arc as the Sun

Naibod in Longitude - The MC's longitude is progressed at the rate of the mean motion of the Sun in longitude (this is 0°59'08'' per day). This method is also widely used.

Naibod in Right Ascension - The MC's right ascension is progressed at the rate of the mean motion of the Sun in right ascension (this is 3m56.5s of arc per day).

Mean Quotidian - The MC is progressed by the same method as the planets, thus moving about 361° per day, as opposed to the Sun's movement of about 1° per day. This method is also known as "Daily Houses".

You can select your desired method from the drop-down list. Any progressed charts or dynamic reports involving progressions that are subsequently calculated will use the newly selected angle progressions method. It is possible to determine which angle progression method has been used in a progressed chart by checking the chart type in the chart details text - the chart type description includes the angle progressions method that was used. Similarly, it is possible to determine which rate was used in a dynamic report by looking at the list of selected events in the report header. This contains a description of the progression type, method and rate.

Rate for User Defined Progs

In addition to the secondary, tertiary and minor rates of progression, it is possible for the user to specify their own rate. The existing rates that are pre-defined are as follows.

Secondary Rate - one day per solar year = 1 / 365.24219907 = .00273790926

Mean Tertiary Rate - one day per lunar cycle = 1 / 27.32158648 = .03660109676

Minor Rate - one lunar cycle per solar year = 27.32158648 / 365.24219907 = .07480402242

You can define your own rate by simply working out the required ratio eg. if you wish to use a lunar progression rate

Lunar Progression Rate = 1 day per lunation cycle = 1 / 29.53059027778 = .033863190359

You can select a previously entered rate from the drop-down list or simply enter a new progression arc rate as a decimal number. The last ten rates that you enter here are stored in the list for easy reselection later.

The progression rate selected here will be used whenever you select to use the **User Progressed** chart method when creating a progressed chart from the **Progressed...** option of the **Charts** menu. This rate is also used in dynamic reports whenever you select **User Rate** from the **Progression Type** option of the "Dynamic Report Selection" screen.

Rate for Primary Directions

When primary directions are calculated in a dynamic report or in a page object, there are several different methods of determining the exact rate of direction. The primary direction rate is always about one year of life per degree of directed arc, but any of the following options may be selected.

1 Year per Degree (Ptolemy) - The progression rate is exactly one degree of arc for each year of life.

Naibod (1 Year for 59'08'') - The progression rate is 59'08'' of arc for each year of life.

Natal Solar Rate - The progression rate is the natal Sun's rate of motion in R.A. for each year of life.

Any dynamic reports or page objects which use primary directions that are subsequently calculated or displayed will use the newly selected calculation method.

Progression Day Type

When charts are progressed by secondary or tertiary rate, it is possible to base the progression rate on either a solar day or a sidereal cycle. (Minor progressions are not based on days, so are not affected by this option). The solar day is the time taken for the sun to move from the Midheaven on one day to the Midheaven on the next day - that is 24hrs. This is the **standard** rate, also known as **Q2**. This is the rate that is in most common use by western astrologers. The sidereal cycle is the time taken for a fixed star to move through 24hrs of arc, which is slightly more than 24hrs of clock time. This is the **Bija** rate, also known as **Q1**. Astrologers who use the sidereal zodiac sometimes use this rate. The ratio of the standard rate to the Bija rate is 0.997269566.

When you change this option, any progressed charts or dynamic reports involving progressions that are subsequently calculated will use the newly selected progression day type. It is possible to determine which progression day type has been used in a progressed chart by checking whether the chart type in the chart details text - this includes either Q1 or Q2 in its name. Similarly, it is possible to determine which rate was used in a dynamic report by looking at the list of selected events in the report header. This contains a description of the progression type, method and rate.

Rate for User Defined Directions

In addition to the solar arc, ascendant arc and vertex arc rates of direction, it is possible for the user to specify their own annual direction rate, for use in casting directed charts or in dynamic reports. The existing arc rates that are pre-defined are as follows.

Solar Arc - the arc of the secondary progressed Sun. This has an average rate of motion of about 1 degree per year.

Ascendant Arc - the arc of the ascendant, as derived from the Midheaven when it is progressed by the secondary progressed solar arc. This has an average rate of motion of about 1 degree per year, but varies somewhat.

Vertex Arc - the arc of the vertex, as derived from the Midheaven when it is progressed by the secondary progressed solar arc. This has an average rate of motion of about 1 degree per year, but varies somewhat.

You can define your own fixed rate in terms of annual longitudinal motion in degrees. You can select a previously entered rate from the drop-down list or simply enter an annual arc rate in degrees and minutes, or in decimal degrees. See Entering Angles for a more detailed descriptive of acceptable formats for entering angles. The last ten angles that you enter here are stored in the list for easy reselection later.

The direction rate selected here will be used whenever you select to use the **User Arc Directed** chart method when creating a directed chart from the **Progressed...** option of the **Charts** menu. This rate is also used in dynamic reports whenever you select **User Arc** from the **Direction Type** option of the "Dynamic Report Selection" screen.

Prog/Dirn Relocation Option

This is a special option that relates to relocating progressed and directed charts. In normal operation, when calculating progressed or directed charts, if a new location is entered by the user, then the resulting chart is calculated as if the natal chart had been relocated to that new location before the progressions or directions are applied. However, when this new option is enabled, the resulting chart is calculated as if the natal chart was relocated only to the latitude of the new location before the progressions or directions are applied (the longitude remains unchanged). This applies to the calculation of progressed and directed charts as well as to the calculation of progressions and directions in the dynamic reports.

Zodiac

Default Zodiac

It is possible to specify which zodiac is used for any chart calculations. Typically, western astrologers use the **Tropical** zodiac, which has its starting point where the Sun is when it crosses the equator northwards. However, many eastern (Vedic) astrologers use a **Sidereal** zodiac that has a starting point that is fixed against the constellations, and is currently roughly 25-30 degrees earlier than the tropical zodiac's starting point. The exact difference depends upon which ayanamsa that is used. The **Draconic** zodiac is used less commonly – it sets the 0 Aries point from position of the moon's north node.

An ayanamsa is the longitudinal difference between the Tropical zodiac and a Sidereal Zodiac. This difference changes with time, due to the precession of the equinoxes, but may be defined as a fixed difference at a specific date, such as 1st Jan 1900. There are certain standard ayanamsas that are used by astrologers, and the most common of these are available for selection from the menu. Any that are not on the menu may be selected by choosing the **Sidereal** / **User Defined** zodiac type, and selecting or entering a value into the Sidereal Vernal Point.

Tropical	Precessing vernal point - Normally used in western astrology
Fagan-Bradley	Standard western astrologers' sidereal ayanamsa
Lahiri	Official Indian government ayanamsa
DeLuce	According to Robert DeLuce in "Constellational Astrology"
Raman	According to B.V.Raman of India
Usha-Shashi	According to Usha-Shashi in "Hindu Astrological Calculations"
Krishnamurti	According to K.S.Krishnamurti
Djwhal Khul	Based on the assumption that the age of Aquarius starts in the year 2117, as proposed by some students of the Ageless Wisdom.
Sri Yukteswar	According to Sri Yukteswar
JN Bhasin	According to JN Bhasin
Larry Ely	According to Larry Ely
Takra I	According to Takra – variant I
Takra II	According to Takra – variant II
Sundara Rajan	According to Sundara Rajan
Shill Pond	According to Shill Pond
User Defined	Allows you to enter your own ayanamsa in terms of the position of the Sidereal Vernal Point at 1st January 1900 for that ayanamsa. Angles may be entered in degrees, minutes and seconds (eg. "334 27 32") or using zodiacal sign (eg. "4 Pi 27 32"). See Entering Angles for more information on entering angles.
Draconic	Based on position of the moon's north node

Any charts subsequently cast will use the newly selected zodiac type. It is possible to see which zodiac has been used in any chart, as it appears as part of the chart details that are displayed in the "Current Chart" box of the main screen.

Note that a few page objects (such as Vedic Dasa tabulations) always use a sidereal zodiac, even when the selected default zodiac is tropical. The sidereal zodiac that is used for these objects is the **Ayanamsa for Sidereal Charts**.

Zodiac Application

• **Use default zodiac only when casting new charts** – When this option is selected, any charts that are opened from chart files will be calculated using the zodiac type with which they were stored. New charts are calculated using the selected default zodiac. This is how previous versions of Solar Fire worked.

• **Use default zodiac for both new and opened charts** - When this option is selected, any charts that are opened from chart files will be calculated using the selected default zodiac type, instead of the zodiac with which they were stored. This effectively overrides the zodiac type stored with charts.

Vedic Warning

This option should be checked unless you deliberately wish to use vedic calculation methods on charts with non-sidereal zodiacs. When it is checked, attempting to use **Charts / Vedic** to calculate a chart with a non-sidereal zodiac will produce a warning message. When it is unchecked, there is no warning message.

Houses

Default House System

You can select a house system which is the one used by default for all new tropical charts in Solar Fire, and optionally also for all re-opened charts as well.

You can also select a second house system which is the one used by default for all new charts which are cast with a sidereal zodiac. This may be the same, or different from the first house system.

The available house systems are as follows.

- **Campanus** - Uses the prime vertical as the fundamental circle, divided into 12 equal lunes. Derived in the 13th century by mathematician Johannes Campanus.

- **Koch** - One of the most commonly used systems. Similar to Alcabitius, except that the degree of the Midheaven is moved back to the ascendant before the ascendant is moved towards the Midheaven. Recently derived (1940s).

- **Meridian** - Also known as the Axial system.

- **Morinus** - Uses the equator as the fundamental circle, divided into 12 equal arcs starting from the projection of the ascendant onto the equator. Attributed to Jean Baptiste Morin in the 17th century.

- **Placidus** - One of the most commonly used systems. Derived by determining the points on the ecliptic whose semi-diurnal arcs exactly trisect their quadrant. Derived by Placidus de Tito in the 17th century.

- **Porphyry** - Each quadrant is dissected by longitude into three equal houses. Originated in the 3rd century AD.

- **Regiomontanus** - Similar to Campanus, but uses the celestial equator as the fundamental circle. Derived by Johannes Muller.

- **Topocentric** - Based on the rotation of the horizon line, cutting the ecliptic at equal spaces in equal time. Recently derived (c 1961) by Vendal Polich and Anthony Page.

- **Equal** - Equal system with the 1st house cusp set to the Ascendant. First described by Ptolemy in his book *Tetrabiblos*.

- **Aries** - Equal system with 1st house cusp set to 0° Aries

- **Solar Sign** - Equal system with 1st house cusp set to 0° of the Sun's sign

- **"*Planet*" on 1st** - Equal systems with 1st house cusp set to that planet's longitude

- **Vertex on 7th** - Equal system with 1st house cusp set opposite to the Vertex

- **MC on 10th** - Equal system with 10th house cusp set to the Midheaven's longitude

- **Whole Signs** - Equal system with 1st house cusp set to 0° of the Ascendant's sign

- **Hindu Bhava** - Based on the Porphyry system, but with the cusps shifted to the midpoints of the Porphyry houses, so that the Ascendant falls in the middle of the first house.

- **Alcabitius** - Time based system, based on the trisection of the diurnal arc of the ascendant traveling towards the Midheaven.

- **Asc in 1st** - Equal system with centre of 1st house set to the Ascendant

Whichever house system you highlight in the list will become the new default house system.

Asc/MC Display Option

Normally, even if the Ascendant and Midheaven are selected as displayed points, they are not shown as chart points inside the chart wheel. The only exceptions to this rule are when these points are not identical to the 1st and 10th house cusps respectively. The reason for this behavior is to avoid putting superfluous information into the chart, thus avoiding clutter. However, there are two options which you may switch on the alter this behavior.

- **Show Asc even when 1st House Cusp** – When switched on, this option ensures that the Ascendant is always displayed in a wheel as a chart point, even when it is also the 1st house cusp.

- **Show MC even when 10th House Cusp** – When switched on, this option ensures that the Midheaven is always displayed in a wheel as a chart point, even when it is also the 10th house cusp.

Composite Chart Houses

This option applies only to the calculation of **Composite – Midpoints** charts. In most cases the calculation of these charts is straightforward, and the house cusps of the chart are simply the midpoints of the same house cusps in the two base charts. However, if the house cusps of the two base charts are almost diametrically opposed, then it is possible that a chart made up of the short-arc midpoints of the base charts' house cusps will have its cusps out of zodiacal order. When this happens, Solar Fire will adjust some of the house cusps to be long-arc midpoints instead of short-arc in order to preserve the correct zodiacal ordering of the houses. This adjustment can be made in any of the three following ways.

- **Auto Anchor** – The 1st and 10th house cusps of the base charts are tested to see which one has the "strongest" composite midpoint, and then that cusp is taken as a short-arc midpoint, and other house cusps adjusted as required to maintain correct zodiacal order of the cusps. The "strongest" midpoint is the one in which the short-arc difference in angle between the cusps on the two base charts is a minimum.

• **Anchor on 1st House** – The 1st house cusp is always taken as the short-arc midpoint, and other house cusps adjusted as required to maintain correct zodiacal order of the cusps.

• **Anchor on 10th House** - The 10th house cusp is always taken as the short-arc midpoint, and other house cusps adjusted as required to maintain correct zodiacal order of the cusps.

House System Application

• **Use this house system only when casting new charts** – When this option is selected, any charts that are opened from chart files will be calculated using the house system with which they were stored. New charts are calculated using the selected default house system (depending on which zodiac they use).

• **Use this house system for both new and opened charts** - When this option is selected, any charts that are opened from chart files will be calculated using the selected default house system, instead of the house system with which they were stored (depending on which zodiac they use). This effectively overrides the house system stored with charts.

Points

You have the ability to select the order in which you prefer the planets to be listed in reports, tabulations and grids.

Highlight a point that you wish to adjust, and then use the **Move Point Up** or **Move Point Down** buttons until it is in the required position in the list.

You can reset the entire list to Solar Fire's initial default order by clicking on the **Reset to Default** button.

View Menu

You can customize the type of astrological data that is displayed from each of the following View menu items.

• Current Chart

- Current Chart+Grid

- Current Grid

- Dual Wheels

- BiWheel

- TriWheel

- QuadriWheel

- QuinquiWheel

- Synastry Grid

The listbox shows which page style is currently selected for each of these menu items.

The purpose of this option is to allow you view your preferred page type for any chart without having to go through extra steps of selecting the page type each time you display a chart. For example, if you usually want to display esoteric astrological information, then you might select "Rays and Rulerships [esot2.pag]" as your selected page style for "Current Chart".

Note that whichever page style you select for "Current Chart" also takes effect whenever you double-click on the list of calculated charts.

>> To select an alternative page style

Select the required menu item from the list

1.   Click on the **Select...** button

2.   Choose a page type from the Page Topic Index dialog, and click on the **OK** button

You can reset all the page styles to their original defaults by clicking on the **Reset to Defaults** button.

Misc

Pluto Glyph

You may select any of three available styles for the Pluto glyph. This style is used in all chart wheels and reports in Solar Fire.

Uranus Glyph

You may select either of two available styles for the Uranus glyph. This style is used in all chart wheels and reports in Solar Fire.

Capricorn Glyph

You may select either of two available styles for the Capricorn glyph. This style is used in all chart wheels and reports in Solar Fire.

Midpoint Trees

There are two options that affect how all midpoint trees are calculated, both in the reports and in the midpoint tree page objects.

• **Allow trees to contain midpoints which include the root planet** – Normally, when midpoint trees are constructed, the root planet for each tree is excluded from calculations of the midpoints which fall under that tree. This can only occur when the root planet is conjunct the other point, and as this can normally be seen easily in the chart itself, it is of less interest than other items in the midpoint trees. However, if you prefer, you can ensure that these entries will appear in the trees by switching this option on.

• **When sorting trees, take into account the sign of the orb** – The entries in midpoint trees can be sorted in two ways: a) according the absolute orb of the contact (disregarding which side it is on), in which case the closest orbs appear at the top of the list, or b) according to the orb and sign, in which case the closest orbs appear in the middle of the list. If you prefer option b), then switch this option on.

Parans

Solar Fire's Star Parans report shows a list of parans for currently selected stars and planets, and parans may also be listed in flexible point's list page objects.

A choice is offered in relation to the format for the parans.

• **Display as Local Clock Time** - The parans are displayed as local clock times. This is useful if you wish to see approximate rise/set clock times.

- **Display as LST Angles** – The parans are displayed as local sidereal time expressed as an angle.

- **Display as LST Times** - The parans are displayed as local sidereal time expressed as a time.

Now Button Precision

When you click on the Now button in Solar Fire's New Chart Data Entry screen (or any other screen with a Now button), the current time is displayed there. You can control whether the time is truncated to the current whole minute, or alternatively to the current second within the current minute.

Sound for Events

The program issues appropriate beeps when any error or information dialog box is displayed, when the "Print" dialog box is displayed and when printing or copying has finished. It is possible to prevent any beeps from being sounded by switching off the sound option.

Angle Rounding

It is possible to display zodiac angles in either of two ways. If the angle rounding option is off, then when angles are displayed they will simply be truncated from their full precision. If the angle rounding option is on, then the displayed angle will be rounded to the nearest displayed unit (ie. to the nearest minute if the angle is displayed in degrees and minutes, or to the nearest second if the angle is displayed in degrees minutes and seconds). The only exception to this rounding rule occurs for zodiacal longitudes just prior to a sign boundary. In this particular case no rounding is applied, to ensure that the displayed angle does not appear to be in the following sign before the ingress actually occurs.

Some examples follow.

Angle	Angle Rounding On	Angle Rounding Off
12° 34' 56.7"	12° 35' or 12° 34' 57"	12° 34' or 12° 34' 56"
23° 59' 59.5"	24° 00' or 24° 00' 00"	23° 59' or 23° 59' 59"

| 29° 59' 59.5" | 29° 59' or 29° 59' 59" | 29° 59' or 29° 59' 59" |

Any charts or reports that are generated display any angles according to the current setting of this option. Note that this option does not affect the way in which angles are calculated or stored internally (they are always stored to a high precision, regardless of this option) - it only affects the manner in which angles are displayed.

Compliments

It is possible to edit the compliments text that appears when most charts and pages are printed. Typically you might want to enter you name, address and telephone number, for the sake of any clients who receive your printed charts. On a single-wheel chart, this text appears on the top right corner of the page; on a biwheel chart it appears at the bottom right; and on a triwheel chart it appears at the bottom left. Compliments text is not normally printed on quadriwheel charts, but can be added to or removed from any page if required, using the Page Editor.

The topmost line of text will always be printed with a bold font (unless it is left blank), and the subsequent lines will be printed in a normal font. Each line of text is justified to the right or the left depending on which part of the chart the text is being printed. This alignment can be changed used the Page Editor.

In some situations you may want to prevent compliments text from appearing eg. if you are producing a large number of charts and pages for publication. In this case, you can check the **Hide compliments text** box. This will prevent the compliments text from appearing on any displayed or printed page. It is not necessary to remove the text itself. Unchecking the box will allow the specified compliments text to be displayed on any subsequently drawn or printed page that includes a compliments text object.

Dates

Window for 2 Digit Year Entry

When you are entering dates into Solar Fire, you can facilitate input by excluding the century number from the year and entering just one or two digits for the year, and allowing the century number to be automatically inserted. For example, entering 3/12/98 might result in the date "3 Dec 1998" being assumed, or 3/12/0 might result in "3 Dec 2000".

This option allows you to specify the 100 year window in which the century number is correctly assumed.

For example, if you enter the window range 1905 (to 2004), then one or two digit year numbers are assumed to be within this year range ie. 0 to 4 are converted to 2000 to 2004, and 5 to 99 are converted to 1905 to 1999.

Note: If you wish to enter a date with any year number which is outside the specified window, then you must enter at least 3 year digits (or a BC date qualifier), including leading zeroes for dates in the first century AD eg. 003 for year 3 AD.

Calendar Style Display Options

• **Never show OS/NS flags – Always use default** – When this option is selected, Solar Fire never displays OS (old style, Julian) or NS (new style, Gregorian) suffixes on its dates. When this option is in effect, any date on or prior to 14 Oct 1582 is an OS date, and any later date is a NS date. This is how earlier versions of Solar Fire always worked.

• **Always show OS/NS flags between years** – When this option is selected, Solar Fire will always display the OS or NS suffix on any chart whose year falls within the specified range.

• **Retain all user entered OS/NS flags** – When this option is selected, Solar Fire remembers whether the date you entered had an OS or NS suffix, and if so, always displays the date with that suffix, and according to that calendar style. For example, if you entered "17 Aug 1753 OS", then that date would always be displayed that way too. However, if you entered "17 Aug 1753 OS" when this option was not selected, then it would be converted into the NS calendar, and displayed as "28 Aug 1753" or "28 Aug 1753 NS".

Interps

The following options apply to textual interpretation reports that Solar Fire generates. You can select which word processor you wish to use when viewing and printing interpretation reports. If you do not select one yourself, then Solar Fire will use the default word processor for your computer system.

• **Use default word processor** – When this option is selected, the report file that Solar Fire generates is launched using whatever word processor has the RTF file type association (for RTF files), or TXT file type association (for TXT files). However, if your computer does not have a file type association, then you will need to use the following option instead.

• **Use specified word processor** – Selecting this option requires you to click on the **Browse...** button to locate your desired word processor program file. You must select a word processor that is capable of opening TXT and RTF files.

• **Apply rich text formatting to report** - Rich Text Format (RTF) is a method of producing formatted reports (ie. with centered text, bold and italics, for example). Without RTF, a report file will contain only plain text in a single font, without any special formatting, and this is much less attractive and harder to read. Solar Fire can produce its interpretations reports either with or without RTF. However, if you use the RTF option, then you must be using a word processor that is capable of understanding the RTF format. MS Word for Windows, WordPerfect and the Windows WordPad can all understand the RTF format. If you have the RTF option switched on, but are using a word processor that does not understand RTF, then you will see a lot of spurious items in the report file that interfere with its normal layout.

Places

This dialog allows you to select a list of "favorite" places, set one of them as your current location, and select which Atlas type to use for place lookups.

Favourite Places

This list can contain the details of up to five places. One of these places must always be your current location, and the other four may be places to which you travel frequently, or places for which you frequently cast charts, for example.

>> To add a favorite place

Click on the **Add...** button.

The will open the Atlas dialog for your currently selected atlas type, from where you can find the required place, or add new place details if you are using the Solar Fire Atlas. See Using Place Databases for more details on selecting a place from the Atlas. When you have selected a place, it is automatically added to the list of favorite places. If your list already has five places on it, then the one at the bottom of the list (the least recently used one) is removed to make way for the new place.

>> To delete a favorite place

Highlight the required place and then click on the **Delete** button.

Current Default Place

The current default place should usually be set to your current location. This is what determines the location details that are displayed on the front screen of Solar Fire.

>> To select a new current default place

Ensure that the place you want is on the list of favorite places (if it is not there then add it).

Highlight the required place

Click on the **Set as Default** button.

The name of the new default place will be updated immediately.

Recently Used Places

In addition to your list of favorite places, Solar Fire also remembers up to 5 other places you have most recently entered or looked up. These places automatically appear on drop-down place selection boxes in the Chart Entry dialog, most subsidiary chart dialogs and others. Having these places listed there makes it easy for users to quickly re-access recently used places that they have not saved to their favorite places list.

However, there are some circumstances in which you may wish to remove those recently used places. For example, if one of those places was looked up in the Solar Fire atlas, it may not have timezone changes associated with it, and you may prefer to look it up via the ACS atlas instead to ensure the correct timezone changes are applied. To do so, you first need to remove it from the list of recently used places. Otherwise Solar Fire will continue to used the recently used place entry instead of looking it up again from the ACS Atlas.

>> To clear the list of recently used places

Click on the **Clear** button.

Lookup timezone on each startup

The default place details also contain the current timezone for that location. If you don't want to have to remember to adjust that timezone for daylight savings yourself, then you can switch on this option, so that every time that Solar Fire starts up, it will check the current timezone according to the Atlas timezone tables, and set it accordingly for the current date.

However, if for any reason the place you have selected as your current default place is not linked to a timezone table, then using this option might result in a warning message each time that Solar Fire starts up, and the timezone will not be updated. In this case you have the option of either switching this option off, or of re-selecting your current location using an Atlas that does has a timezone table link.

Atlas to Use

Solar Fire contains a built-in copy of the ACS Atlas. It also has the capability of linking to a standalone ACS PC Atlas, if you have one installed on your computer.

Solar Fire also contains its own atlas, but this is only included for backward compatibility, and it is recommended that you use the ACS Atlas instead.

After you set this option, whenever the atlas is accessed either directly (by clicking on a **Place...** button) or indirectly (by using the Autolookup feature), the chosen atlas is accessed.

Refresh Index

This button is only accessible when the Solar Fire atlas is selected. The Solar Fire atlas contains an index of country and places that greatly speeds up lookups.

If you only ever add, edit or delete places to this atlas via Solar Fire, then the index will be maintained automatically.

However, if you were to add or install new atlas files, or make other changes to atlas files via the operating system, then these index files might no longer be up-to-date, and you might fail to find new information. In this case you can select this button to invoke a re-indexing of the files, thus ensuring that the atlas has access to all new information in it.

Charts

Chart Conversion to SFv6/v7 Format

This version of Solar Fire uses a chart file format that is different from that of version 5 and earlier. This new file format has advantages over the old format, but it is not compatible with earlier versions. However, this version of Solar Fire is able to read all older version chart files, and is also able to save chart files to the SFv5 or SFv3/4 file format if required.

However, when saving to a SFv5 or earlier version chart file, life events are not saved. Also, when saving to a SFv3/4 chart file, any chart rating and source notes that you have entered, along with the chart event type or gender are not saved, and it is not possible to save any charts other than natal types charts.

• **Always automatically convert older charts** – When this option is selected, any time that you select an old version chart file (SFv1/2/3/4/5) to open, it will automatically be converted into a new version chart file, and a backup copy of the old version file will be stored into the OLDCHART sub directory of the main Solar Fire Charts folder. This option is recommended if you do not need to maintain compatibility with other software that is unable to read the new Solar Fire chart file format.

• **Prompt me whether or not to convert each older chart file** - When this option is selected, any time that you select an old version chart file (SFv1/2/3/4/5) to open, you will be prompted whether or not allow it to be converted into a new version chart file. If you consent, then it is converted and a backup copy of the old version file will be stored into the OLDCHART sub directory of the main Solar Fire Chart folder. If you do not consent, then it is left unchanged.

• **Never convert – keep all older format chart files** – When this option is selected, any old version chart file that you open remains unchanged. However, this means that you will not have the advantages of the new chart file format features.

Auto Chart Save

Any new charts that are created by the program, plus any charts which are edited instead of being opened, must be saved to a chart database if you wish to use them again in later sessions with the program.

It is possible to save a chart by manually selecting Save options within the program, or alternatively any new charts can be saved automatically whenever they are created by switching this option on.

For more information on saving charts see Saving Charts to a File.

Chart Data Email Options

Solar Fire allows you to create emails that automatically include details of any charts that you have selected, either as attached chart files and comment files, or within the body of the message itself. You can also automatically create emails that include chart page graphics as attached files. This should greatly facilitate the exchange of astrological data.

In order to use these email options, you must have a MAPI compliant email program. See About MAPI for more information, and for a full explanation of the various email options that you can set after clicking on the **Edit Options** button.

AutoRun

Solar Fire can automatically run a set of Astrologer's Assistant tasks every time that it starts up. For example, you may want Solar Fire to generate a chart of current transits whenever it starts up, or to open your own chart, and then view it in a triwheel with the current progressions and transits around it.

If a task file has already been selected for AutoRun, then the file name and its title and description will be displayed in the text boxes.

If you wish to create a new task file, then see Using the Astrologers Assistant for further instructions.

>> To select a task file to run on startup

Click on the **Select...** button and choose an existing task file from the list of available task files.

>> To prevent a task file from running on startup

Click on the **Clear** button.

Ephemerides

Solar Fire installs a copy of the Swiss Ephemeris into a standard location in the Program Files folder. However, it is possible that you already have a copy of the Swiss Ephemeris in another location on your computer. In this case you can avoid keeping multiple copies of the Swiss Ephemeris files by directing Solar Fire to use the copy in the other location.

>> To select an alternative location of the Swiss Ephemeris

Click on the **Browse...** button and choose the folder in which the Swiss Ephemeris resides.

Once you have chosen a new directory, Solar Fire attempts to connect to the ephemeris files at the new location. If you specified a folder that does not contain the correct Swiss Ephemeris files, then you will see an error message, and the location will revert to its original value.

After you have successfully specified an alternative location, you may delete the ephemeris files from Solar Fire's old Swiss Ephemeris folder, in order to free up disk space, if you wish.

Note: Swiss Ephemeris asteroid ephemerides must always reside in subdirectories of the main Swiss Ephemeris directory. If you use this option to change locations, then you must ensure that any extra asteroid ephemerides you have are also present in the new location, or you will lose access to them. See Using More Asteroids.

Stations

A planet or point is stationary only instantaneously ie. not for any finite length of time. Hence, in normal usage, a point referred to as being stationary in a chart actually means that it is *near* a station, rather than truly being stationary.

There are a number of possible ways of defining the criteria for how near a point must be to a station in order to be considered "stationary", and Solar Fire offers four such options, from which the user may select one.

• Within this timespan of exactness - the user may specify the number of days and/or hours, within which the point is considered stationary

• Within this distance of exactness - the user may specify the orb as a distance in longitude (celestial), within which the point is considered stationary

• When actual speed is less than - the user may specify a daily rate of motion (in zodiacal longitude per day), below which the point is considered stationary

• When speed relative to average is less than - the user may specify a percentage of the typical speed, below which the point is considered stationary

>> To shows stations on chart wheels

Ensure that the **Show Stations with "S"** option is checked.

When this option is switched on, any chart which normally has space to display a retrograde symbol will display an "S" in that space if that point is within orb of a station according to the option selected above. If colors are enabled in the chart, then a stationary point which is retrograde will have the "S" shown in the retrograde color, or if the point is direct then in normal text color.

Eclipses

Maximum eclipse is defined as the instant when the Moon passes closest to the axis of Earth's shadow, or when the Moon' shadow passes closest to the Earth's centre.

The exact lunar phase (ie. exact conjunction of Sun and Moon around a solar eclipse or their exact opposition around a lunar eclipse) is defined by their exact aspect in longitude alone.

The time of maximum eclipse is generally different from the exact time of the associated lunar phase. However, because the Moon generally has non-zero latitude, the time of closest approach between the two bodies (maximum eclipse) is slightly different. The difference between the time of maximum eclipse and exact lunar phase can vary by 15 minutes or more.

Solar Fire offers the choice of which time to use for its eclipse calculations

- **Use exact lunar phase** - when this option is selected, eclipse titles always have "(NM)" or "(FM)" as a suffix to indicate that they are the times of the exact new moon or full moon respectively eg. "Solar Partial Eclipse (NM)"

- **Use maximum eclipse time** - when this option is selected, there is no suffix on eclipse titles eg. "Solar Partial Eclipse"

Note: Earlier versions of Solar Fire only calculated maximum eclipse times, and did not have an exact lunar phase option. Hence if you keep the default setting of using exact lunar phase, the eclipse times you obtain will be different from the eclipse times in earlier versions. If you want to replicate the results from earlier versions, select the maximum eclipse time option.

Editing the Toolbar Buttons

The toolbar contains a range of graphical buttons that provide shortcuts to various items within Solar Fire. It may be customized by changing the selection or ordering of the buttons it contains.

>> To customize the toolbar

Select the **Edit Toolbar...** item from the **Preferences** menu, or double-click the mouse on any blank area of the toolbar.

This will display the toolbar customization dialog, which display a list of available toolbar buttons on the left, and current toolbar buttons on the right. You can manipulate buttons and separators (ie. blank spaces) as follows.

>> To add a button

1.   In the current toolbar buttons list, select the button above which you wish to insert the new button.

2.   In the available toolbar buttons list, select the required new button.

3.   Click on the **Add** button.

>> To remove a button

1.   In the current toolbar buttons list, select the button you wish to remove.

2.   Click on the **Remove** button.

>> To change the order of buttons

1.   In the current toolbar buttons list, select the button you wish to move.

2.   Click on the **Move Up** or **Move Down** buttons as required.

>> To restore your previous button selection

Click on the **Reset** button.

This will restore the order of buttons to the way it was when you opened this dialog box.

Viewing Panels on the Main Screen

The panels on the main screen which may be turned on or off from the **Preferences** menu are as follows.

- Toolbar

- Date and place

- Current Settings

- Solar Live Bar

- Planet Bar

See Solar Fires Main Screen for a detailed description of what each of these items contains.

Chapter 32: Editing a Wheel Design File

This section describes how to edit files that contain wheel or dial designs which may be used in Solar Fire's chart or dial displays and printouts.

>> To edit a particular wheel or dial design

Select one of the **Wheel Styles...** or **Dial Styles...** options from the **Chart Options** menu, or from a button on the View Chart screen.

From the file manager, select the required file from the list of file names, and select the **Edit...** button

>> To start up the wheel designer directly from Windows

From the Windows group containing Solar Fire program icons, double-click on the **Wheel Designer** icon.

If you have started the wheel designer via Solar Fire's file manager, then when the screen first appears, the current design file will be open. You may simply wish to examine or edit this file, but you may also use the available menu options to open and edit other wheel or dial design files or to create new ones.

The displayed wheel or dial is not that of a true chart - its planetary positions are fictitious and fixed, and are shown purely for convenience of getting a rough idea of how the design will look when used with a real chart. In order to see the design with a real chart, you will need to use it in Solar Fire to display a chart.

Setting All Line Colors

Sometimes you may wish to create a chart with colored circles, cusp lines etc. You can do this by editing the color properties of each object of the design. However, you can also set all the lines colors at once, if you prefer.

>> To set all the wheel's line colors to a selected color

Select the **Set All Line Colors...** item from the **Edit** menu

Select the required color from the color selection dialog.

Chapter 33: Backing Up and Restoring Chart Files

Most files in Solar Fire can be easily re-installed or fairly readily reconstructed if should you experience serious problems with your computer's hard disk or operating system. However, chart files cannot be reconstructed unless you keep some sort of copy of all the charts that you cast or import. Therefore, it is wise to make backups of your chart data on a regular basis. Visit www.alabe.com/astrobackup to download a free utility that will automate your file transfers and backups. Or:

>> To backup your data to any other location on your computer or network (eg. a USB Flash Drive)

For Chart Files only: Select the **Backup Chart Files...** item from the **Utilities** menu.

For All User Files: Select the **Backup All User Files...** item from the **Utilities** menu.

You will be prompted to select a drive or location to save the backup files to.

If you want to create a backup copy that you can keep separately from your computer, then you should choose an external drive, but you can also save copies to another directory or disk on your computer, or to another computer linked to yours on a network.

>> To find your Solar Fire User Files folder

Select the **Open User Files Folder...** item from the **Utilities** menu.

>> To restore your backup chart data

Copy the chart files from their backup location into the Charts subfolder under the Solar Fire User Files folder.

>> To restore your back user files

Copy the files from their backup location into the Solar Fire User Files folder.

Chapter 34: Using Birthday Reminders

The birthday reminders feature enables you to save a birthday reminder for any person for whom you have already cast a chart.

Solar Fire can optionally check for any birthdays which are forthcoming (or overdue) each time it is first run on any given day.

Adding New Birthday Reminders

You can add a birthday reminder for any chart which is already in your list of calculated charts, or from any chart which is stored in a chart file. The reminder is created using the day and month of the chart's birth date.

>> To add a birthday reminder for one or more chart in the calculated chart list

From the main screen, select one or more charts from the list of "Calculated Charts"

Then do either of the following

• Select the **Add to Birthday Reminders...** item from the Chart menu

• Use a right hand mouse click over one of the selected charts, and select the **Add to Birthday Reminders...** item from the pop-up menu

>> To add a birthday reminder from the Chart Open dialog

Select the required chart/s from the list of charts in the current chart file

Click on the Send/Add... button

Select the **Add to Birthday Reminders...** item from the drop-down menu

Once you have added reminders, you can view them at any time. See Viewing Birthday Reminders

Viewing Birthday Reminders

>> **To view the birthday reminders dialog**

Select the **Birthday Reminders...** item from the Utilities menu

This will display the **View Birthday Reminders** dialog.

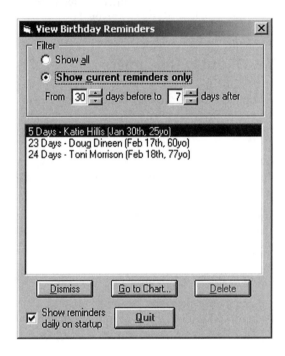

You can use either of the following **Filter** options.

• **Show all** - use this to see a list of all stored reminders, regardless of whether they are current or not

• **Show current reminders only** - use this to display only those reminders for birthdays which occur within the given range of days, and which have not already been dismissed for the current year's birthday

>> **To dismiss a reminder until next year's birthday**

1.   Highlight the required reminder entry

2.   Click on the **Dismiss** button

Dismissing a reminder does not remove the reminder altogether, but simply prevents any further reminders for it from appearing as a "current reminder" until next year. Dismissed reminders remain visible when the **Show All** option is being used with the postfix "[Dismissed]", but will no longer appear when the **Show current reminders only** is being used (until next year).

>> To restore a dismissed reminder

1.   In the **Show All** view, highlight the dismissed reminder entry

2.   Click on the **Restore** button

>> To permanently remove a reminder from the list

1.   Highlight the required reminder entry

2.   Click on the **Delete** button

This permanently removes the reminder from all reminder lists. You cannot retrieve a removed reminder. Instead you must re-add it from a chart.

>> To find the source chart for this reminder

1.   Highlight the required reminder entry

2.   Click on the **Go To Chart...** button

This will display the **Chart Open** dialog, with the source chart's file open, and the chart itself highlighted. From there you can open it, view, add comments etc.

>> To get an automatic reminder pop-up as birthdays approach

Ensure the **Show reminders daily on startup** option is checked.

When this option is switched on, Solar Fire checks the list of birthday reminders within a few seconds of starting up, on the first occasion it runs on each calendar day. If there are any reminders which fall within the specified range of days leading up to or following a birthday, then this dialog pops up, listing the current reminders.

If you quit without dismissing or removing any reminders, then the same reminders will be shown to you again on the following day (as long as they still fall within the specified range of days.)

Chapter 35: Text and Data Supplied with Solar Fire

Solar Fire includes data and interpretations from a variety of sources. This data is immediately available to the user once Solar Fire is installed.

Chart Data

Solar Fire includes a number of chart databases with a total more than 2000 charts, from several sources - The Clifford Data Compendium and the Australian Data Collection, and a collection of other charts from Sy Scholfield.

All of the chart data has been supplied by reputable specialist data collectors, and has been rated for accuracy using Rodden Rating system.

Rodden Rating

- **AA** - Data from Birth Certificates (BC), hospital or governmental birth records (BR), notes from Vital Statistics/Registries, family bibles, baby books, family written records. This is the best evidence of data accuracy available.

- **A** - Data from the person, family member, friend or associate. Also included are newspaper birth announcements. Times given within a 'window of time' of thirty minutes (eg. "between 3.30pm and 4.00pm") are presented here.

- **B** - Data from biographies and autobiographies where no other source is given.

- **C** - Caution, data not validated. No source, vague, rectified/speculative data, "personal" ambiguous sources, approximate birth times (eg. "early morning", "around lunchtime").

- **DD** - Dirty Data. Two or more unsubstantiated quotes of time, place or data (perhaps rectified without designation). Any unverified data that are contradicted by another source.

The Scholfield Collection

This collection consists of about 1200 charts categorized into the following chart files

- Corporate.SFcht

- Entertainment.SFcht

- Infamous.SFcht

- Literature.SFcht

- Miscellaneous.SFcht

- Politics.SFcht

- Royalty.SFcht

- Science.SFcht

- Sports.SFcht

- Visual Arts.SFcht

About the Author

Sy Scholfield (a.k.a. Simon Astley Scholfield) is a British-Australian astro-data collector based in Brisbane, Queensland. His online collections include "Aussie Stars: Astrological Profiles of Famous Australians" (www.aussie-stars.com) and "Queer Stars: Astrology Charts for Gay, Lesbian, Bisexual and Transgender celebrities" (www.astroqueer.com/charts.html). Selections of Scholfield's data have also been published in Lois Rodden's *Data News* and *AstroDatabank* website & CDs; Frank C. Clifford's book, *British Entertainers: The Astrological Profiles;* and Grazia Bordoni's *Data Notizie* newsletters. For more information see his official website (www.syscholfield.com).

The Clifford Data Compendium

The Clifford Data Compendium presents the birth data of 500 famous individuals in a number of areas from entertainment to sport, politics to religion. It incorporates some of the most accurate data of leading figures found in other collections whilst including many data collected by the author, and some never before published.

The charts are contained in the file *clif2000.SFcht.*

Each data entry has notes presented in the following format:

Source - Details of where the data originated from (if not from the author's archives) and the classification of the data is in brackets (see Data Accuracy below)

Real Name - If available and differing from name given

Profession - The various vocations for which the individual is primarily known

Biography - A short biography, including a few dates for further study

Some entries incorporate birth details of related individuals.

Data Accuracy

It is vital any data collections presented to the astrological community be as accurate and fully sourced as possible. There may, however, be the occasional update to this collection, and the author welcomes any corrections or additions.

All data are classified using the simple Rodden Rating system. All data presented in this collection are of AA, A or B standard. Unverified data have not been included.

Abbreviations found in the Notes section:

FCC - Author Frank C. Clifford

RR - Rodden Rating - a data classification system (see above)

GBAC - The Gauquelin Book of American Charts

CAH - Contemporary American Horoscopes

Data Bibliography

Most of the data presented have been personally checked by the author himself, and in most cases the actual Birth Certificate or Birth Record/Note is in hand. Many thanks to my international colleagues for sharing data and collected BCs and BRs over the last few years, including Thelma & Tom Wilson, Dana Holliday, Edwin Steinbrecher, David Fisher, Sally Davis, Francoise Gauquelin, Tashi Grady, Linda Clark, Caroline Gerard, Lois Rodden, Marion March, and Grazia Bordoni.

The Gauquelin Book of American Charts (ACS, 1982). Accurate BC data by Michel & Francoise Gauquelin

The House of Commons (1992-7) by Caroline Gerard. Available from: 6 Belford Mews, Dean Village, Edinburgh EH4 3BT, Scotland (£8).

The Astro-Data series. Five volumes and Data News by Lois Rodden, covering a variety of data.

Contemporary American Horoscopes. BC data from Janice Mackey and Jessica Saunders, 1990. Available on computer disk from Astrolabe.

A special thank you to Edwin Steinbrecher for providing access to his database and BRs. The Steinbrecher Data Collection is a comprehensive database of 20,000 timed data (+ 6000 noon charts). See the website: http://www.dome-igm.com/dome/

About the Author

Frank C. Clifford is an astrologer, palmist and data collector. His data interests include running the Data Exchange Network to swap data with international collectors, working with the Astrological Association's Data Section, and checking data/biography for many magazines and books. His non-astrological work includes script-writing, broadcasting and researching. Frank lives in London and can be contacted via Flare Publications. His first data book "British Entertainers: The Astrological Profiles" is available from Flare Publications (SF), P.O. Box 10126, London NW3 7WD, England, UK. UK orders - cheques or postal orders for £11.50; International orders - an International Money Order for £17. All prices include p&p. Please do not send cash, unless by guaranteed/registered delivery.

The Australian Data Collection

This is a collection of 370 charts of famous Australians (and immigrants) and Australian events, all sourced, and some with biographical notes and important dates. This data was compiled by Australian astrologer Stephanie Johnson, with contributions from other astrologers around the world.

The charts are contained in the file *aus2008.SFcht*.

Chart Art
The "Chart Art" background graphics included in Solar Fire were provided by 3 different Australian artists/designers.

- **Kay Steventon** - Art_Angel.jpg, Art_Angel2.jpg, Art_Angel3.jpg, Art_Planets.jpg, Art_Sunmoon.jpg

- **Eila Laurikainen** - Art_Fire_Frame.jpg, Art_Earth_Frame.jpg, Art_Earth_Frame_Ltr.jpg, Art_Air_Frame.jpg, Art_Water_Frame.jpg

- **Celine Lawrence** - Art_Air_Dark.jpg, Art_Air_Dark2.jpg, Art_Fire_Dark.jpg, Art_Fire_Light.jpg, Art_Fire_Red.jpg, Art_Stars_Dark.jpg, Art_Water_Dark.jpg, Art_Water_Light.jpg, Art_Water_Light2.jpg

These graphics are copyright (2008), and permission is required to use them for any purpose other than within pages generated by Solar Fire.

Interpretations Text

The interpretations text in Solar Fire was written by Stephanie Johnson Dip FAA of Esoteric Technologies Pty Ltd. Text Copyright © 1994-2008 Esoteric Technologies Pty Ltd.

The Sabian Symbols and wording of the symbols are from "The Sabian Symbols in Astrology" by Dr. Marc Edmund Jones (c) The Marc Edmund Jones Literary Trust. First published in 1993 by Aurora Press, PO Box 573, Santa Fe, New Mexico 87504, USA.

The parts of the body for each degree of the zodiac are from "A Handbook of Medical Astrology" by Jane Ridder-Patrick (c). Published by Penguin/Arkana 1990 ISBN 0-14-019214-X. Website: www.janeridderpatrick.com

The interpretations in the file STANDARD.INT relate to natal geocentric charts. It can also be used fairly effectively with various other types of charts, such as return charts or progressed charts, provided that the reader bears in mind the original purpose of the text, and adapts it to the new context. For example, the interpretation of the Sun in the 5th house in a return chart will only apply for a period of 1 year, whereas the text was written to refer to enduring traits that would result from this placement in a natal chart.

The interpretations in the file TRANSITS.INT relate to transits to a natal chart.

The interpretations in the file PROGRESS.INT relate to progressions to a natal chart.

The interpretations file SYNASTRY.INT relates to synastry between two natal charts.

The interpretations file CALENDAR.INT relate to transits to a natal chart.

The interpretations file FIRDARIA.INT relates to firdaria planetary periods in relation to a natal chart.

Not all possible categories of interpretations are covered in these files given the vast number of possible combinations that need to be potentially catered for. For example there is no text relating to aspects between the TransNeptunians and planets.

You are, however, free to add you own text to either of these files, or to create your own interpretations files from scratch, by using the Interpretations Compiler supplied with Solar Fire.

Copyright Restrictions

All text included with Solar Fire is copyrighted, but the licensed owner of Solar Fire is granted permission to use any output printed or exported from Solar Fire for the purpose of providing astrological charts and reports generated by Solar Fire to friends or clients. This text must not otherwise be reproduced or copied without the express permission of the copyright holder. This text may also be edited before distribution, provided that the copyright of any portions of original text is respected and acknowledged where appropriate.

If you print reports using text supplied with Solar Fire, then you should ensure that Esoteric Technologies' copyright notice appears on the report.

If you have added some of your own text, then you might like to add a copyright notice that applies to the text you have written yourself, for example

Main Text (c) 1993-2004 Esoteric Technologies Pty Ltd

Portions of Text (c) 2005 Susan Smith

If you are printing reports that use your own text exclusively, then there is no need to include any copyright notice relating to Esoteric Technologies.

Fixed Stars Data and Text

The fixed star file BRADY.FST contains data and interpretations for 50 fixed stars. This file was compiled by Bernadette Brady Dip. (FAA) from her work in progress "Fixed Stars and Stained Glass". Bernadette has done all her research on fixed stars working with parans, so she suggests that the best results can be achieved with this star file by using the Star Parans report rather than the Star Aspects report in Solar Fire. She recommends using an orb of 15 to 20 minutes of arc when using the Star Paran report. She has included coding of + and - signs with some star names to indicate stars which are especially positive (+++) and those that may prove very difficult (---). Text Copyright © 1995 Bernadette Brady.

The fixed star file PTOLEMY.FST contains a number of stars that were commonly used in the era of Ptolemy. This file was also compiled by Bernadette Brady. The keyword text for each star in this file identifies its nature in terms of planetary symbolism (eg. Jupiter for a star which has a Jupiterian nature), and its long text identifies which position in its zodiacal symbol this star takes. Text Copyright © 1995 Bernadette Brady.

The fixed star file ALLSTARS.FST contains data on about 290 of the most commonly used stars, but has no interpretations text. It was generated by importing the fixed star file that is supplied with the NOVA program, and is included by permission of Astrolabe, Inc.

Arabic Parts

The Arabic Parts file supplied with Solar Fire contains all the Arabic Parts that were supplied with the NOVA program, and is included by kind permission of Astrolabe, Inc.

Asteroids

Solar Fire is supplied with ephemerides for more than 1000 asteroids and minor planets. The ephemerides cover the period 1500 to 2100.

It is possible to obtain additional asteroid ephemerides from the Astrodienst web site at http://www.astro.ch/swisseph/

Eclipses

Solar Fire's eclipse data has been extracted from Fred Espenak's (NASA/GSFC) web pages at http://sunearth.gsfc.nasa.gov/eclipse/eclipse.html, which include comprehensive and accurate astronomical eclipse data covering many millennia.

Appendix A: Bibliography

Those who are interested in reading further may wish to refer to some of the following publications. There are, of course, many other high quality astrological publications available, and this list is simply intended to be a starting point for those wishing to know more.

General Astrology

Alan Oken's Complete Astrology - Alan Oken - Publ. Bantam Books

Choice Centered Astrology - Gail Fairfield - Publ. Ramp Creek Publishing, Inc.

Synastry - Penny Thornton - Publ. The Aquarian Press

The Astrologer's Companion - John Filbey & Peter Filbey - The Aquarian Press

The Twelve Houses - Howard Sasportas - Publ. The Aquarian Press

Predictive Astrology

Planets in Transit - Robert Hand - Publ. Whitford Press

Solar and Lunar Returns - John Filbey - Publ. Aquarian Press

The Eagle and the Lark - Bernadette Brady - Publ. Samual Weiser, Inc.

The Progressed Horoscope - Alan Leo - Publ. Destiny Books

Locational Astrology

Planets in Locality - Steve Cozzi - Publ. Llewellyn

Planets on the Move - Maritha Pottenger and Zipporah Dobyns - Publ. ACS Publications

The Geodetic World Map - I. I. Chris McRae - Publ. American federation of Astrologers Inc.

Medieval & Classical Astrology

Carmen Astrologicum - Dortheus of Sidon - Translated D.Pingree - Publ. Ascella Publications

Christian Astrology - William Lilly - Publ. Regulus Publishing Company Ltd

Classical Astrology for Modern Living - Dr J. Lee Lehman - Publ. Whitford Press

Essential Dignities - J. Lee Lehman Ph.D. - Publ. Whitford Press

Night and Day: Planetary Sect in Astrology - Robert S. Hand - Publ. ARHAT and Golden Hind Press

Tetrabiblos - Ptolemy - Translated F.E.Robbins - Publ. Harvard Uni. Press

Three Books on Nativities – Omar of Tiberias – Translated R. Hand – Publ. Project Hindsight (Latin Track Volume XIV)

Esoteric Astrology

Esoteric Astrology - Alice A. Bailey - Publ. Lucis Publishing Company

Soul-Centered Astrology - Alan Oken - Publ. Bantam Books

The Best of Charles Jayne - Charles Jayne - Publ. American Federation of Astrologers Inc.

The Labours of Hercules - Alice A. Bailey - Publ. Lucis Publishing Company

The Sabian Symbols as an Oracle - Lynda Hill & Richard Hill - Publ. White Horse Books

The Prenatal Epoch - E.H. Bailey - Publ. Samuel Weiser Inc.

The Sabian Symbols in Astrology - Marc Edmund Jones - Publ. Aurora Press

Transpersonal Astrology - Errol Weiner - Publ. Element, Inc.

Other Specialised Topics

Asteroid Goddesses - Demetra George - Publ. ACS Publications, Inc.

A Handbook of Medical Astrology - Jane Ridder-Patrick - Publ. Penguin/Arkana

Finding Our Way Through the Dark: The Astrology of the Dark Goddess Mysteries - Demetra George - Publ. ACS Publications Inc.

Natural Fertility - Francesca Naish - Publ. Sally Milner Publishing

Planets in Composite - Robert Hand - Publ. Whitford Press

The Black Moon Book - F. Santoni & Demetra George - Publ. Sum Press.

The Combination of Stellar Influences - Reinhold Ebertin - Publ. American Federation of Astrologers Inc.

The Lunation Cycle - Dane Rudhyar - Publ. Aurora Press

Interpreting the Eclipses – Robert Carl Jansky – Publ. Astro Computing Services

Lunar Shadows, The Lost Key to the Timing of Eclipses - Dietrich Pessin

Delineation With Astrodynes - Ken Stone - Publ. American Federation of Astrologers Inc.

Astrodyne Manual - Elbert Benjamine - Publ. Church of Light

How To Read Cosmodynes - Doris Chase Doane - Publ. American Federation of Astrologers Inc.

Astronomical Calculations and Computing

Astronomical Algorithms - Jean Meeus - Publ. Willman-Bell, Inc.

Astronomical Formulae for Calculators - Jean Meeus - Publ. Willman-Bell, Inc.

Mathematical Astronomy Morsels – Jean Meeus – Publ. Willman-Bell, Inc.

Horoscope Calculation - J.A.Eshelman - Publ. American Federation of Astrologers, Inc.

Planetary Programs and Tables from -4000 to +2800 - P.Bretagnon & J-L.Simon - Publ. Willman-Bell, Inc.

Appendix B: Changes from Version 6.x to Version 7

Following is a list of the major and most notable changes that have been made for the Gold (v7) version of Solar Fire. A large number of smaller changes have also been made, but have been excluded from this list for the sake of clarity and brevity.

Encyclopedia - Addition of an Encyclopedia of Astrology

Chart Art - Addition of new "Chart Art" pages – a selection of artistic page backgrounds for printed wheels – ideal for client work

New Chart Collections - Addition of new chart databases with about 1000 charts, compiled by expert data collectors

14 New Standard Chart Points - various chart angles and zodiac points plus Selena (White Moon), Sedna and Eris

New Calendar module – to generate customized astro-calendars for a day, week or month in relation to any natal chart, with popup interpretations (containing some newly written additions) and ability to send data directly to MS Outlook or export to other calendar applications

New Birthday Reminders - a popup utility – no need to ever miss your friends or clients birthday's again

New Tabulations - New range of tabulations to complement the existing reports for any chart/s

New Firdaria Interpretations - new reports interpreting current or full-life firdaria periods for any chart

Enhanced Dynamic Reports – all events may be now calculated with fullest possible accuracy and displayed to the nearest second of time, and daylight savings now automatically adjusted as required. Also events in orb at beginning of report may now shown, ensuring no long term transits missed in short reports, report columns are user configurable, and daylights savings adjustments may be applied automatically in reports

Improved Electional Searches – shows exact aspect hits, allows searches for events relating to natal charts, new midpoint searches, allows searches for chart shapes, allows bracketing of conditions

Improved Chart Searches - allows searches for charts with aspects or synastry placements in relation to any given natal chart, allows searches for chart shapes, allows bracketing of conditions

New Wheel Style Preview - allowing user to browse through wheel or dial styles before choosing one

Stationary Points - Identification of stationary points, in both charts and reports, with user-definable station parameters

Page Print Preview – so that you can now easily see exactly what will be printed

Astrodynes/Cosmodynes – presented in the new tabulation module, or may be added to user-defined pages

File Locations - now uses standard Microsoft folder locations for all its files, ensuring better compatibility with newer operating systems, and making data backup easier

Stellarium - Now links to impressively featured open source planetarium program, in addition to Solar Fire's built-in planetarium

House systems - user may select different default house system for Vedic charts, and Sidereal/Tropical toggle now also toggles house system

Retained Charts - can now add single retained charts instead of having to retain all charts at once

Reports - added house modality emphasis, added planetary stations, now show speed to nearest sec arc if rate below 1deg/day

Page Designer - simpler flexible list editing, simplified menus and various new object alignment options

Quinquiwheels - Additional of ability to display 5 ringed charts

Extra Point Wheels - can now show aspects between extra points

ACS Atlas - Ability for user to add own places

Planetary Status Bar - Pop-up hints have improved format , and nearest phases and eclipses have been added

ChartView, ReportView - addition of new Chart Selection dialog allowing quick selection of (or preview for multiple) alternative charts

Appendix C: Technical Support

If you are having a problem running your software, please don't hesitate to contact our technical support team.

Most technical problems can be resolved quickly. We understand that we provide software for astrologers, not computer experts. We can help with the basics.

The best method of contact is by email, using **Technical Support** item from Solar Fire's **Help** menu. This automatically generates an email for you containing information about your operating system and program version. All you have to do is add a clear description of your problem, and then send the email when you are ready.

However, we realize that not everyone will have access to email. In this case you can contact us by mail, fax or telephone.

Here's a checklist to help you help us when you run into a problem.

If the problem you are having is procedural, go to the documentation first.

Know what program you're using. This program is **Solar Fire Gold**.

Know what equipment you're using. Use this space to keep your hardware brand information handy.

Computer: eg. Pentium IV 433Mhz, Core 2 Duo

Windows Version: eg. Windows 98, Windows NT, Windows 20000, Windows XP, Windows Vista, SoftWindows on MacIntosh

RAM: eg. 128MB, 512MB, 2GB

Printer: eg. HP Laserjet 1200, Epson Stylus Pro, Canon 4000

As soon as you receive an error message, write it down. This can tell us exactly what the problem is.

What job were you working on? Were you entering data for a natal chart, or printing out a chart wheel or experimenting with some other option? Were you importing Nova-type chart files? Have you used that part of the program before?

With all this information at hand, contact Astrolabe technical support by phone at 508-896-5081 between 10 am and 4 pm United States Eastern time, by fax at 508-896-5289, in writing at PO Box 1750, Brewster MA 02631 or by email at support@alabe.com.

Index